Managing and Using
Information Systems:
A Strategic Approach

Managing and Using Information Systems: A Strategic Approach

Keri E. Pearlson

JOHN WILEY & SONS, INC.
New York / Chichester / Weinheim / Brisbane / Singapore / Toronto

Acquisitions Editor *Beth Lang Golub*
Editorial Assistant *Jennifer Battista*
Marketing Manager *Jessica Garcia*
Senior Production Editor *Michael Farley*
Cover Designer *Harry Nolan*
Production Management Services *Argosy Publishing*

This book was set in New Caledonia by Argosy Publishing and printed and bound by Courier/Westford. The cover was printed by Lehigh Press. This book is printed on acid-free paper.

Library of Congress Cataloging-in-Publication Data

Pearlson, Keri.
  Managing and using information in the digital economy / Keri E. Pearlson.—1st ed.
    p. cm.
  Includes bibliographical references.
  ISBN 0-471-32001-3 (paper: alk. paper)
  1. Knowledge management. 2. Information technology—Management. 3. Management information systems. 4. Electronic commerce. I. Title.

  HD30.2 .P4 2001
  658.4'038—dc21

                                                                                    00-067457

ISBN 0-471-32001-3

Printed in the United States

10 9 8 7 6 5 4 3 2

To Yale & Hana

Acknowledgments

Books of this nature are written only with the support of many individuals. I would like to personally thank several individuals who helped with this text. While I've made every attempt to include everyone who helped make this book a reality, there is always the possibility of unintentionally leaving someone off. I apologize in advance if that is the case here.

Early versions of the chapters of this book were researched and drafted by students from the Information Management (IM) program at the University of Texas at Austin Graduate School of Business. These amazingly bright students provided incredible inspiration for this book, and several of them pitched in to help write initial drafts of some of the chapters. Specifically, I'd like to acknowledge and thank W. Thomas Cannon, Jeff Greer, David K. Wolpert, Matthew Spafford Sumsion, David M. Zahn, Ben Ballengee, Arthur (Jamie) Ebersole, and Vince Cavasin. Thank you also to the University of Texas MSIS department and to the Business school faculty and staff for their support.

Case studies included with this text came from MIS colleagues all over the globe. A special acknowledgment goes to Professor Jonathan Trower at Baylor University who spent many hours managing the cases for this text. Thank you to Janis Gogan, Ashok Rho, Yvonne Lederer Antonucci, E. Jose Proenca, Bruce Rollier, Dave Oliver, Celia Romm, Ed Watson, D. Guiter, S. Vaught, Kala Saravanamuthu, Ron Murch, Tom Rohleder, Sam Lubbe, Thomas Kern, and Mark Dekker for sending us such great cases.

Several other individuals helped with research and with managing the details of this project. These folks also provided much of the on-line research that helped keep this manuscript, and the supplemental materials, current. Thank you to Tom Cannon, Anthony Paulson, Mik Nielsen, Jason Frederick, Liz Brown, Alicia Harrison, Andres Barcenos, and Eva Chiang. Outstanding editorial comments were made by Justin Harmon, a professional editor, who helped sculpt each individual chapter into a coherent book.

An early version of the manuscript of this book was tested by Dr. Kathy Hurtt, of the University of Wisconsin. Her students read each chapter, and sent me comments which helped fine-tune the manuscript. In alphabetical order, those first students were Amanda Brent, Tanate Charuchaimontri, Drew Colbett, Brad Gibbs, Jingfang Guan, David Hills, Ching-Hsi Hsieh, Chuan-Yen Hu, Kyungmi Jeon, Johanna Jonung, Samuel J. Lex, Wilfung Martono, Jeremy Menard, Brent Miller, Taylor Miller, Jody Moser, Brook Nienhaus, Esmeralda Sanchez, Shana Sparber, Michelle Thomas, Emilia Todorova-Raymond, Brent Williams, Raymond Young, Peter Zakrajsheck, Huachun Zhai, and Lulu Zhang. Later drafts of the manuscript were used by Dr. Kay Nelson at the University of Utah, Dr. John Butler at Ohio

State, and Dr. Carol Saunders at University of Oklahoma. Dr. Nelson also provided minicases that were useful for the ethical use of information chapter. And several anonymous reviewers gave us suggestions which helped improve our manuscript. Thanks!

This book would not have been started were it not for the initial suggestion of a wonderful editor at Wiley and Sons, Beth Lang Golub. Her persistence and patience have helped shepherd this book through many months of creation, modification, evaluation, and production. Thanks also to Samantha Alducin, Alicia Wrobleski, Jeanine Furino, Cecelia Musselman and her team at Argosy, and Fred Courtright (the PermDude) and his team at the Permissions Company. Others at Wiley and at partner companies have provided valuable help.

And thank you to my husband, Dr. Yale Pearlson, and my daughter, Hana Pearlson. Their patience with me while I worked on this project was incredible. And they celebrated and commiserated the ups and downs that came with the process of writing this book. I love you guys!

Preface

"Information technology is a business force now. It amounts to one-half of U.S. firms' annual capital expenditures and increasingly affects how firms organize, do business, and compete. Business managers who choose not to reckon with it do so at their and their firm's peril."

Peter G. W. Keen
in *Every Manager's Guide to Information Technology*

"I'm not hiring MBA students for the technology you learn while in school, but for your ability to learn about, use and subsequently manage new technologies when you get out."

John Post
Federal Express

Give me a fish and I eat for a day; Teach me to fish and I eat for a lifetime.

Proverb

Managers are no longer able to afford the luxury of abdicating participation in information systems decisions. Managers who choose to do so risk having their business decisions compromised. With the proliferation of web and e-business, information systems are at the heart of virtually every business interaction, process, and decision. Managers who let someone else make decisions about their information systems are letting someone else make decisions about the foundation of their business. This is a textbook about using and managing information, written for current and future managers.

The goal of this book is to assist managers in becoming knowledgeable participants in information systems decisions. Becoming a knowledgeable participant means learning the basics and feeling comfortable enough to ask questions. No text will provide managers with everything they need to know to make important information systems decisions. Some texts instruct on the basic technical background of information systems. Some texts discuss applications and their life cycle. Some texts take a comprehensive view of the MIS field and offer the reader snapshots of current systems along with chapters describing how those technologies are designed, used, and integrated into business life.

This book takes a different approach. This text is intended to provide the reader with a foundation of basic concepts relevant to using and managing information. It is not intended to provide a comprehensive treatment on any one aspect of MIS, for certainly each aspect is itself a topic for many books. It is not intended to provide the reader with enough technological knowledge to make them MIS experts.

It is not intended to be a source of discussion of any particular technology. This textbook is written to help managers begin the discussion of how information systems will help, hinder, and create opportunities for their organizations.

The idea for this text grew out of discussions with colleagues in the MIS area. Many faculty use a series of case studies and current readings from trade and popular press sources to teach their core MIS courses. Others simply rely on one of the classic texts, which include dozens of pages of diagrams, frameworks, and technologies. This text is based on a core MIS course taught for over 5 years at the University of Texas at Austin. The course was an "appetizer" course, a brief introduction into the world of MIS for MBA students, lasting only 10 class sessions. The course had two main topics: using information and managing information. And the course was structured around providing the general MBA with enough knowledge of the field of MIS so they could recognize opportunities to use the rapidly changing technologies in new and creative ways. The course was an appetizer to the "main dish" of a host of specialty courses that went much deeper into the topics. But completion of this course meant that students were able to feel comfortable listening to, contributing to, and ultimately participating in decision information systems.

This book includes an introduction, 11 chapters of text, and a set of case studies and supplemental readings on a website. The introduction makes the argument that managers must be knowledgeable participants in information systems decisions. The first few chapters build a basic framework of the relationship between a business strategy, an information systems strategy, and an organizational strategy. The links of these strategies are explored in subsequent chapters on the relationship between information technology and, respectively, the organization, the individual, and the strategy. Readers will also find a chapter on how information technology relates to business transformation.

General managers will find it difficult to discuss their creative applications for information technology without some foundation of how it is managed in organizations. Therefore, the remaining chapters describe the basics of an information architecture, e-business and the Internet, the organization of the MIS function, the management of knowledge, project management, and moral/ethical implications of using information and information systems.

This text is written to be used with supplemental materials and case studies. In order to keep the case studies current, they were not printed in the text itself, but are available without additional charge to those who have the textbook. For this edition of the book, the cases are available on the web. These cases come from all over the globe and are written about many different managerial situations. Each provides a rich contextual setting for the discussion of several issues raised in the book chapters. Please visit the book's website at www.wiley.com/college/pearlson for more information on the cases.

No text in the field of MIS is current. The process of writing the chapters, coupled with any publication process, makes the text somewhat out of date prior to delivery to its audience. With that thought in mind, this text is written to summarize the "timeless" elements of using and managing information. And this text was written to be supplemented with a series of case studies, current readings, and web links. The format of this text is such that each chapter provides the basic language used for a set of important management issues. Cases take these issues and put them in a business example for discussion by students. Current readings and web links bring the foundation issues up-to-date with examples of how successful managers implement these ideas.

Who should read this book? General managers interested in participating in information systems decisions will find this book a good reference resource for the language and ideas of MIS. Managers in the information systems field will find this book a good resource for beginning to understand the general manager's view of how information systems can affect their business decisions. And MIS students will be able to use the readings and concepts in this book as a beginning point in their journey to become informed and productive business people in the 21st century.

The information revolution is here. Where do you fit in?

Keri E. Pearlson

About the Author

Dr. Keri E. Pearlson is the President of KP Partners, a consultancy to both small and large businesses in the area of strategic use of information systems and organizational design. She is also the President of the Zero Time Institute, dedicated to researching and coaching businesses in successful strategies for the new economy. She specializes in executive education programs, seminars, briefings, and management coaching.

Dr. Pearlson has held various positions in academia and industry. From 1992–2000, she was a member of the information systems faculty at the Graduate School of Business at the University of Texas at Austin, where she taught management information systems courses to MBAs and executives. She was also a research affiliate with CSC-Research Services, where she conducted a study of the design and execution of mobile organizations. She has also held positions at the Harvard Business School, CSC-Index's Prism Group, AT&T, and Hughes Aircraft Company.

Her research activities involve topics spanning management of information systems and organizational design. She is co-author of *Zero Time: Providing Instant Customer Value—Every Time, All the Time* (Wiley and Sons, July 2000) and has published articles and case studies on a variety of MIS issues, including mobility, telecommuting, virtual organizations, business process redesign, outsourcing, and customer service support systems. Her work has been published in Sloan Management Review, Academy of Management Executive, Information Resources Management Journal, and Beyond Computing. Many of her case studies have been published by Harvard Business School Publishing.

She serves on the board of directors of I-Teams.com and Intelligent Learning Systems.

Dr. Pearlson holds a Doctorate in Business Administration (DBA) in Management Information Systems from the Harvard Business School and both a Masters Degree in Industrial Engineering Management and a Bachelors Degree in Applied Mathematics from Stanford University.

Contents

▶ **CHAPTER 2** Organizational Impacts of Information Systems Use   **33**

▶ **CHAPTER 3** Information Technology and the Design of Work   **53**

▶ **CHAPTER 4** Strategic Use of Information Resources   **71**

▶ **CHAPTER 8**   The Management Information Systems Organization   161

► **CHAPTER 9**   Knowledge Management   **189**

▶ CHAPTER 10   Project Management   217

▶ CHAPTER 11   Using Information Ethically   246

Glossary   262

Index   272

INTRODUCTION

Why do managers need to understand and participate in the information decisions of their organizations? After all, most corporations maintain entire departments dedicated to the management of their information systems (IS). These departments are staffed with highly skilled professionals devoted to the field of technology. Shouldn't managers rely on experts to analyze all the aspects of IS and to make the best decisions for the organization? The answer to that question is no. Managing information is a critical skill for success in today's business environment. All decisions made by companies involve, at some level, the management and use of IS. And managers today need to know about their organization's capabilities and uses of information as much as they need to understand how to obtain and budget financial resources. The explosive growth of personal computers and the Internet has highlighted this fact, since together they form the backbone for virtually all new business models. A manager who doesn't understand the basics of managing and using information cannot be successful in this business environment.

Consider the now historic rise of companies such as Amazon.com, and e-Toys. Amazon.com started out as an online bookseller and rapidly outpaced traditional brick and mortar businesses like Barnes and Noble, Borders, and Waterstones. Management at the traditional companies responded by having their IS support personnel build websites to compete. But upstart Amazon.com had moved on, keeping its leadership position on the Web by leveraging its new business model into other marketplaces, such as music, electronics, health and beauty products, lawn and garden products, auctions, tools and hardware, and more. Likewise, e-Toys was just another toy store to executives at traditional toy stores such as Toys-R-Us. Traditional toy stores also built websites to have a presence on the Web. But that was not enough. When it came time to sell toys for the busy Christmas season in 1999, e-Toys outsold all traditional toy stores. Again, the upstart led the traditional businesses. E-businesses were able to succeed where traditional companies were not in part because their management understood the power of information, IS, and the Internet. They did not succeed because their managers could build web pages or assemble an IS network. Quite the contrary. The executives in these new businesses understood the fundamentals of managing and using information and could marry that knowledge with a sound, unique business vision to achieve domination of their intended market spaces.

The goal of this book is to provide the foundation for making the general business manager a knowledgeable participant in IS decisions, since any IS decision in which the manager does not participate can greatly affect the organization's ability to succeed in the future. This chapter outlines the fundamental reasons for taking the initiative to participate in IS decisions. Moreover, because effective participation requires a particular set of managerial skills, this chapter identifies the most important ones, recognizing that they will be helpful not just in making IS decisions, but all business decisions. This chapter describes how a manager should participate in the decision-making process, and outlines how the remaining chapters of this book develop this point of view. Finally, this chapter presents current models for understanding the nature of a business and that of an information system in order to provide a framework for the discussions that follow in subsequent chapters.

▶ THE CASE FOR PARTICIPATING IN DECISIONS ABOUT INFORMATION SYSTEMS

Experience has shown that business managers have no problem participating in most organizational decisions, even those outside their normal business expertise. For example, ask a plant manager about marketing problems and the result will probably be a detailed opinion on both key issues and recommended solutions. Dialogue among managers routinely crosses all business functions in formal as well as informal settings, with one general exception: IS. Management continues to tolerate ignorance in this area relative to other specialized business functions. Culturally, managers can claim ignorance of IS issues without losing prestige among colleagues. On the other hand, admitting a lack of knowledge regarding marketing or financial aspects of the business will earn colleagues' contempt.

These attitudes are attributable to the historic role that IS have played in businesses. For many years, technology was regarded as a support function and treated as administrative overhead. Its value as a factor in important management decisions was minimal. And it often took a great deal of technical knowledge to understand even the most basic concepts. However, in today's business environment maintaining this view of technology is certain to cost market share and could ultimately lead to the failure of the organization. Technology has become entwined with all the classic functions of business—operations, marketing, accounting, finance—to such an extent that understanding its role is necessary for making intelligent and effective decisions about any of them. Therefore, understanding basic fundamentals about using and managing information is worth the investment of time. Furthermore, a general understanding of key IS concepts is now possible without the extensive technological knowledge required just a few years ago.

A Business View

Information technology (IT) is a critical resource for today's businesses. If a majority of a firm's business is online, as it is for all banks and airlines, most manufacturers and retailers, and many insurance firms, the company's business strategy suddenly becomes totally irrelevant when the network is down. And Allen Alter reports in *Computerworld* that a worldwide benchmarking study found that prior to the growth of the Internet, the 500 U.S. companies that generate the most revenue spent more than $6,000 per employee on average for IT. This investment totaled a staggering $100 billion. The use of the Internet has already doubled this, and investments are expected to grow exponentially.

The implication of these statements is clear. Technology both supports and consumes a significant amount of an organization's resources. The trends show that high-growth firms are increasing their investments in IT. These resources must return value, or they will be invested elsewhere. The business manager, not the IT specialist, decides which activities receive funding and develops metrics for evaluating the performance of the investment. Therefore, the business manager needs a basic grounding in managing and using information.

People and Technology Work Together

In addition to financial issues, a manager must know how to mesh technology and people to create effective work. Technology facilitates the work that people do. Correctly incorporating IT into the design of a business enables people to focus their time and resources on issues that bear directly on customer satisfaction and other revenue and profit-generating activities. But adding IT to an existing organization requires the ability to manage change. The skilled business manager must balance the benefits of using new technology with the costs associated with changing existing behaviors of people in the workplace. Making this assessment does not require a detailed technical knowledge. However, it does require an understanding of what the consequences are likely to be and why adopting new technology may be more appropriate in some instances than in others. Understanding these issues also helps managers know when it may prove effective to replace people with technology at certain steps in a process.

Rapid Change in Technology

The proliferation of new technologies has created a business environment filled with opportunities. Even today, new uses of the Internet produce new types of e-businesses which keep every manager and executive on alert. Competitors are coming from unexpected places, and new business opportunities are springing up with little advanced warning. The manager's role is to frame these opportunities so that others can understand them, to evaluate them against existing business needs and possible new directions, and finally to pursue any that fit with an articulated business strategy. The quality of the information at hand will affect the quality of both the decision and its implementation. Managers must develop an understanding of what information will be crucial to the decision, how to get it, and how to use it. This *information model* can then be used to discuss specific issues with co-workers, customers, and others. Without a coherent information model, credibility is at risk. Lost credibility compromises the manager's ability to persuade others to pursue the opportunities that have been identified.

What If a Manager Doesn't Participate?

Decisions about IS have a direct impact on the profits of a business. The basic formula PROFIT = REVENUE − EXPENSES can be used to evaluate the impact of these decisions. Adopting the wrong technologies can cause a company to miss business opportunities and any revenues they would generate. Inadequate IS can cause a breakdown in servicing customers, which directly impacts sales. On the expense side, a poorly calculated investment in technology can lead to overspending and excess capacity. Inefficient business processes sustained by ill-fitting IS also increase expenses. Lags in implementation or poor process adaptation each reduce profits and therefore growth. IS decisions can dramatically affect the bottom line.

Failure to consider IT strategy when planning business strategy and organizational strategy leads to one of three business consequences: IS that fail to support business goals, IS that fail to support organizational systems, and a misalignment between business and organizational strategies. These consequences are discussed briefly in this section and in more detail in later chapters. While examining IT-related consequences in greater detail, consider their potential effects on an organization's ability to achieve its business goals. How would each consequence change the way people work? Which customers would be most affected and how? Would the organization still be able to implement its business strategy?

Information Systems Must Support Business Goals

IS are a major investment for any firm in today's business environment. Yet poorly chosen IS can actually become an obstacle to achieving business goals. If the systems do not allow the organization to realize its goals, or if the IS lack the capacity needed to collect, store, and transfer critical information for the business, the results can be disastrous. Customers will be dissatisfied or, worse, lost. Production costs may be excessive. And, worst of all, management may not be able to pursue desired business directions that are blocked by inappropriate IS. Toys-R-Us found that out when its well-publicized website was unable to process and fulfill orders fast enough. It not only lost those customers, it had a major customer relations issue to manage as a result. Consider the well-intended web designer who was charged with building a website to disseminate information to investors, customers, and potential customers. If the business goal is to do business over the Web, then the decision to build an informational website, rather than a transactional website, is misdirected and could potentially cost the company customers by not taking orders online. And while it is possible to redesign the website, even that will require expending additional resources that might have been saved if business goals and IS strategy were discussed together.

Information Systems Must Support Organizational Systems

Organizational systems represent the fundamental elements of a business—its people, work processes, and structure—and the plan that enables them to work efficiently to achieve business goals. If the company's IS fail to support its organizational systems, the result is a misalignment of the resources needed to achieve its goals. It seems odd to think a manager might put a computer on the desk of every employee without providing the training these same employees need to use the tool effectively, and yet this mistake—and many more costly ones—get made in businesses every day. Managers make major decisions such as switching to new, major IS without informing all the affected staff of necessary changes in their daily work. For example, when companies put in an enterprise resource planning (ERP) system, the system often dictates how many business processes are executed. Deploying technology without thinking through how it actually will be used in the organization—who will use it, how they will use it, how to make sure the applications chosen actually accomplish what is intended—results in significant expense without a lot to show for it. The general manager, who, after all, is charged with ensuring that company resources are used effectively, must ensure that the company's IS support its organizational systems and that changes made in one system are reflected in other, related systems. For example, a company that plans to institute a wide-scale telecommuting program will need an information system strategy compatible with that organization strategy. Desktop PCs located within the corporate office are not the right solution for a telecommuting organization. Laptop computers, applications that are accessible anywhere and anytime, and networks that facilitate information sharing are needed. If the organization only allows the purchase of desktop PCs and only builds systems accessible from desks within the office, the telecommuting program is doomed to failure.

▶ WHAT SKILLS ARE NEEDED TO PARTICIPATE EFFECTIVELY IN INFORMATION TECHNOLOGY DECISIONS?

Participating in IT decisions means bringing a clear set of skills to the table. Many have discussed what skills are required for success as a manager. Figure I.1 lists basic skills required of managers who wish to participate in key IT decisions. This list emphasizes understanding, organizing, planning, and solving the business needs of the organization. Individuals who want to develop as managers will find this an excellent checklist for professional growth.

These skills may not look much different from those required of any successful manager. That is the main point of this book: General managers can be successful participants in IS decisions without an extensive technical background. General managers who understand a basic set of IS concepts and who have outstanding managerial skills, like those in Figure I.1, are ready for the digital economy.

How to Participate in Information Systems Decisions

Technical wizardry is not required to become a knowledgeable participant in the IS decisions of a business. What is needed is curiosity, creativity, and the confidence to question in order to learn and understand. A solid framework that identifies key management issues and relates them to aspects of IS gives the background needed to participate.

Focus on business solutions—The ability to bring experience with operations and external customers to bear on current opportunities.
Curiosity—The ability to question and learn about new ideas, applications, technologies, and business models.
Creativity—The ability to transform resources and create something entirely new to the organization.
Project management—The ability to plan, organize, direct, and control company resources to effectively complete a project.
Communication—The ability to share thoughts through text, images, and speech and to gather the thoughts of others through listening, reading, and observing.
Interpersonal skills—The ability to cooperate and collaborate with others on a team, among groups, or across a chain of command to achieve results.
Analytical skills—The ability to break down a whole into its elements for ease of understanding and analysis.
Organizational skills—The ability to bring together distinct elements and combine them into an effective whole.
Planning skills—The ability to develop objectives and to allocate resources in such a manner as to ensure that they are achieved.
Flexibility—The ability to change rapidly and effectively, such as by adapting work processes, shifting perspectives on an issue, or adjusting a plan to achieve a new goal.

FIGURE I.1 Skills of successful managers.

The goal of this book is to provide this framework. The way in which managers use and manage information is directly linked to business goals. And business strategy drives both organizational and IS decisions. Business, organizational, and information strategies are fundamentally linked. This is called the Information Systems Strategy Triangle. Failing to understand this relationship is detrimental to a business. And failing to plan the consequences in all three areas can cost a manager his or her job. This book provides managers with a foundation for understanding business issues related to IS from a managerial perspective.

Organization of the Book

In order to be a knowledgeable participant, managers must know about both using information and managing information. The chapters in this text begin with that basic assumption. Chapter 1 explains the Information Systems Strategy Triangle and provides a brief overview of relevant frameworks for business strategy and organizational strategy. It is provided as background for those who have not formally studied organization theory or business strategy. For those who have studied these areas, this chapter is a brief refresher of major concepts used throughout the remaining chapters of the book. Subsequent chapters provide frameworks and sets of examples for understanding the links between IT and organizational forms (Chapter 2), individual work (Chapter 3), business strategy (Chapter 4), and business transformation (Chapter 5).

The remainder of the chapters look at issues related to building IS strategy itself. Chapter 6 provides a framework for understanding the four components of IS architecture: hardware, software, networks, and data. Chapter 7 is about e-commerce, e-business, and the Internet. Chapter 8 looks at ways in which people are organized to run an IS department. Chapter 9 provides an overview of how to manage knowledge and why managing knowledge is different from managing information. Chapter 10 discusses what IS projects are, why they need managing, and how to manage them. Finally, Chapter 11 discusses some of the ethical issues that should be considered.

▶ BASIC ASSUMPTIONS

Every book is based on certain assumptions, and understanding those assumptions makes a difference in the interpretation of the text. The first assumption made by this text is that managers must be knowledgeable participants in the IS decisions made within and affecting their organizations. That means that the general manager must have a basic understanding of the business and technology issues related to IS. Since technology changes rapidly, this text also assumes that the technology of today is different from the technology of yesterday, and, most likely, the technology available to readers of this text today differs significantly from that available when the text was written. Therefore, this text focuses on generic concepts that are, to some extent, technology independent. It provides a framework on which to hang more current information such as new uses of the Internet or new networking technologies. It is assumed that the reader will seek out current sources to learn about the latest and greatest technology.

In this text a distinction is made between the role of the general manager and the role of IS manager within a business. The general manager must have a basic knowledge of IS in order to make decisions that may have serious implications for the business. The IS manager must have a more in-depth knowledge of technology in order to manage the IS and to be of assistance to general managers who must use the information. Assumptions are also made about how business is done, and what IS are in general. Knowing what assumptions are made about each will support an understanding of the material to come.

Assumptions about Management

The classic view of managing describes four activities, each dependent on the others: planning, organizing, leading, and controlling (see Figure I.2). A manager performs these activities with the people and resources of the organization in order to attain the established goals of the business. Conceptually, this simple model provides a framework of the key tasks of management, which is useful for both general business as well as IS management activities. While many books have been written describing each of these activities, organizational theorist Henry Mintzberg offers a view that most closely details the perspective relevant to IS management.

Mintzberg's model describes management in behavioral terms by categorizing the three major roles a manager fills: interpersonal, informational, and decisional

Classic Management Model	
Planning	Managers think through their goals and actions in advance. Their actions are usually based on some method, plan, or logic, rather than a hunch or gut feeling.
Organizing	Managers coordinate the human and material resources of the organization. The effectiveness of an organization depends on its ability to direct its resources to attain its goals.
Leading	Managers direct and influence subordinates, getting others to perform essential tasks. By establishing the proper atmosphere, they help their subordinates do their best.
Controlling	Managers attempt to assure that the organization is moving toward its goal. If part of their organization is on the wrong track, managers try to find out why and set things right.

FIGURE I.2   Classic management model. Adapted from James A. F. Stoner, *Management*, 2nd edition. Englewood Cliffs, N.J.: Prentice–Hall, 1982.

(see Figure I.3). This model is useful because it describes the chaotic nature of the environment in which managers actually work. Managers rarely have time to be reflective in their approaches to problems. Thus, quality information becomes ever more crucial to effective decision making.

Assumptions about Business

Everyone has an internal understanding of what constitutes a business, which is based on readings and experiences in different firms. This understanding forms a model that provides the basis for understanding actions, interpreting decisions, and communicating ideas. Managers use their internal model to make sense of otherwise chaotic and random activities. This book will make use of several conceptual models of business. Some of them take a functional view and others take a process view.

Functional View
The classical view of a business is based on the functions that people perform, such as accounting, finance, marketing, operations, and human resources. The business organizes around these functions to coordinate them and to gain economies of scale within specialized sets of tasks. Information first flows vertically up and down between line positions and management; after analysis it may be transmitted across other functions for use elsewhere in the company (see Figure I.4).

Process View
Michael Porter of Harvard University describes a business in terms of the primary and support activities that are performed to create, deliver, and support a product or service (see Figure I.5). The primary activities of inbound logistics, operations, outbound logistics, marketing and sales, and service are chained together in

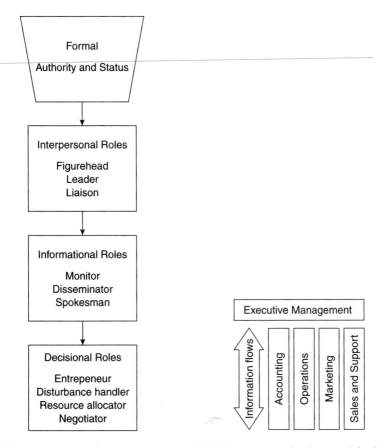

FIGURE I.3 Manager's roles.
Source: H. Mintzberg, *The Nature of Managerial Work*, pp. 59. New York: Harper & Row, 1973.

FIGURE I.4 Hierarchical view of the firm.

sequences that describe how a business transforms its raw materials into value-creating products. This value chain is supported by common activities shared across all the primary activities: for example, general management and legal services are distributed among the primary activities. Improving coordination among activities increases business profit. Organizations that effectively manage core processes across functional boundaries will be winners in the marketplace. IS are often the key to this process improvement and cross-functional coordination.

Both of these views are important to understanding IS. The functional view is useful when similar activities must be explained, coordinated, executed, or communicated. For example, understanding a marketing information system means understanding the functional approach to business in general and the marketing function in particular. The process view, on the other hand, is useful when

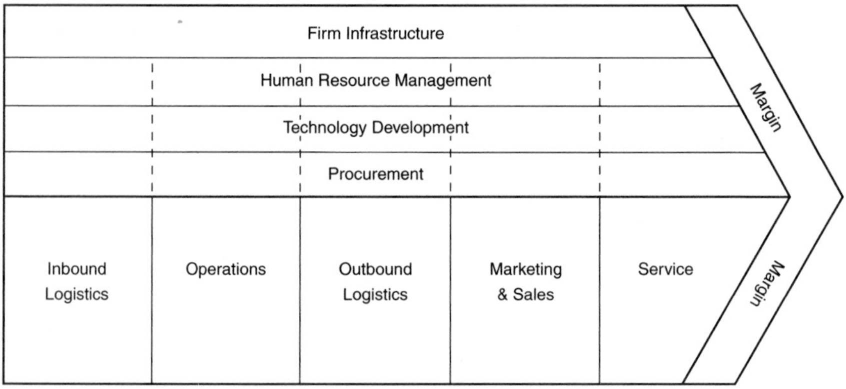

FIGURE I.5 Process view of the firm: the value chain. Source: M. Porter, *Competitive Advantage*. New York: Free Press, 1985.

examining the flow of information throughout a business. For example, understanding the information associated with order fulfillment or product development or customer service means taking a process view of the business. This text makes the assumption that both views are important for participating in IS decisions.

Assumptions about Information Systems

Consider the components of an information system from the manager's viewpoint, rather than from the technologist's viewpoint. Both the nature of information and the context of an information system must be examined to understand the basic assumptions of this text.

Information Hierarchy

The terms "data," "information," and "knowledge" are often used interchangeably, but have significant and discrete meanings within the knowledge management domain. Tom Davenport, in his book *Information Ecology*, points out that getting everyone in any given organization to agree on common definitions is difficult. However, his work (summarized in Figure I.6) provides a nice starting point for understanding the subtle, but important differences.

The information hierarchy begins with *data*, or simple observations. Data is a set of specific, objective facts or observations, such as "inventory contains 45 units." Standing alone, such facts have no intrinsic meaning, but can be easily captured, transmitted, and stored electronically.

Information is data endowed with relevance and purpose.[1] People turn data into information by organizing it into some unit of analysis: e.g., dollars, dates, or customers. Deciding on the appropriate unit of analysis involves interpreting the

---

[1] Peter F. Drucker, "The Coming of the New Organization." *Harvard Business Review*, January–February 1988, p. 45–53.

Data	Information	Knowledge
Simple observations of the state of the world:	Data endowed with relevance and purpose:	Information from the human mind (includes reflection, synthesis, context):
• Easily structured • Easily captured on machines • Often quantified • Easily transferred	• Requires unit of analysis • Need consensus on the meaning • Human mediation necessary	• Hard to structure • Difficult to capture on machines • Often tacit • hard to transfer

FIGURE I.6   Source: Thomas Davenport, *Information Ecology*. New York: Oxford University Press, 1997.

context of the data and summarizing it into a more condensed form. Consensus must be reached on the unit of analysis.

Knowledge is information synthesized and contextualized to provide value. It is information with the most value. Knowledge is a mix of contextual information, values, experiences, and rules. It is richer and deeper than information, and more valuable because someone has thought deeply about that information and added his or her own unique experience, judgment, and wisdom. Knowledge also involves the synthesis of multiple sources of information over time.[2] The amount of human contribution increases along the continuum from data to information to knowledge. Computers work well for managing data, but are less efficient at managing information.

System Hierarchy

An information system comprises three main elements: technology, people, and process (see Figure I.7). When most people use the term "information system," they actually refer only to the technology element. In this text, however, the term *infrastructure* is used to mean hardware, software, data, and network components, while *architecture* refers to the strategy implicit in these components. These ideas will be discussed in greater detail in Chapter 6. The term *information system* is used in this text to refer to the combination of technology (the "what"), people (the "who"), and process (the "how") which, in turn, facilitates the communication of data, information, and knowledge throughout an organization. This text uses the terms *information system*, to mean this combination and *information technology* (IT) to refer to the actual technical devices, concepts, and tools used in the system.

Above the information system itself is management, which oversees the design and structure of the system and monitors its overall performance. Management develops the business requirements and the business strategy that the information system is meant to satisfy. The system's architecture provides a blueprint that translates this strategy into components, or infrastructure.[3]

---

[2] Thomas H. Davenport, *Information Ecology*. New York: Oxford University Press, 1997, p. 9–10.

[3] Gordon Hay and Rick Muñoz, "Establishing an IT Architecture Strategy." *Information Systems Management*, Summer 1997.

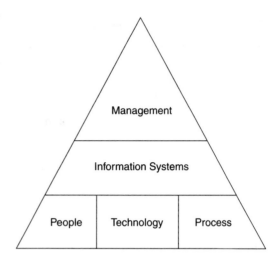

FIGURE I.7 System hierarchy.

▶ SUMMARY

The explosive growth of Internet-based businesses has highlighted the need for all managers to be skilled in managing and using IS. It is no longer acceptable to delegate IS decisions to the Management Information Systems (MIS) department alone. The general manager must be involved in order to both execute business plans and protect options for future business vision. This chapter makes the case for general managers' full participation in strategic business decisions concerning IT. It outlines the skills required for such participation, and it makes explicit certain key assumptions about the nature of business, management, and IS that will underlie the remaining discussions. Subsequent chapters are designed to build on these concepts by addressing the following questions:

- How should information strategy be aligned with business and organizational strategies? (Chapter 1)
- What does it mean to align IT decisions with organizational decisions? (Chapter 2)
- How is the job of the individual in an organization affected by decisions concerning IS? (Chapter 3)
- How can a business achieve competitive advantages using its IS? (Chapter 4)
- How might IS enable business transformation? (Chapter 5)
- What are the components of an IT architecture? (Chapter 6)
- How can electronic commerce contribute to business goals? (Chapter 7)
- What is an IS organization? What are the components of IS strategy? How can a manager effectively manage IS? (Chapter 8)
- How should knowledge be managed within an organization? (Chapter 9)
- What does it mean to manage a project? (Chapter 10)
- What ethical and moral considerations bound the uses of information in business? (Chapter 11)

► *CASE STUDY I-1*

Pat Cannon, MBA°

Pat Cannon was a typical MBA. He was about to graduate from a top-10 business school with an MBA and a desire to change the world while growing a significant savings account. Pat was debating between three job opportunities, all of which would be a big step up the professional latter from the associates job he held when working for Impressive Consulting Group (ICG), the job held right before returning to get an MBA. But Pat wasn't sure which job to take, in part because he didn't feel the MBA classes at the business school had been enough preparation in information systems.

Pat had come to business school with 4 years' experience at Impressive Consulting Group (ICG), a global consulting organization with practices in virtually every major city in the world. Pat worked in the Dallas office as an associate right out of undergraduate school. Pat's undergraduate degree was in business, concentrating in marketing, and he had worked on a number of interesting strategic marketing projects while at ICG. Pat was just completing a standard MBA program after two years of full-time study, and spent the summer in between working for MFG corporation, a large manufacturing company in the Midwestern U.S. The internship at MFG corporation involved working with the new Web marketing group, which Pat choose in order to see just how a company like MFG takes advantage of the Web; at the same time, Pat hoped to become more proficient in Web and Internet technologies. But the experience at MFG's Web marketing group made Pat more anxious, highlighting to him how much more there was to information systems and to the Web than he had previously thought. Pat returned to business school in the fall of the second year wondering just how much information systems knowledge would be needed in future jobs. Further, he felt that becoming a knowledgeable participant in information decisions was critical to success in the fast-paced Internet-based business world awaiting after graduation.

There were three jobs Pat was considering upon graduation. Pat wondered just what type of information systems knowledge was needed for each. All three jobs involved reasonable enough salary, signing bonus, and stock/retirement benefits, so the decision was strictly regarding knowledge needed to be a success on the job. The three jobs are summarized below.

1. Return to ICG as a consultant. This job was attractive to Pat because it meant returning to his former employer, which Pat departed from in good standing. Pat liked the company who rewarded innovation and supported learning and growth among consultants. Pat figured a partnership was easily in the future if he joined ICC after business school. As a consultant, Pat could live wherever he desired, and travel to the client site 4 days a week. The 5th day each week, Pat would be able to work at home, or if desired, in a company office. As a consultant, Pat initially thought engagements in strategic marketing would be most interesting. And ICG had a strong programming group that was brought into each engagement to do the programming and systems analysis work. The consultant role was really one of understanding client concerns, and assisting in building a marketing strategy. Virtually all of the projects would have some Internet component, if not

---

°The names in this case are fictitious. Any resemblance to real individuals or organizations is just coincidental. This case is written simply to highlight administrative issues relevant to general managers.

entirely about building an Internet presence. This was of interest to Pat. But based on the experience this past summer, he was wondering just how much technical skill would be required of the consultants in this arena.

2. Join start-up InfoMicro. Several of Pat's friends from business school were joining together to form a new start-up company on the Internet. This business plan for this company projected that InfoMicro would be one of only 2 Internet start-ups in their marketplace, giving the company good position and great opportunity for growth. The business plan showed the company intending to IPO as early as 3 years after inception, and Pat believed they could do it. Pat would join as VP of Marketing, supplementing the other 3 friends who would hold President, VP Finance and VP Operations positions. The friends who would be President and VP Finance were just completing a techno-mba at Pat's school, and were providing the technical competence needed to get InfoMicro on the Web. Pat would be focusing on developing customers and setting marketing strategy, eventually building an organization to support that operation as necessary. But since InfoMicro was a Web-based business, Pat felt a significant amount of information systems knowledge may be required to successfully be the marketing executive.

3. The final offer was from Pat's internship company, MFG Corp. The job would be to join the marketing department as a manager responsible for new customer development. Many of MFG corporation's customers were older, established companies like MFG Corporation, but new customers were likely to be start-ups, newer, up-and-coming companies, or highly successful new companies like Cisco or Dell. Pat felt that some knowledge of information systems may be necessary simply to provide innovative interaction mechanisms such as customer Web pages. And Pat knew that discussions with the MFG information systems group would be necessary in order to build these new interfaces. How knowledgeable must Pat be of information systems issues in order to hold this job?

As spring break approached, Pat knew a decision had to be made. Recruiters from all three companies had given Pat a deadline of the end of break week, and Pat wasn't at all sure which job to take. All sounded interesting, and all were reasonable alternatives for Pat's next job.

Discussion Questions

1. For each job Pat is considering, what do you think would be the types of knowledge Pat would need, relative to information systems?

2. How could Pat be a knowledgeable participant in each of the three jobs? What would it mean to be a knowledgeable participant in each job? Give an example for each job.

3. As a marketing major and an MBA, is Pat prepared for the work world awaiting? Why or why not?

CHAPTER 1

THE INFORMATION SYSTEMS STRATEGY TRIANGLE

In 1991, National Linen Service, a supplier of linen for restaurants and hotels, found itself facing poor earnings due to increased competition and a weak economy. The company decided to install a strategic systems department in an attempt to increase its competitiveness and lower costs. The new systems department installed a program called Boss. Unfortunately, rather than notifying the contract department when customer contracts expired, Boss was programmed to simply drop expired customers off the database. Needless to say, National Linen's bottom line worsened. National Linen Service failed to take into account the unintended consequences of installing an information system on its business strategy and organizational design.

This case underlines the point made in the Introduction: It is imperative that a general manager take a role in decisions about information systems (IS). While it is not necessary for a general manager to understand all technologies, it is necessary to aggressively seek to understand the consequences of using technologies relevant to the business's environment. General managers who leave the information technology (IT) decisions solely up to their IT professionals often put themselves and their companies at a disadvantage. While IT can facilitate the movement and exchange of information, IT that is inappropriate for a given operating environment can actually inhibit and confuse that same exchange. Management information systems (MIS) is not an island within a firm. MIS manages an infrastructure which is essential to the firm's functioning.

This chapter introduces a simple framework for understanding the impact of IS on organizations. This framework is called the Information Systems Strategy Triangle because it relates business strategy with IS strategy and organizational strategy. This chapter also presents key frameworks from organization theory that describe the context in which MIS operates, as well as the business imperatives that MIS supports.

A word of explanation is needed. This chapter, and the subsequent chapters in this book, will address questions of IS strategy squarely in the context of business strategy. Studying business strategy alone is something better done in other texts and courses. However, to provide foundation for IS discussions, this chapter summarizes several key business strategy frameworks. Studying IS alone does not provide general managers with the appropriate perspective. In order to be effective, managers need a solid sense of how IS are used and managed within the organization. Studying details of technologies is also outside the scope of this text. Details of the technologies are important, of course, and it is important that any organization maintain a sufficient knowledge base to plan for and operate applications. But because technologies change so rapidly, keeping a text current is impossible. Therefore this text has taken the perspective that understanding what questions to ask is a skill more fundamental to the general manager than understanding any particular technology. This text provides readers with an appreciation of the need to ask questions, a framework from which to derive the questions to ask, and a foundation sufficient to understand the answers received. Chapter 1 seeks to root this foundation in an understanding of business strategy and organizational theory. To that end, this chapter summarizes several of the key managerial frameworks in these areas. Students with extensive background in organizational behavior and business strategy will find this a useful review of key concepts. This chapter also presents a simple framework for designing IS strategy in this chapter. The remaining chapters all build on these foundations.

This chapter begins with a simple framework for relating business strategy to organizational and IS decisions. The Information Systems Strategy Triangle is shown in Figure 1.1.

The first point derived from this simple model is that successful firms have an overriding business strategy that drives both organizational strategy and IS strategy. The decisions made regarding the structure, hiring practices, and other components of the organizational strategy, as well as decisions regarding applications, hardware, and other IS components, are all driven by the firm's business objectives, strategies, and tactics. Successful firms have these three strategies in balance—they have purposefully designed their organization and their IS strategies to complement their business strategy.

Second, as this model also suggests, IS strategy can itself affect and is affected by changes in a firm's business and organizational strategies. That means in order to perpetuate the balance needed for successful operation, changes in the IS strategy must be accompanied by changes in both the organizational and overall business strategy.

FIGURE 1.1 The Information Systems Strategy Triangle.

And third, IS strategy always has consequences—intended or not—on business and organizational strategies. Avoiding unintended consequences means remembering to consider business and organizational strategies when designing IS deployment. For example, placing computers on employee desktops, without an accompanying set of changes to job descriptions, process design, compensation plans, and business tactics will fail to produce the anticipated productivity improvements. Success can only be achieved by purposefully designing all three components of the Strategy Triangle.

Setting business and organizational strategies, in general, are topics covered very well in many other texts and, therefore, are outside the scope of this text. However, the rest of this chapter will provide some important background on current frameworks for understanding business and organizational strategies, so as to ground the discussions of IS strategy that will ensue throughout this text. Further, these frameworks summarize key concepts for two of the points in the Strategy Triangle.

► BRIEF OVERVIEW OF BUSINESS STRATEGY FRAMEWORKS

A strategy is a plan. It is a well-articulated vision of where a business seeks to go and how it expects to get there. It is the form in which a business communicates its goals. This plan is constructed in response to market forces, customer demands, and organizational capabilities. Market forces create the competitive situation for the business. Some markets, such as those faced by airlines, makers of personal computers, and issuers of credit cards, are characterized by many competitors and a high level of competition such that product differentiation becomes increasingly difficult. Other markets, such as those for package delivery, automobiles, and petroleum products, are similarly characterized by high competition, but product differentiation is better established. Customer demands comprise the wants and needs of the individuals and companies who purchase the products and services available in the marketplace. And organizational capabilities include the skills and experience that give the corporation a currency that can add value in the marketplace.

There are several well-accepted models which frame discussions of business strategy. We will review three models: first, the Porter generic strategies framework and three variants of the differentiation model it presents; second, D'Aveni's hypercompetition model; and, finally, Brandenburger and Nalebuff's co-opetition model.[1] The end of this section introduces key questions a general manager must answer in order to understand the strategy of the business.

The Generic Strategies Framework

Companies sell their products and services in a marketplace populated with competitors. Michael Porter's framework helps managers understand the strategies they

---

[1] Another popular model by Michael Porter, the value chain, is a useful model for discussing internal operations of an organization. Some find it a useful model for understanding how to link two firms together. This framework is used in Chapter 4, to examine business process design. For further information, see Michael E. Porter, *Competitive Advantage*. New York: Free Press, 1985.

may choose in order to build a competitive advantage. In his book *Competitive Advantage*, Porter claims that the "fundamental basis of above-average performance in the long run is sustainable competitive advantage."[2] Porter identifies three primary strategies for achieving competitive advantage: cost leadership, differentiation, and focus. These advantages derive from the company's relative position in the marketplace, and they depend on the strategies and tactics employed by competitors. Figure 1.2 summarizes these three strategies for achieving competitive advantage.

Cost leadership means the organization aims to be the lowest-cost producer in the marketplace. The organization enjoys above-average performance by minimizing costs. The product or service offered must be comparable in quality to those offered by others in the industry in order that customers perceive its relative value. Typically, there is only one cost leader. If more than one organization seek advantage with this strategy, a price war ensues, which eventually may drive the organization with the higher cost structure out of the marketplace.

Differentiation means the organization qualifies its product or service in a way that allows it to appear unique in the marketplace. The organization has identified which qualitative dimensions are most important to its customers, and it has found ways to add value along one or more of those dimensions. In order for this strategy to work, the price charged customers by the differentiator must seem fair relative to the price charged by competitors. Typically, multiple firms in any given market will employ this strategy.

Focus means the organization limits its scope to a narrower segment of the market and tailors its offerings to that group of customers. This strategy has two variants: *cost focus*, in which the organization seeks a cost advantage within its segment, and *differentiation focus*, in which it seeks to distinguish its products or services within the segment. This strategy allows the organization to achieve a local competitive advantage, even if it does not achieve competitive advantage in the marketplace overall. As Porter explains:

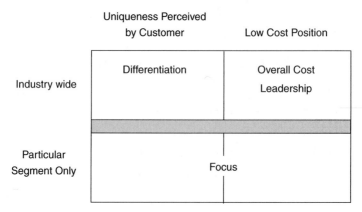

FIGURE 1.2 Three strategies for achieving competitive advantage. Source: M. Porter, *Competitive Strategies*. New York: Free Press, 1998.

[2] Michael E. Porter, *Competitive Advantage*. New York: Free Press, 1985.

The focuser can thus achieve competitive advantage by dedicating itself to the segments exclusively. Breadth of target is clearly a matter of degree, but the essence of focus is the exploitation of a narrow target's differences from the balance of the industry. Narrow focus in and of itself is not sufficient for above-average performance.[3]

Variants on the Differentiation Strategy

Porter's generic strategies are fundamental to an understanding of how organizations create competitive advantage. Several variants of his differentiation strategy are useful for further analyzing sources of advantage. These are the shareholder value model, the barriers to entry model, and the unlimited resources model. D'Aveni also describes these "arenas of competition" as the timing and knowledge advantage, the stronghold advantage, and the deep pockets advantage.

Shareholder value model. William Fruhan[4] described this model, which holds that the timing of the use of any specialized knowledge can create advantage as long as the knowledge remains unique. This model suggests that customers buy products or services from an organization in order to have access to its unique knowledge. This knowledge and the timing of its use differentiate among competitors. As D'Aveni observes, however, such an advantage is static, rather than dynamic, since the purchase is a one-time event.

Barriers to entry model. Another well-accepted model suggests that firms create barriers to potential competitors' entry into a market based on an assessment of the competitive threats in that market. This assessment flows from another Porter model known as the five forces, which identifies five potential sources of threat to competitive advantage in any given market, all of them players who might take market share: suppliers, buyers, substitutes, industry competitors, and new entrants. The five forces model (discussed more fully in Chapter 4) suggests that an organization can differentiate itself by offering products or services that are difficult to displace in the eyes of customers because of features that appear unique. According to D'Aveni, this strategy provides the organization with the advantage of a relative stronghold in the marketplace.

Unlimited resources model. This differentiation strategy utilizes a large base of resources that allow an organization to outlast competitors. An organization with greater resources can manage risk and sustain losses more easily than one with fewer resources. According to D'Aveni, this deep-pocket strategy provides a short-term advantage only; if a firm lacks the capacity for continual innovation, it will not sustain its competitive position over time.

The Porter models and their variants are useful for diagnostics, or understanding how a business seeks to profit in its chosen marketplace, and for prescriptions, or building new opportunities for advantage. However, the Porter models were developed at a time when competitive advantage was sustainable because the rate of change in any given industry was relatively slow and manageable. Since the

---

[3] Michael E. Porter, *Competitive Strategies.* New York: Free Press, 1998.

[4] William E. Fruhan, Jr., "The NPV Model of Strategy—The Shareholder Value Model." In *Financial Strategy: Studies in the Creation, Transfer, and Destruction of Shareholder Value.* Homewood, IL: Richard D. Irwin, 1979.

late 1980s when this framework was at the height of its popularity, several newer models have been described that take into account the increasing turbulence and velocity of the marketplace. Two such frameworks are discussed below.

Hypercompetition and the New 7-S's Framework

Discussions of *hypercompetition*[5] take a very different perspective. Whereas the previous models focus on the creation and sustaining of advantage, hypercompetition models suggest that the speed and aggressiveness of the moves and countermoves in any given market create an environment in which advantages are "rapidly created and eroded."[6] This perspective works from the following assumptions:

Every advantage is eroded. Advantages only last until competitors have duplicated or out-maneuvered them. Once an advantage is no longer an advantage, it becomes a cost of doing business.

Sustaining an advantage can be a deadly distraction. Some companies can extend their advantages and continue to enjoy the benefits, but sustaining an advantage can become a distraction from developing new ones.

The goal should be disruption, not sustainability, of advantage. A company seeks to stay one step ahead through a series of temporary advantages that erode competitors' positions, rather than by creating a sustainable position in the marketplace.

Initiatives are achieved with a series of small steps. Competitive cycles have shortened, and new advantages must be achieved quickly. Companies focus on creating the next advantage before the benefits of the current advantage erode.

D'Aveni identified four arenas in which firms seek to achieve competitive advantage under hypercompetition: cost/quality, timing/know-how, strongholds, and deep pockets. His framework suggests seven approaches an organization can take in its business strategy. Figure 1.3 summarizes this model.

D'Aveni's model describes the strategies companies can use to disrupt competition, depending on their particular capabilities to seize initiative and pursue tactics that can create a series of temporary advantages. For the purposes of this book, we have briefly summarized his new 7-S's[7] in Figure 1.4.

The 7-S's are a useful model for identifying different aspects of a business strategy and aligning them to make the organization competitive in the hypercompetitive arena of business in the millenium. This framework can be used to assess competitors' strengths and weaknesses, as well as to build a roadmap for the company's strategy itself. Using this model, managers are able to identify new organizational

---

[5] R. D'Aveni, *Hypercompetition: Managing the Dynamics of Strategic Maneuvering*. New York: Free Press, 1994.

[6] Ibid.

[7] The "old" 7-S's of competitive advantage—structure, strategy, systems, style, skills, staff, and superordinate goals—entered business literature in a paper by R. Waterman, T. Peters, and J. Phillips, "Structure Is Not Organization," in *Business Horizons* (June 1980). D'Aveni used these as a point of reference in deriving his "new" 7-S's under hypercompetition.

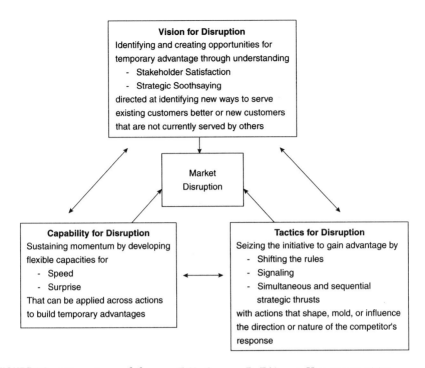

FIGURE 1.3 Disruption and the new 7-S's. Source: R. D'Aveni, *Hypercompetition: Managing the Dynamics of Strategic Maneuvering.* New York: Free Press, 1994.

Approach	Definition
Superior stakeholder satisfaction	Understanding how to maximize customer satisfaction by adding value strategically
Strategic soothsaying	Seeking out new knowledge that can predict or create new windows of opportunity
Positioning for speed	Preparing the organization to react as quickly as possible
Positioning for surprise	Preparing the organization to respond to the marketplace in a manner that will surprise competitors
Shifting the rules of competition	Finding new ways to serve customers which transform the industry
Signaling strategic intent	Communicating the intended actions of a company, in order to stall responses by competitors
Simultaneous and sequential strategic thrusts	Taking a series of steps designed to stun and confuse competitors in order to disrupt or block their efforts

FIGURE 1.4 D'Aveni's new 7-S's.

responses to their competition, and to identify new opportunities that extend their current strengths. This model is particularly useful in markets where the rate of change makes sustaining a business strategy very difficult. It suggests that a business strategy must be continuously redefined in order to be successful.

Co-opetition

Another popular contemporary strategy is *co-opetition*. As defined by Brandenburger and Nalebuff in their book of the same name, co-opetition is a strategy whereby companies cooperate and compete at the same time. It is different enough from the generic strategies proposed by Porter to merit discussion here.

Co-opetition describes the mindset for the set of players in what Brandenburger and Nalebuff call the *value net*.[8] The value net includes a company and its competitors and complementors, as well as its customers and suppliers, and the interactions among all of them. A *complementor* is a company whose product or service is used in conjunction with a particular product or service to make a more useful set for the customer. For example, Goodyear is a complementor to Ford and GM because tires are a complementary product to automobiles. Likewise, as suggested in the book by Brandenburger and Nalebuff, hardware and software companies are complementors.

Co-opetition, then, is the strategy for creating the best possible outcome for a business by optimally combining competition and cooperation. Brandenburger and Nalebuff build such a strategy using modeling. For our purposes, the concept of co-opetition is important in that it defines a strategic direction that has implications for the Information Systems Strategy Triangle; i.e., how to decide what IS to build, how to use them, and which industry players will be important to involve.

Why Are Strategic Advantage Models Essential to Planning for Information Systems?

A general manager who relies solely on IS personnel to make IS decisions gives up not only any authority over IS strategy, but also leeway that may be crucial to future business decisions. Poorly chosen IS infrastructure can hamper successful implementation of business strategy. In fact, business strategy should drive IS decision making, and changes in business strategy should entail reassessments of IS. Moreover, changes in IS potential should trigger reassessments of business strategy—as in the case of the Internet, where companies who failed to understand or consider its implications for the marketplace were quickly outpaced by competitors who had. For the purposes of our model, the Information Systems Strategy Triangle, understanding business strategy means answering the following questions:

1. What is the business goal or objective?
2. What is the plan for achieving it? What is the role of IS in this plan?

[8] A. Brandenburger and B. Nalebuff, *Co-opetition*. New York: Doubleday, 1996.

3. Who are the crucial competitors and cooperators, and what is required of a successful player in this value net?

The frameworks previously presented will be useful in the discussion of the incorporation of IS into business strategy; they will be revisited over the course of the next few chapters. They will be particularly important in the discussion of the role of IS in building and sustaining competitive advantages (Chapter 4). Three main frameworks of business strategy and their usefulness to the discussion of IS are summarized in Figure 1.5. The next section of this chapter establishes a framework for understanding organizational strategy.

► BRIEF OVERVIEW OF ORGANIZATIONAL STRATEGIES

Organizational strategy includes the organization's design, as well as the choices it makes that define, set up, coordinate, and control its work processes. The organizational strategy is a plan that answers the question: "How will the company organize in order to achieve its goals and implement its business strategy?" There are many models of organizational strategy, a few of which are reviewed in this section.

A simple framework for understanding the design of an organization is the *business diamond*, introduced by Leavitt and embellished by Hammer and Champy.[9] Shown in Figure 1.6, the business diamond identifies the crucial components of an organization's plan as its business processes, its values and beliefs, its management control systems, and its tasks and structures.

This simple framework is useful for designing new organizations and for diagnosing organizational troubles. For example, organizations that try to change their cultures but don't change the way they manage and control will not be effective.

Framework	Key Idea	Usefulness in Information Systems Discussions
Porter's generic strategies framework	Firms achieve competitive advantage through cost leadership, differentiation, or focus.	Understanding which strategy is chosen by a firm is critical to choosing IS to complement that strategy.
D'Aveni's hypercompetition model	Speed and aggressive moves and counter-moves by a firm create competitive advantage.	The 7-S's give the manager suggestions on what moves and countermoves to make and IS are critical to achieve the speed needed for these moves.
Brandenberg and Nalebuff's co-opetition model	Companies cooperate and compete at the same time.	Being cooperative and competitive at the same time requires IS that can manage these two roles.

FIGURE 1.5 Summary of key strategy frameworks.

[9] M. Hammer and J. Champy, *Reengineering the Corporation*. New York: HarperBusiness, 1994.

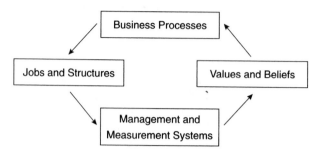

FIGURE 1.6 The business diamond. Source: M. Hammer and J. Champy, *Reengineering the Corporation.* New York: HarperBusiness, 1994.

A complementing framework for the business diamond identifies conventional organization design variables and IT design variables. Lucas and Baroudi[10] have categorized these variables, which is summarized in a list in Figure 1.7. Their work provides a useful list of organizational variables including structure, work processes, communications and interorganizational relationships. These are components of an organization that can change by managerial decision. For example, managers decide on the organizational subunits, and can change them as their organizational strategy changes. But further, this list identifies IT design decision points and links those variables with their corresponding organizational variable.

A more comprehensive framework for organizational design can be found in the book by Cash, Eccles, Nohria, and Nolan, *Building the Information Age Organization.*[11] This framework, shown in Figure 1.8, suggests that the successful execution of a business's organizational strategy comprises the best combination of organizational, control, and cultural variables.

Organizational variables include decision rights, business processes, formal reporting relationships and informal networks. Control variables include the availability of data, the nature and quality of planning, and the effectiveness of performance measurement and evaluation systems and incentives to good work. Cultural variables comprise the values of the organization. Figure 1.9 contains a table summarizing these variables.

The objective is to give the manager a set of frameworks to use in evaluating various aspects of organizational design. Using these frameworks, the manager can review the current organization and assess which components may be missing and

---

[10] H. Lucas and J. Baroudi, "The Role of Information Technology in Organization Design." *JMIS* Spring 1994, vol 10, No. 4.

[11] Cash, Eccles, Nohria, and Nolan, *Building the Information Age Organization.* Homewood, IL: Richard D. Irwin, 1994.

Class of Variable	Conventional Design Variable	IT Design Variable
Structural	Definition of organizational subunits	Virtual components
	Determining purpose, output of subunits	
	Reporting mechanisms	
	Linking mechanisms	Electronic linking
	Control mechanisms	
	Staffing	Technological leveling
Work process	Tasks	Production automation
	Workflows	Electronic workflows
	Dependencies	
	Output of process	
	Buffers	Virtual components
Communications	Formal channels	Electronic communications
	Informal communication	Technology matrixing collaboration
Interorganizational	Make vs. buy decisions	Electronic relations customer/supplier relationships
	Exchange of materials	Electronic customer/supplier relationship
	Communications	Electronic linking mechanism

Source: H. Lucas and J. Baroudi, "The Role of Information Technology in Organization." *JMIS*, Spring 1994, pp. 9–23.

FIGURE 1.7 Conventional and IT design variables.

what options are available looking forward. Understanding organizational strategy means answering the following questions:

1. What are the important structures and reporting relationships within the organization?
2. What are the characteristics, experiences, and skill levels of the people within the organization?
3. What are the key business processes?
4. What control systems are in place?
5. What is the culture of the organization?

The answers to these questions will inform any assessment of the organization's use of IS. Chapters 2 and 3 will use these organizational theory frameworks, summarized in Figure 1.10, to assess the impact of MIS on the firm.

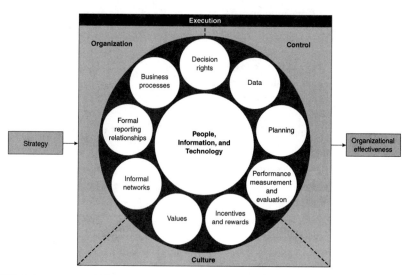

FIGURE 1.8 Managerial levers. Source: Cash, Eccles, Nohria, and Nolan, *Building the Information Age Organization*. Homewood, IL: Richard D. Irwin, 1994.

Variable	Description
Organizational variables	
Decision rights	Authority to initiate, approve, implement, and control various types of decisions necessary to plan and run the business.
Business processes	The set of ordered tasks needed to complete key objectives of the business.
Formal reporting relationships	The structure set up to ensure coordination among all units within the organization.
Informal networks	Mechanism, such as ad hoc groups, which work to coordinate and transfer information outside the formal reporting relationships.
Control variables	
Data	The information collected, stored, and used by the organization.
Planning	The processes by which future direction is established, communicated, and implemented.
Performance measurement and evaluation	The set of measures that are used to assess success in the execution of plans and the processes by which such measures are used to improve the quality of work.
Incentives	The monetary and nonmonetary devices used to motivate behavior within an organization.
Cultural variables	
Values	The set of implicit and explicit beliefs that underlie decisions made and actions taken.

Source: Cash, Eccles, Nohria, and Nolan, *Building the Information Age Organization*. Homewood, IL: Richard D. Irwin, 1994.

FIGURE 1.9 Organizational Design Variables.

Framework	Key Idea	Usefulness in IS Discussions
Business diamond	There are 4 key components to an organization: business processes, values and beliefs, management control systems, and tasks and structures.	Using IS in an organization will affect each of these components. Use this framework to identify where these impacts are likely to occur.
Managerial levers	Organizational variables, control variables, and cultural variables are the levers managers can use to affect change in their organization.	This is a more detailed model than the Business diamond and gives specific areas where IS can be used to manage the organization and to change the organization.

FIGURE 1.10   Summary of organizational strategy frameworks.

▶ BRIEF OVERVIEW OF INFORMATION SYSTEMS STRATEGY

IS strategy is the plan an organization uses in providing IS. (See Figure 1.11.) MIS is a means by which a company implements its business strategy. Business strategy is a function of competition (what does the customer want and what does the competition do?), positioning (in what way does the firm want to compete?), and capabilities (what can the firm do?); MIS helps determine the company's capabilities. While an entire chapter is devoted to IT architecture, for now a more basic framework will be used to understand the decisions related to IS that an organization must make.

The purpose of this matrix is to give the manager a high-level view of the relation between IS infrastructure and the other resource considerations that are key to IS strategy. This infrastructure, shown in Figure 1.11, includes hardware components, such as desktop units and servers. It also includes software, such as the programs used to do business, to manage the computer itself, and to communicate between systems. The third component of IS infrastructure is the network, which is the physical means by which information is exchanged among hardware components, such as through a modem and dial-up network (in which case the service is actually provided by a vendor such as AT&T), or through a private digital network (in which case the service is probably provided by an internal unit). Finally, the fourth part of the infrastructure is the data itself. The data is the actual information, the bits and bytes stored in the system. In current systems, the data is not necessarily stored alongside the programs that use it; hence, it is important to understand what data is in the system and where it is stored. There are many more detailed models of IS infrastructure, and there are dozens of books to which the interested reader may refer. For the purposes of this text, the matrix will provide sufficient information to allow the general manager to assess the critical issues in information management.

	What	Who	Where
Hardware	List of physical components of the system	Individuals who use it Individuals who manage it	Physical location
Software	List of programs, applications, and utilities	Individuals who use it Individuals who manage it	What hardware it resides upon and where that hardware is located
Networking	Diagram of how hardware and software components are connected	Individuals who use it Individuals who manage it Company from whom service is obtained	Where the nodes are located, where the wires and other transport media are located
Data	Bits of information stored in the system	Individuals who own it Individuals who manage it	Where the information resides

FIGURE 1.11 Information systems strategy matrix.

▶ FOOD FOR THOUGHT

The Information Systems Strategy Triangle suggests the following management principles:

1. Business strategy drives organizational strategy and IS strategy. It is important to design the organization and its IS in such a way as to support clearly defined business goals and objectives.

2. Organizational strategy must complement business strategy. The way a business is organized either supports the implementation of its business strategy or it gets in the way.

3. Likewise, IS strategy must complement business strategy. When IS support business goals, the business appears to be working well.

4. Organizational strategy and information strategy must complement each other. They must be designed so that they support, rather than hinder each other.

5. If a decision is made to change one corner of the triangle, it is necessary to evaluate the other two corners to ensure that balance is preserved. Changing business strategy without thinking through the effects on the organizational and IS strategies will cause the business to struggle until balance is restored. Likewise, changing IS or the organization alone will cause an imbalance.

The chapters that follow examine in further detail the links between organizational strategy and information strategy (Chapters 2 and 3), and the links between business strategy and information strategy (Chapter 4). The links between business and organizational strategies are left to other courses of study.

► SUMMARY

The Information Systems Strategy Triangle represents a simple framework for understanding the impact of IS on businesses. It relates business strategy with IS strategy and organizational strategy and suggests the balance that must be maintained in business planning.

In an organization that operates successfully, an overriding business strategy drives both organizational strategy and information strategy. As the triangle model also suggests, information strategy can itself affect and is affected by changes in a firm's business and organizational strategies. Moreover, information strategy always has consequences—intended or not—on business and organizational strategies.

Many models exist that frame strategies for achieving competitive advantage in business. The basic models—the traditional models by Porter, the hypercompetitive model by D'Aveni, and the co-opetition model by Brandenburger and Nalebuff—describe approaches for achieving competitive advantage under market conditions that vary in their complexity and volatility.

By organizational strategy, we mean the organization's design, as well as the choices it makes that define, set up, coordinate, and control its work processes. There are many models of organizational strategy, including the business diamond, which identifies crucial components of an organization plan; the organizational design variables described by Lucas and Baroudi; and the framework by Cash, Eccles, Nohria, and Nolan for combining organizational, control, and cultural variables.

IS strategy is the plan the organization uses in providing information services. A basic framework for understanding IS decisions considers the relation of architecture (the "what") and the other resource considerations ("who" and "where") that represent important planning constraints.

► DISCUSSION QUESTIONS

1. Why is it important for Business strategy to drive organizational strategy and IT strategy? What might happen if business strategy was not the driver?

2. Suppose managers in an organization decided to hand out laptop computers to all sales people, with out making any other formal changes in organizational strategy or business strategy. What might be the outcome? What unintended consequences might occur?

3. Consider a traditional manufacturing company who wanted to take advantage of the internet and the web. What might be an reasonable business strategy and how would organizational and IT strategy need to change?

4. This chapter describes key components of an IS strategy. Describe the IS strategy of a consulting firm using the matrix framework.

CISCO SYSTEMS*

Cisco Systems, Inc. was one of the early successes from the Internet. Cisco makes the routers, switches and other technologies necessary to make the Internet work. They provide products and services to customers who want to build their own networks or who want to connect to others. Customers include large enterprises with complex networking needs, service providers who provide network, cable, or other telecommunication services, and smaller businesses who want to connect to the Internet. And they have been quite successful, growing from revenues of $1.3 billion in 1994 to $12.2 billion in 1999, and their stock is up more than 2,300% in the same time period.

In order to fuel the explosive growth, Cisco executes a business strategy of acquiring companies to complement their core strengths. As of October 1999, Cisco had acquired 43 companies (the latest was just hours before this case was written) in fields related to their goal: Be the biggest supplier of equipment needed to build, run, and manage the Internet. The acquisitions provided Cisco with immediate infrastructure, technology, and smart people. John Chambers, the CEO and President of Cisco since 1991, described his strategy to *Business Week* magazine as,

> [Mergers and acquisitions] are a requirement, given how rapidly customer expectations change. The companies who emerge as industry leaders will be those who understand how to partner and those who understand how to acquire. Customers today are not just looking for pinpoint products, but end-to-end solutions. A horizontal business model always beats a vertical business model. So you've got to be able to produce that horizontal capability in your product line, either through your own R&D, or through acquisitions.

Cisco is not only a vendor of components for the Internet, they run their business on the Internet. Their business strategy has been to build the "ultimate model of an efficient Net company," and to do so, they use the Internet for connecting to customers, suppliers, and other stakeholders.

Cisco connects to customers though a series of Web pages that allow customers to read and learn about products and services. In addition, like many companies, customers can learn about Cisco, order products, seek support and service, and contract for training. However, unlike many companies, Cisco sells more than 75% of their products over the Net, which amounts to about $30 million a day. And almost 80% of customer support issues are handled this way. There are several benefits to this method of doing business. First, that gives the customer control over part of the ordering process because they can choose and enter exactly what they want. Second, Cisco instantly gives them back information regarding availability and delivery, often without a person intervening. It means Cisco can respond instantly to a customer order by accepting and managing the electronic order. And it means that response is less costly to Cisco than to competitors where human intervention is needed.

*Adapted from: "Meet Mr. Internet," *Business Week*, Sept. 13, 1999, pg. 128-140, from Cisco website, www.cisco.com on October 28, 1999, and from "John Chambers: The Art of the Deal," *Business 2.0*, October 1999, website: www.business2.com/articles/1999/10/text/chambers.html

But Cisco's interaction with customers is only part of their success. Cisco has built an extensive network of suppliers, partners, resellers, and contractors who are also connected directly to Cisco. An order received by Cisco is sent to suppliers who manufacture some of the products for Cisco. The suppliers, in turn, are able to provide exactly what Cisco's customers want to Cisco. And this is done automatically by the information system.

In order to accomplish this e-business, Cisco has about 19,000 employees all over the world. Employees, too, interact with the Internet for much of their business. Recruiting and candidate screening is done on the network. Managers have access to staff records on the network. Information on competitors is available on the network. And all financial information is gathered and stored on the network, making it possible to virtually "close" business on any day of the quarter. That means they can accurately evaluate their entire company's financial performance on any day of the year. Processes are virtually paper-free, where just about anything that can be done on the Net is done on the net. And Cisco's success internally only provides additional fuel for their story externally: Doing business on the Internet is the only way to go.

Questions for Discussion:

1. How does the business strategy affect information systems and organizational systems decisions?
2. Why does Cisco management insist on putting all of their business processes on an internal network?
3. How does candidate screening on a network support their business strategy?
4. What options does Chambers, CEO of Cisco, have other than to use the Internet so aggressively?

CHAPTER 2

ORGANIZATIONAL IMPACTS OF INFORMATION SYSTEMS USE

At Diamond Technology Partners, a management consulting firm headquartered in Chicago, Illinois, everyone in the organization can and does use a computer since the integration of information systems (IS) is fundamental to every job in the organization. Every consultant has a laptop with applications that allow him or her to tap into the company databases, complete administrative functions, work on projects, and communicate with others. Every staff member also has a computer at his or her disposal. Using the computer is fundamental to the way the company is organized since every piece of information generated by every person in the organization is created, stored, and retrieved from the IS. Everyone has access to the work done by everyone else, regardless of position or status in the company. Information needed to do a task is available to whoever needs it at the time and place they need it. For example, a consultant working with a major bottling company in Florida can access computer routines developed for a similar project for a utility company in Oregon. IS are integrated into every work function, enabling Diamond Technology Partners to operate under a very different organizational form than its low-tech counterparts. Employees can sustain organizational activities usually reserved for colleagues collocated at the same physical site even when they are traveling around the world. They also can share information as if everyone was in the same office.

Consider another example. One of the earliest companies to make use of IS as part of designing its organization was Mrs. Fields Cookies. In the early 1980s, this company was managing cookie and bakery stores all over the world with a fraction of the management staff of other fast-food chain stores. Every store had a computer system that told the manager how many cookies batches to make, when to bake them, and when they would lack sufficient freshness for sale. The effect was a control mechanism similar to having founder Debbie Fields in each store ensuring the quality of her cookies. But the information system went further. It allowed Mrs. Fields to hire people whose skills were in selling cookies and not worry about whether those people could calculate baking cycles. The money spent for labor at Mrs. Fields stores paid for sales skills, not for baking skills. And with store controllers at the headquarters offices in Park City, Utah, examining the numbers for each store within 12 hours of the end of each business day, the computer system helped frame an organizational design that gave Mrs. Fields the ability to sell gourmet cookies at a reasonable price.

The point is simple: Incorporating IS as a fundamental organizational component affects the way managers design their organizations. And when used appropriately, IS and information technology (IT) leverage human resources, capital, and materials to create an organization that optimizes performance. There is a synergy to designing organizations with IT in mind that cannot be achieved when IT is just added on.

Chapter 1 introduced a simple framework for understanding the impact of IS on organizations. The Information Systems Strategy Triangle relates business strategy with IS strategy and organizational strategy. In an organization that operates successfully, an overriding business strategy drives both organizational strategy and information strategy. Information strategy itself affects and is affected by changes in a firm's business and organizational strategies. The most effective businesses optimize the interrelationships between the organization and IT, maximizing efficiency and productivity.

Organizational strategy includes the organization's design, as well as the managerial choices that define, set up, coordinate, and control its work processes. As discussed in the last chapter, there are many models of organizational strategy, such as the business diamond that identifies four primary components of an organization: its business processes, its tasks and structures (or organizational design), its management control systems, and its values and culture. Figure 2.1 summarizes these design variables. Optimized organizational design and management control systems support optimal business processes, and they, in turn, reflect the firm's values and culture.

This chapter builds on these models. Of primary concern is the ways in which IT can improve organizational design and management control systems. This chapter will consider how IT can best affect such organizational variables as decision rights, business processes, formal reporting relationships, and informal networks. In addition, it will examine IT in relation to management control variables, including data, planning, performance measurement and evaluation, and incentives. This chapter will look at some innovative organizational designs that have made extensive use of IT and will conclude with some ideas about how organizations of the future will organize with the increasingly widespread use of the Internet and electronic linkages with suppliers, customers, and the world. This chapter addresses the organizational level issues and complements it with a discussion of the individual worker issues in the next chapter.

Variable	Description
Organizational variables	
Decision rights	Authority to initiate, approve, implement, and control various types of decisions necessary to plan and run the business.
Business processes	The set of ordered tasks needed to complete key objectives of the business.
Formal reporting relationships	The structure set up to ensure coordination among all units within the organization.
Informal networks	Mechanism, such as ad hoc groups, which work to coordinate and transfer information outside the formal reporting relationships.
Control variables	
Data	The information collected, stored, and used by the organization.
Planning	The processes by which future direction is established, communicated, and implemented.
Performance measurement and evaluation	The set of measures that are used to assess success in the execution of plans and the processes by which such measures are used to improve the quality of work.
Incentives	The monetary and nonmonetary devices used to motivate behavior within an organization.
Cultural variables	
Values	The set of implicit and explicit beliefs that underlie decisions made and actions taken.

Source: Cash, Eccles, Nohria, and Nolan, *Building the Information Age Organization*. Homewood, IL: Richard D. Irwin, 1994.

FIGURE 2.1 Organizational design variables.

► INFORMATION TECHNOLOGY AND ORGANIZATIONAL DESIGN

This section examines how IT affects organizational design. It looks at how IT changes the way a company hires people and how it changes the structure of the organization.

Information Technology Allows Companies to Hire Differently

The organization that optimizes its use of IT hires different people, designs jobs differently, and utilizes a different organizational structure. Its workers communicate differently with each other. They are better able to work together across functions and even at a geographic remove. They have better access to the data that can enable them to work effectively and thus often enjoy greater autonomy.

Why do IT-savvy firms hire differently? First, workers must either know how to use the technologies that support the work of the firm before they are hired, or they must be trainable in the requisite skills. Hiring procedures incorporate activities that determine the skills of applicants. For example, a company may ask a candidate to sit at a computer in order to answer a basic questionnaire, take a short quiz, or simply browse the Web in order to evaluate the applicant's skill level or they may only accept applications submitted to a website. Second, IT utilization affects the array of nontechnical skills needed in the organization. Certain functions—many clerical tasks, for example—can be handled more expeditiously, so fewer workers adept in those skills are required. IT-savvy companies can eliminate clerical capabilities from their hiring practices and focus on more targeted skills. Third, IT can serve to leverage managerial effectiveness, allowing a single manager to track and supervise the work of a greater number of employees. Thus, the ratio of supervisors to regular workers can often be reduced, which directly impacts the number of people a company needs to hire. IT often allows centralization of certain managerial functions within even the most diffuse organization, realizing economies of scale and changing the firm's expectations for local managers. For example, in a restaurant where using the computer is part of the work tasks, potential hires are not only interviewed to understand their people skills, but they are asked to sit at a computer to complete an electronic application to make sure they are comfortable using the computer. In this way, candidates uncomfortable with computers are screened out before hiring offers are made.

The design of the organization is a function of the skill mix required for the firm's work processes and of the flow of those processes themselves. Thus, an organization that infuses technology effectively and employs a workforce with a high level of IT skills will necessarily design the organization differently from an organization that does not. As previously discussed, the skill mix required by an IT-savvy firm will reflect greater capacity for using the technology itself. It will require less of certain clerical and even managerial skills that are leveraged by technical capacity. And, it may deploy skills according to different ratios in central and local units. In Mrs. Fields' case, IT skills were more necessary in the central organization, but much less necessary in the stores—sales skills became the point of focus for new hires locally. In addition, the very process of job design is likely to be different in an IT-savvy firm: because it must reflect an organization-wide strategy for optimizing the array of skills, as well as the requirements of a process-driven production environment, job design is more likely to be driven centrally but with the participation of process partners across the organization. Thus, Mrs. Fields uses feedback from store managers in designing the job descriptions for branch employees, and store managers use hiring tools that have been rendered strictly consistent from store to store. Chapter 3 will more fully explore how jobs and tasks themselves are designed with IT.

These crucial differences in skill mix and job design imply a different structure for the IT-savvy organization. First, because technical capacity must be incorporated as fully as possible into all work processes that can benefit, the firm must adopt an integrative approach to IT management and then organize itself accordingly. The IT function must be represented high on the organization chart; its own design must fully reflect the firm's driving business strategy, and its functioning must integrate fully with non-technical units according to the requisites of optimal process design. Second, outside the IT unit, the apt utilization of technology alters work and managerial processes in such a way as to affect organizational structure. IT increases managerial leverage, easing certain management tasks, such as tracking work flow and measuring productivity.

Information Technology Allows Organizations to Be Structured Differently

Traditional organization structures are hierarchical, flat, or matrixed (see Figure 2.2). Hierarchical structures are those where individuals are part of a bureaucracy in which each person has a single supervisor, who in turn has a supervisor, and so on. When work is to be done, it typically comes from the top and is segmented into smaller and smaller pieces until it reaches the level of the business in which it will be done. Middle managers do the primary information processing and communication function, telling lower subordinates what to do and telling senior managers the outcome of what was done. IS are used typically to store and communicate information along the lines of the hierarchy and to support the information management function of the managers.

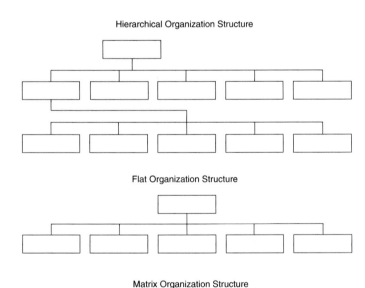

FIGURE 2.2 Hierarchical, flat, and matrix organization structures.

In contrast, the flat structure is one in which everyone does whatever needs to be done in order to complete business. Entrepreneurial organizations are often like this because they typically have fewer employees, and even when they grow they initially build on the premise that everyone must do whatever is needed. As the work grows, new individuals are added to the organization, and eventually a hierarchy is formed where divisions are responsible for segments of the work processes. Many companies strive to keep the "entrepreneurial spirit," but in reality work gets done in much the same way as with the hierarchy described above. Flat organizations often use IS to off-load certain routine work in order to avoid hiring additional workers. As a hierarchy develops, the IS become the glue tying together parts of the organization that otherwise would not communicate.

The third popular form, the matrix organization, typically assigns workers to two or more supervisors in an effort to make sure multiple dimensions of the business are integrated. For example, a staff member in marketing would have a supervisor for his region and a different supervisor for his product line. He would report to both, and both would be responsible in some measure for his performance. In some cases the matrix reflects a third dimension (or more), such as the customer relations segment. IS reduce the operating complexity of matrix organizations by allowing information sharing among the different managerial functions. For example, a salesperson's sales would be entered into the information system and appear in the results of all of the managers to whom he or she reports.

But matrix organizations often fail to enable managers to achieve their business strategies. Applegate, McFarlan, and McKenney describe the problem as follows:

> The inability to cope with the increased information processing demands was a major cause of the failure of the matrix organization. In the 1960s, mainframe system architectures, with their centralized control of information processing, mirrored the centralized intelligence and control of the hierarchy. The microcomputer revolution of the 1980s provided tools to decentralize information processing control that mirrored organizational attempts to decentralize decision authority and responsibility to small entrepreneurial units. While these decentralized IT resources helped improve local decision making, the debates and conflicts concerning whether to centralize or decentralize IT resource management reflected organizational arguments concerning the centralization or decentralization of organizational decision authority. However, the network revolution of the 1990s enables distributed information processing and intelligence that make the IT centralization/decentralization debates of the 1980s irrelevant.[1]

Made possible by new IS, a fourth type of organizational structure emerged: the networked organization (see Figure 2.3). Networked organizations characteristically feel flat and hierarchical at the same time. An article published in the

---

[1] Applegate, L. M., McFarlan, W., and McKenney, J., "Corporate Information Systems Management: Text and Cases," 4th Edition. Boston: Richard D. Irwin, Inc., 1996.

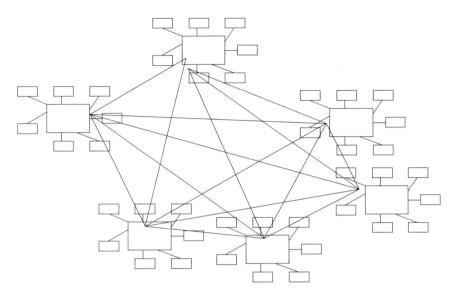

FIGURE 2.3 The networked organization form.

Harvard Business Review describes this type of organization: "Rigid hierarchies are replaced by formal and informal communication networks that connect all parts of the company. . . . [This type of organizational structure] is well known for its flexibility and adaptiveness."[2]

Networked organizations are those that utilize distributed information and communication systems to replace inflexible hierarchical controls with controls based in IS. Networked organizations are defined by their ability to promote creativity and flexibility while maintaining operational process control. IS are fundamental to process design; they improve process efficiency, effectiveness, and flexibility. As part of the execution of these processes, data is gathered and stored in centralized data warehouses for use in analysis and decision making. In theory at least, decision making is more timely and accurate because data is collected and stored instantly. And the extensive use of communications technologies and networks renders it easier to coordinate across functional boundaries. In short, the networked organization is one in which IT ties together people, processes, and units.

When IT is used primarily as a communication vehicle, the organization feels flat. Traditional hierarchical lines of authority are used for tasks other than communication since everyone can, in theory, communicate with everyone else. However, IT can be used to replace organizational components, in addition to communications lines. That results in a form called the *T-form organization*.

---

[2] Applegate, L. M., Cash, J. I., and Mills, D. Q., "Information Technology and Tomorrow's Manager." *Harvard Business Review*, November–December 1988, pp. 128–136.

T-form Organization

Further collaboration between IT and organizational design has resulted in the T-form organization.[3] The "T" stands for "technology-based" or "technology-oriented," and the design variables discussed in Chapter 1 differ accordingly. In the T-form organization, conventional design variables, such as organizational sub-units, reporting mechanisms, flow of work, tasks, and compensation are combined with technology-enabled components, such as electronic linking, production automation, electronic work flows and communications, and electronic customer/supplier relationships. While the original theory was developed long before the Internet was popular, the structure of the T-form organization informs many Internet-based companies today.

The T-form organization typically feels flat. The term used is *technological leveling*, because the technology allows individuals from all parts of the organization to reach all other parts of the organization. While the structure may not look flat on paper, technologies such as e-mail and voice mail make it very easy for anyone in the organization to communicate with anyone else.

Unfettered access to shared information means that supervision of and interaction between employees must be based at least somewhat on mutual trust. There are fewer face-to-face meetings in the T-form organization. As with the networked organization, individuals tend to use electronic means to communicate with each other, but they additionally keep work in a central repository. For example, many consulting firms use Lotus Notes as an infrastructure for their client projects. Notes is a group support tool that houses information, applications, and data and is easily accessible on virtually any type of computer. Typically, the consultant downloads the Notes databases needed for his or her project, then "replicates" them with the central network copies at the end of the work day. The consultant uses information in Notes often without knowing exactly who put it in. And he or she enters information without knowing precisely who will access it later. Thus, organizations that support the use of tools such as Notes often have parallel cultures that encourage trust and foster integrity in the shared information.

Work is often coordinated automatically in the T-form organization. Systems make it possible to move information freely across organizations and between individuals. Thus, decisions can be made wherever they are needed, rather than only at the senior levels of the organization. And consequences of the decisions are known faster across the organization. The example of a large national mortgage company illustrates how IS can help coordinate work. A sales representative for the mortgage company has a territory in Illinois, while a loan coordinator works in Rhode Island, several hundred miles away. Once the sales representative interests a customer in a mortgage, he or she enters the requisite paperwork in the company database and instantly sends it to the loan coordinator. The loan coordinator then mails a letter of introduction to the customer, with instructions for preparing

---

[3] Lucas, H. C., *The T-Form Organization: Using Technology to Design Organizations for the 21st Century*. San Francisco: Jossey Bass Publishers, 1996.

to close the loan. Although the sales representative and the coordinator may not know each other and may not ever have worked together, IS makes it possible to coordinate work efficiently and to provide seamless services to the customer.

A T-form organization's business processes are designed differently—tasks typically encompass more inclusive responsibilities. IS can supplement work, enabling an individual to take on more steps of the process. For example, at Ford Motor Company, clerks at the receiving dock initiate the accounts payable process. When a shipment comes in, the clerk uses IS to indicate what was received, and, in most cases, that step alone is sufficient to trigger payment to the supplier. The clerk's area of responsibility is much broader than simply receiving boxes at the dock, yet he or she does not have to learn in depth about accounts payable to be able to initiate payment to vendors.

Increasingly, T-form organizations have broadened their electronic networks to include links with suppliers. Suppliers can access T-form organizations' computers to see what parts are needed, to check inventory levels of parts, and to assist with services. For example, Proctor and Gamble works very closely with Wal-Mart to make sure the shelves of the giant retailer are stocked with Proctor and Gamble products. When the inventory dips below a set level, an order is automatically placed. When the goods ship to Wal-Mart, Proctor and Gamble sends an electronic invoice, which is handled directly by Wal-Mart's systems. Very few individuals are needed to make this process work. Wal-Mart needs a worker at the dock to handle the shipment when it arrives, but typically the rest of the process is automatic.

Likewise, T-form organizations seek to connect with customers electronically. For example, FedEx, the shipping organization, allows customers to link directly with its operational systems to track packages. And American Airlines, Continental Airlines, and other airlines allow customers to link with their scheduling and ticketing systems. T-form organizations build IS that connect with customers in an effort to increase responsiveness, improve service, and decrease costs. These changes affect the design of marketing and sales organizations. For example, e-Toys, an online toy store, allows customers to browse an electronic catalog that resides on the company computer system. A customer can place an order, enter credit card information, and check availability online. The system accepts the order, runs a credit check, and initiates a packing slip for the item selected. The product arrives at the customer's door via whatever delivery option he or she selects. The customer need not talk with a staff member unless there is a problem, and the cost of toy sales is greatly reduced. The linking of these supply chains is characteristic of the T-form organization.

▶ INFORMATION TECHNOLOGY AND MANAGEMENT CONTROL SYSTEMS

Not only does IT change the way organizations are structured, it also profoundly affects the way managers control their organizations. By control, we mean how people and processes are monitored, evaluated, given feedback, and compensated or rewarded. Figure 2.4 summarizes the activities of management control.

Control Activites	Brief Definition
Monitoring	Observing and keeping track of the progress, quality, cost, time, and other relevant parameters.
Evaluating	Comparing the data collected through monitoring to standards or historical data.
Providing Feedback	Communicating the results of evaluation to the individuals responsible for the activities and tasks.
Compensating	Deciding on salary or other forms of payment to those individuals who performed the tasks.
Rewarding	Deciding and delivering bonuses, recognition, or other types of prize for exemplary work.

FIGURE 2.4 Model of management control activities.

Traditional hierarchical organizations require managers to tightly control operating processes. To do so, they must understand the standard operating procedures for the primary activities of the organization.[4] The complexity of the activities is handled by creating divisions and subdivisions and dividing the work among them. The subdivision continues until individual jobs are specified and tasks are assigned to individual workers. Then begins the work of the control systems: to insure that the work is done on time, properly, and on budget.

IS play three important roles in management control processes:

1. They enable the collection of information that may not be collectable other ways.

2. They speed the flow of information from where it is generated to where it is needed.

3. They facilitate the analysis of information in ways that may not be possible otherwise.

We will examine these three characteristics of IS in the context of the management control activities we outlined in Figure 2.4.

Information Technology Changes the Way Managers Monitor

Monitoring work can take on a completely new meaning with the use of information technologies. IS make it possible to collect such data as the number of keystrokes, the precise time spent on a task, exactly who was contacted, and the specific data that passed through the process. For example, a call center that handles customer service telephone calls is typically monitored by an information system that collects data on the number of calls each representative received and the length of time each representative took to answer each call and then to respond to the

[4] Simons, Robert, *Levers of Control: How Managers Use Innovative Control Systems to Drive Strategic Renewal.* Boston: Harvard Business School Press, 1995.

question or request for service. Managers at call centers can easily obtain statistics on virtually any part of the process. And data collection is built into the system, making it unintrusive. In contrast, a manager of field representatives might also use IS to monitor work, but the use may be more obvious and thus present an intrusion. For example, having field sales personnel complete documents detailing their progress adds work for them.

The organizational design challenge is to embed monitoring tasks within everyday work. Workers perceive their regular tasks as value-added but tasks completed simply to provide information for management control as non-value-added. Often these tasks are avoided, or worse, data recorded is inaccurate, falsified, or untimely. Collecting monitoring data directly from work tasks—or embedding the creation and storage of performance information into software used to perform work—renders it more reliable.

Information Technology Changes the Way Managers Evaluate

IS make it possible to evaluate data against reams of standard or historical data as desired. Models can be built and simulations designed. Thus, managers can more easily and completely understand the progress and performance of work. In fact, the ready availability of so much information catches some managers in "analysis paralysis": analyzing too much or too long. In our example of the call center, a manager can compare a worker's output to that of his colleagues, to his own earlier output, to historical outputs reflecting similar work conditions at other times, etc.

While evaluation constitutes an important use of IS, how the information is used has significant organizational consequences. Information collected for evaluation may be used to provide feedback so the worker can improve his performance; it also can be used to determine rewards and compensation. The former use—for improvement in performance—is nonthreatening and generally welcome. But using the same information for determining compensation or rewards can be threatening. Suppose the call center manager is evaluating the number and duration of calls service representatives answer on a given day. The manager's goal is to make sure all calls are answered quickly, and he or she has communicated that goal to his or her staff. Now think about how the evaluation information is used. If the manager simply provides the workers with information about numbers and duration, then the evaluation is not threatening. Typically, each worker will make his or her own evaluation and respond by improving call numbers and duration. A discussion may even occur in which the service representative describes other important dimensions, such as customer satisfaction and quality. Perhaps the representative takes longer than average on each call because of the attention devoted to the customer. On the other hand, if the manager uses the information about number of calls and duration to rank workers so that top workers are rewarded, then workers may feel threatened by the evaluation and respond accordingly. The representative not on the top of the list may shorten calls, deliver less quality, or cause a decrease in customer satisfaction. The lesson for managers is to take care concerning what is monitored and how the information the systems make available is used.

Information Technology Changes the Way Managers Provide Feedback

As previously discussed, how information is used affects the organization. Using evaluation information for rewards will drive behavior accordingly. But how feedback is communicated to the organization also plays a role in affecting behavior.

Some feedback can be communicated via IS themselves. A simple example is the feedback built into an electronic form that will not allow it to be submitted until it is properly filled out. But for more complex feedback, IS may not be the appropriate vehicle. For example, no one would want to be told they were doing a poor job over e-mail or voice mail. Negative feedback of significant consequence often is best delivered in person or over the telephone in real time.

IS can allow for feedback from a variety of participants who otherwise could not be involved. Many companies do a "360-degree" feedback, into which the individual's supervisors, subordinates, and coworkers all provide input. IS makes it relatively easy to solicit feedback from anyone who has access to the system. Since that feedback is received more quickly, improvements can be made faster.

Information Technology Changes the Way Managers Compensate and Reward

Compensation and rewards are the ways organizations create incentives to good performance. A clever reward system can make employees feel good without paying them more money. IS can affect these processes, too. Some organizations use their websites to recognize high performers. Others reward them with new technology. At one organization, top performers get new computers every year, while lower performers get the "hand me downs."

IS make it easier to design complex incentive systems such as shared or team-based incentives. An information system facilitates keeping track of contributions of team members and can allocate rewards according to complex formulas.

Information Technology Changes the Way Managers Control Processes

The above section primarily addresses controlling individuals. But the manager also needs to control work done at the process level. At the individual level, IS can streamline the process of monitoring, evaluating, and compensating. Process control is a different matter.

Process control refers to the levers available to a manager to insure that operational processes are carried out appropriately. A percentage of that control lies in making sure that individuals perform appropriately. But the process itself needs continuous improvement. While the various methods of process improvement lie outside the scope of this book, it is important to understand that IS can play a crucial role. IS provide decision models for scenario planning and evaluation. For example, the airlines routinely use decision models to study the effects of changing routes or schedules. IS collect and analyze information from automated processes, and they can be used to make automatic adjustments to the processes. For example, a paper mill uses IS to monitor the mixing of ingredients in a batch of paper and to add more ingredients or change the temperature of the boiler as necessary. While IS collect, analyze, and move information, managers are free to make decisions.

▶ VIRTUAL ORGANIZATIONS

The virtual organization provides a clear example of how organizations can be designed differently using information. Chapter 3 goes into more detail on this subject when it examines the design of work. In this chapter, the virtual organization is considered from a structural perspective. IT has made it possible for individuals to work for an organization and live anywhere. The Internet and corporate intranets have created the opportunity for individuals to work from anyplace they can access a computer. Individuals work from home, or even such remote locations as satellite offices, customer sites, and hotel rooms.

For work that can be done on a computer or work that makes extensive use of telecommunications, technologies such as ISDN, the Internet, Lotus Notes, and Microsoft Outlook make it possible to design a work environment anywhere. For example, all graduate students at the University of Texas Graduate School of Business (and many other schools) buy laptop computers as part of their program. Students use them everywhere. They can access the school's network from within and outside the campus. Within the campus, they can plug into the network in common areas and in classrooms. Outside the campus, they dial in over traditional telephone lines or use more expensive high-speed ISDN lines (see Chapter 6 for a discussion of technologies). In essence, they form a virtual organization. They work in teams with individuals whom they rarely meet face to face. They complete joint assignments using the systems. They can work from anyplace and at any time. Instructors need not gather everyone in one place to meet.

The structure of a virtual organization is networked. Everyone has access to everyone else using the technology. Hierarchy may be present in the supervisory roles, but work is done crossing boundaries. E-mail is the most widely used means of communication, making it possible for even the newest member of a team to communicate with the most senior person in the organization. The basis of success in a virtual organization is the amount of collaboration that takes place between individuals. In a traditional organization, individuals mainly collaborate by holding face-to-face meetings. They use IS to communicate and to supplement these meetings, but the culture requires "looking at eyeballs" to get work done. By contrast, a virtual organization uses its IS as the basis for collaboration. For example, the consulting firm discussed earlier, which uses Lotus Notes as the basis for collaborative work, gives its consultants access to the entire knowledge of the organization from the "portal" of their computers.

In the virtual organization, management processes, support processes, and business processes are designed differently. These processes must reflect the assumption that not everyone will be in the office when they happen. For example, a bigger office may not be a useful reward for an employee in such an organization, so the reward system may have to be different. In fact, all management processes must be reexamined. If managers require personal observation to conduct evaluations, then the process may have to change. Managers in a virtual organization often monitor results, rather than the process. It becomes the responsibility of the individual worker to keep the manager informed of problems and to seek assistance. Managers must design ways to monitor performance electronically.

Support functions also differ. For example, a virtual organization might not require individuals to fill out paper expense forms, but rather electronic forms that are accessible from anywhere. IT support might not mean bringing a broken system to the technicians or a visit from the technicians. Instead, technical support might comprise a website with a chat room or a posting of frequently asked questions. Or, the virtual worker can call a toll free support center. Also, virtual companies can hire firms to provide on-site service to their workers.

Business processes themselves must be accessible anyplace and any time. Often they are built on the Internet or made accessible on company computers using other forms of telecommunication. For example, an insurance company has put its customer service and ordering processes online so that its teleworkers can take calls and complete these processes from anywhere. Many of its representatives now work from home.

VeriFone, a leading manufacturer of credit verification systems, is well known for its virtual organization.[5] The company was founded in 1981 by an entrepreneur who hated bureaucracy. By 1990, it was the leading company for transaction automation with products and services used in over 80 countries. VeriFone has an office building in northern California which houses a nominal corporate headquarters, as well as several plants around the world where its processing systems are actually made or where distribution centers facilitate rapid delivery to customers. But most corporate functions run decentrally out of multiple global locations including Texas, Hawaii, India, and Taiwan. The company sought to put its people in close proximity to customers and emerging markets, which resulted in about a third of the employees traveling roughly half of the time. This strategy gave VeriFone first-hand information about business opportunities and competitive situations worldwide.

At the heart of the company culture is constant and reliable sharing of information. Everyday the Chief Information Officer (CIO) gathers yesterday's results and measures them against the company's plans. Using IS for simulation and analysis, he pulls together information from databases around the company for an e-mail newsletter to everyone in the company. The newsletter describes the latest products, competitive wins, and operating efficiencies. The top 15 sales people are often listed, along with their sales figures. More than just managing the IS, VeriFone's CIO provides the "information glue" that holds the virtual organization together.

A story is told of a new salesperson who was trying to close a particularly big deal. He was about to get a customer signature on the contract when he was asked about the competition's system. Being new to the company, he did not have an answer. But he knew he could count on the company's information network for help. He asked his customer for 24 hours to research the answer. He then sent a note

---

[5] Galal, Hossam, Stoddard, Donna, Nolan, Richard, and Kao, Jon, "VeriFone: The Transaction Automation Company." Harvard Business School case study 195–088.

to everyone in the company asking the questions posed by the customer. The next morning, he had several responses from others around the company. He went to his client with the answers and closed the deal.

What is interesting about this example is that the "new guy" was treated as a colleague by others around the world, even though they did not know him personally. And further, he was able to collaborate with them instantaneously. It was standard procedure, not panic time, because of the culture of collaboration in this virtual organization. The information infrastructure provided the means, but the organization built on top of it consisted of processes designed for individuals at a geographical remove.

One last comment: The "virtual organization" is not to be confused with a similar concept referred to as the "virtual corporation," which nonetheless features some similar characteristics. The virtual corporation describes a business strategy for allying with complementary businesses so that the combined businesses respond to customers as if they were a single entity. Each of the companies in the virtual corporation bring a set of strengths to the combined group, and rely on the other partners for their core strengths, and each company alone would be at risk if other partners did not provide the complementary strengths. The virtual corporation is also made possible by extensive use of IS, since instantly connecting the partners is critical to their functioning as a virtual whole. Chapter 4 discusses the virtual corporation as a strategic use of IS.

▶ FOOD FOR THOUGHT: IMMEDIATELY RESPONSIVE ORGANIZATIONS

A series of ideas are floating around centered on the immediacy of responses that IS makes possible and the organizational forms that result (see, for example, the popular books *Blur*,[6] *Real Time*,[7] *Corporate Kinetics*,[8] *Adaptive Enterprise*,[9] and *The Horizontal Organization*.[10] These ideas suggest that the increased use of IS in general, and the Internet in particular, have made possible the ability to respond instantly to customer demands, supplier issues, and internal communication needs. IS are enabling even more advanced organization forms such as the adaptive organization, the horizontal organization, and a relatively new form, the zero time organization.[11] Common to all of these designs is the idea of agile, responsive organizations that can configure their resources and people quickly and are flexible enough to sense and respond to changing demands.

[6] Davis, Stan, and Meyer, Christopher, *Blur*. Reading, MA: Perseus Books, 1998.

[7] McKenna, Regis, *Real Time*. Boston: Harvard Business School Press, 1997.

[8] Fradette, Michael, and Michaud, Steve, *Corporate Kinetics*. New York: Simon and Schuster, 1998.

[9] Haeckel, Stephan H., and Slywotzky, Adrian J., *Adaptive Enterprise: Creating and Leading Sense-and-Respond Organizations*. Boston: Harvard Business School Press, 1999.

[10] Ostroff, Frank, *The Horizontal Organization: What the Organization of the Future Actually Looks Like and How It Delivers Value to Customers*. New York: Oxford University Press, 1999.

[11] Yeh, R., Pearlson, K, and Kozmetsky, G, *ZeroTime: Providing Instant Customer Value Everytime—All the Time*. New York: Wiley, 2000.

The zero time organization, for example, describes the concept of instant "customer-ization," or the ability to respond to customers immediately. In order to accomplish this goal, the organization must master five disciplines:

- **Instant value alignment:** understanding the customer so well that the company anticipates and is therefore ready to provide exactly what the customer wants.

- **Instant learning:** building learning directly into the company's tasks and processes and making sure that requisite information is readily at hand when it is needed.

- **Instant involvement:** using IS to communicate all relevant information to suppliers, customers, and employees and making sure everyone is prepared to deliver their products, services, or information instantly.

- **Instant adaptation:** creating a culture and structure that enable all workers to act instantly and to make decisions to respond to customers.

- **Instant execution:** building business processes so that they have as few people involved as possible (no touch), electronically cross organizational boundaries, and result in cycle times so short that they appear to execute instantly when the customer needs their outputs.

Building in the capability to respond instantly means designing the organization so that the key structural elements are able to respond instantly. For example, instant learning means building learning into the business processes. And that means using IS to deliver small modules of learning directly to the point where the process is being done. For example, at Dell Computers, assembly line workers have access to a terminal directly above their workstations. As an assembly comes to their stations, the instructions are displayed instantly on the terminal. The worker does not have to ask for the instructions, nor go anyplace to find them. IS allows this to happen. As the assembly travels to the workstation, its bar code tells the information system what type of assembly it is and which instructions to display. When the assembly reaches the table, the instructions are already there.

Very few companies are zero time organizations. Since IS are becoming ubiquitous, and since customers increasingly demand instant service, ZeroTime characteristics will be increasingly emerging in business.

▶ SUMMARY

Incorporating information systems as a fundamental organizational design component is critical to company survival. Organizational strategy includes the organization's design, as well as the manager's choices that define, set up, coordinate, and control its work processes. Organizational designers today must have a working knowledge of what information systems can do and how the choice of information system will affect the organization itself.

Information technology affects organizational design in several ways. It allows companies to hire differently, since information systems can be incorporated into the actual work processes. It also allows organizations to be structured differently. Information flows can facilitate or inhibit organizational structures. And new, information technology intensive organizations are increasingly appearing. Forms such as the flat, hierarchical and matrix organization are being enhanced by information technology resulting in networked organizations, t-form organizations and virtual organizations.

Information technology affects managerial control mechanisms. Traditional hierarchical organizations require managers to tightly control operating processes. Control systems insure that work is done on time, properly, and on budget. Control activities such as monitoring, evaluating, providing feedback, compensating, rewarding, and motivating are all affected by the use of information systems. It is the job of the manager to insure the proper control mechanisms are in place and the interactions between the organization and the information systems do no undermine the managerial objectives.

▶ DISCUSSION QUESTIONS

1. IT allows companies to hire differently. Think about a job you have had and describe the hiring process. How might information technology change the type of person hired for that job?

2. How might IT change a manager's job?

3. Is monitoring an employee's work on a computer a desirable or undesirable activity from a manager's perspective? From the employee's perspective? Defend your position

4. E-mail has made communications between individuals much easier. Give an example of a type of communication that would be inappropriate if it only took place over e-mail. What is an example of an appropriate communication for e-mail?

5. Consider the brief description of the zero time organization. What is an example of a control system that would be critical to manage for success in the zero time organization? Why?

▶ *CASE STUDY 2-1*

Mary Kay, Inc.°

Mary Kay, Inc. sells facial skin care products and cosmetics around the globe. The business model is to provide one-on-one, highly personalized service, and the company had sales of more than $2 billion in 1998. Over 500,000 Independent Beauty Consultants (IBCs) sell in 29 markets worldwide. Each IBC runs his or her own business, in which he or she develops a client base, then provides services and products for sale to that client base. The IBCs are, themselves, entrepreneurs who build their own business.

The business strategy has evolved to include e-commerce. According to Kregg Jodie, senior Vice President and CIO, "E-commerce has enabled us to develop a high-tech strategy to conduct business more efficiently and retain our unique focus on high-touch, personalized service."

The e-commerce system put in place had two major components: mymk.com and Mary Kay InTouch. Mymk.com gave IBCs the ability to create instant online sites where customers can shop anytime directly with their personal IBC. Mary Kay

---

° Adapted from "Mary Kay, Inc." *Fortune Magazine,* November 8, 1999, Microsoft supplement, p. 5.

InTouch streamlined the ordering process by automatically calculating discounts, detecting promotion eligibility, and providing a faster way to transact business with the company. Jodie explained, "Consultants can now conduct business with the company at a time convenient for them. The product catalog is always up to date and inventory data is accessed in real time so backorders are noted during the order process." The system is also integrated with the supply chain management system, giving greater visibility to the manufacturing process of demand patterns.

Discussion Questions:

1. The case describes the business strategy and IS. If these systems were put in place without changing any of the organizational systems, what would you expect to happen? Would the systems be used by IBCs without specific motivation to do so? Why?

2. What changes would you suggest Mary Kay, Inc. managers make in their management systems order to realize the intended benefits of the new systems? Specifically, what types of changes would you expect to make in the evaluation systems, the reward systems, the training systems, and the hiring systems?

3. What business processes are affected by the new systems? How will they be affected?

Characteristics of an Information Age Organization

In 1988, three professors at the Harvard Business School predicted what the key characteristics would be for the information age organization, and they were very close to what has happened. Below is a summary of these characteristics related to three dimensions: organizational structure, management processes, and human resources.

These characteristics, shown in Figure 2.5, help a manager understand how information systems have impacted organizations. Information age organizations have a different organization structure because they achieve benefits of small and large scale simultaneously, because they have flexible structures, because they blur the lines of controls, and because they focus on projects and processes. They have different management processes because they have designed these processes with information systems in mind. Control is separated from reporting relationships, keeping information flowing throughout the organization. Decision making and creativity are supported by information systems, which retain corporate history, experiences, and expertise in ways non-information-based organizations cannot achieve. Finally, human resources are different because individuals are better trained and therefore are able to work more autonomously. The work environment is increasingly engaging and exciting, due art to the velocity at which business happens. Management is not seen as the goal to which all workers aspire, and that does not detract from the workers' value, ambition, or abilities.

Understanding the information age organization will help general managers become better managers. These characteristics speak to a very different organization than the ones existing in the past. And with the explosion of the Internet and Web applications, newer organization models are sure to come.

Dimension	Characteristics
Organizational Structure	Companies have benefits of small scale and large scale simultaneously.
	Large organizations adopt flexible and dynamic structures. The distinctions between centralized and decentralized control blur.
	Focus is on projects and processes instead of tasks and standard procedures.
Management Processes	Decision making is well understood.
	Control separated from reporting relationships.
	Computers support creativity at all levels of the organization.
	Information systems retain corporate history, experience, and expertise.
Human Resources	Workers are better trained, more autonomous, and more transient.
	The work environment is exciting and engaging.
	Management is a shared, rotated, and sometimes part-time job.
	Job descriptions tied to narrowly defined tasks are nonexistent.
	Compensation is tied directly to contribution.

Source: Applegate, Cash, and Mills, "Information Technology and Tomorrow's Manager." *Harvard Business Review,* November–December 1988. pp. 128–136.

FIGURE 2.5 Key characteristics for the information age organization.

CHAPTER 3

INFORMATION TECHNOLOGY AND THE DESIGN OF WORK*

In her book, *In the Age of the Smart Machine: The Future of Work and Power*, Shoshana Zuboff studied the effects on data clerks of a new computer system that automated insurance claims processing. Before the implementation, clerks processed claims by hand using paper, pencils, and ledger books. After the information technology (IT) system was implemented, the clerks used only computer keyboards and telephones—and the latter only occasionally, when they needed to call customers for clarifications.

The new IT system created confusion and workers felt distanced from the work process. The clerks did not fully understand where the data on their screens came from, or what it meant. The sensory satisfaction gained from handling paper forms and writing in ledger books was missing. The information with which the clerks worked became nothing more than streams of data, without apparent meaning or importance. Zuboff found that the clerks were "frustrated by the loss of the concreteness that had provided for them a sense of certainty and control."[1] As one benefits analyst explained, "Now we have numbers without names—no ledgers, no writing, no history, no paper. The only reality we have left is when we get to talk to a customer."

The clerks actually lost skills. A manager described the new system as requiring "less thought, judgment, and manual intervention" than the manual system it had replaced. This sentiment was echoed by a benefits analyst who prided himself on knowing, through memorization and experience, a variety of claims limitations that his job previously required him to know. After the implementation, he noted: "The computer system is supposed to know all the limitations, which is great because I no longer know them. I used to, but now I don't know half the things I

---

* The author wishes to acknowledge and thank David K. Wolpert MBA '99 for his help in researching and writing early drafts of this chapter.

[1] Zuboff, Shoshana, *In the Age of the Smart Machine: The Future of Work and Power*. New York: Basic Books, 1988. All quotes in this section are from pp. 130–135.

53

used to. I feel that I have lost it—the computer knows more." New clerks, when hired, were chosen for their ability to use the computer, not for their ability to understand the processes of the insurance business.

The work itself became more routine and mechanical. One analyst distilled his work description down to "pushing buttons." Other employees observed that whereas they used to work with or for their supervisors, they now worked mainly with machines. The decreased level of human interaction was upsetting to many employees, and some resisted the change imposed upon them.

Although the automation of work may increase productivity and cut costs, it can also lower morale and job satisfaction and cause employees to lose skills. These drawbacks can themselves cause additional problems, such as increased employee turnover or absenteeism, which ultimately may lead to dropping productivity.

In Chapter 1, the Information Systems Strategy Triangle suggested that changing information systems (IS) would result in changes in organizational characteristics. The clerical work described above is an example of that. While the deployment of IS was done for business reasons, there were consequences in the organization that were not anticipated. Workers' skills were underutilized in some ways and workers were not skilled in using the IS. They were unable to successfully do the automated job. Instead, they preferred the manual methods. The managers of this implementation did not make adequate changes in the organizational strategy to support the changes made in the IS.

Chapter 2 explored how IT influences the design of organizations. This chapter examines how IT affects work at an individual—rather than an organizational—level. It explores issues of changing the nature of work, IT's impact on different types of workers, and the rise of new work environments. This chapter looks at how IT has enabled and facilitated a shift toward work that creates, disseminates, and applies knowledge. It will examine how work is changed, where work is done, and how work is managed. The terms IS and IT are used interchangeably in this chapter, and only basic details are provided on technologies used. The point of this chapter is to look at the impact of IS on the way work is done by individual workers. This chapter should help managers understand the challenges in designing technology-intensive work and develop a sense of how to address these challenges.

▶ JOB DESIGN FRAMEWORK

A simple framework can be used to assess how emerging technologies may affect work. As suggested by the Information Systems Strategy Triangle (in Chapter 1), this framework links the organizational strategy with IS decisions. This framework is useful in designing key characteristics of jobs by asking key questions and helping identify where IS can impact the performance, effectiveness, and satisfaction of the worker. Consider the following questions:

- **What tasks will be performed?** Understanding what tasks are needed to complete the process being done by the worker requires an assessment of the specific outcomes that are needed, the inputs that are given, and the transformation needed to turn outputs into inputs.

- **How will the work be performed?** Some things are best done by people and other things are best done by computer. For example, dealing directly with customers is often best done by people, since the unpredictability of the interaction may make for a complex set of tasks that cannot be automated. Further, most people want to deal directly with other people. On the other hand, computers are much better at keeping track of inventory, calculating compensation, and many other repetitious tasks that are opportunities for human error.

- **Who will do the work?** If a person is going to do the work, this assessment is about who that person should be. What skills are needed? What part of the organization will do it and who is in that group? Will the entire group do the work?

- **Where will the work be performed?** With the increasing availability of networks and the Internet, managers can now design work for workers who are not physically near them. Will the work be performed locally? Remotely? By a geographically dispersed work group?

- **How can IS increase performance, satisfaction, and effectiveness of the workers doing the work?** Once the job tasks and the individuals doing the job are identified, the creativity begins. How can IS be used in concert with the person doing the task? How can these two resources help each other? What is the best arrangement for using IS to support the human work?

Figure 3.1 shows how these questions can be used in a framework to incorporate IS into the design of work.

► HOW INFORMATION TECHNOLOGY IS CHANGING THE NATURE OF WORK

Advances in IT have provided an expansive set of tools that make individual workers more productive and broaden their capabilities. They have transformed the way work is performed—and the nature of the work itself. This section examines three ways in which new IT alters employee life: by creating new ways to do traditional work, by creating new types of work, and by presenting new challenges in managing workers brought about by the use of IS.

New Ways To Do Traditional Work

IT has changed the way work is done. Many traditional jobs are now done by computers. For example, computers can check spelling of documents, whereas traditionally that was the job of an editor or writer. Jobs that were once done by art and skill are often greatly changed by the introduction of IT, such as the jobs described at the beginning of this chapter. Workers at one time had to have an understanding of not only what to do, but how to do it; now they often only have to make sure the computer is working because the computer does the task for them. Workers

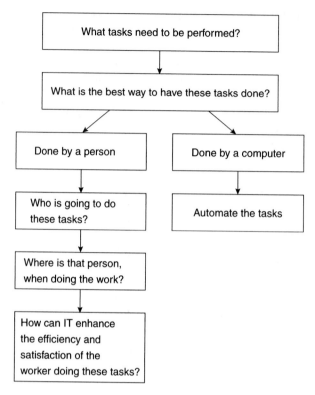

FIGURE 3.1 Framework for job design impacts.

once had to be familiar with others in their organization because they passed work to them; now they may never know those coworkers because the computer routes the work. In sum, the introduction of IT into an organization can greatly change the day-to-day tasks done by the workers in the organization.

Zuboff describes a paper mill, where paper makers' jobs were radically changed with the introduction of computers.[2] The paper makers mixed big vats of paper and knew when the paper was ready by the smell, consistency, and other subjective attributes of the mixture. For example, one worker could judge the amount of chlorine in the mixture by sniffing and squeezing the pulp. While they were masters at their craft, they were not able to explicitly describe to anyone else exactly what was done to make paper. The company, in an effort to increase productivity in the paper-making process, installed an information and control system. Instead of the workers looking and personally testing the vats of paper, the system continuously tested parameters and displayed the results on a panel located in the control room. The paper makers sat in the control room, reading the numbers, and making decisions on how to make the paper. Many found it much more difficult, if not impossible, to make the same quality paper when watching the control panel instead of personally testing, smelling, and looking at the vats. The introduction of the informa-

[2] Ibid.

tion system resulted in very different skills needed to make paper. The entire process had been abstracted and displayed on electronic readouts, and that required skills to interpret the measurements, conditions, and data generated by the new computer system.

IT change the communication patterns of workers. Workers who sit at terminals communicate with a computer for the bulk of the work day. For example, a bank clerk who sits at a terminal processing loan applications has little reason to communicate with coworkers who sit at their terminals doing the same thing. Prior to the computer terminals, the clerks sat at desks from which they could pass paper personally through the process and communicate with coworkers.

Workers who use portable computers while in the field have a different experience than their counterparts without portable systems. For example, one team of repair personnel were given portable data terminals that were connected by radio to the corporate network. They were able to send and receive short messages, as well as tap into company databases to get current customer information. Before visiting a customer, they could look at the service history and, therefore, were better prepared to fix the current problem. Likewise, when they completed their service call, they entered the information into their data terminals, which helped keep the database current and changed their job from one of simply doing services to one that included small amounts of data entry. Needless to say, the dozens of data entry personnel, whose job had been to read the data entry sheets and type the information into the computer, were no longer necessary. The data entry clerk's job was eliminated with the introduction of the field data terminals.

IT change the amount and type of information available to workers. As previously described, the service force had access to company records from their portable terminals. Accessing this information while out in the field gave the service personnel much more current information than they had previously had. In addition, they were able to get any information recorded in the database, whereas prior to the data terminals, they only would have access to whatever they brought with them. IS gave them real time access to the entire database.

In another example, salespeople had portable terminals that not only kept track of inventory, but helped them in the selling function. Prior to the information system, the salespeople used manual processes to keep track of inventory in their trucks. When visiting customers, it was only possible to tell them what was missing from their shelves and to replenish any stock they wanted. With IS, the salespeople became more like marketing and sales consultants, helping the customers with models and data of previous sales, floor layouts, and replenishment as well as forecasting demand based on analysis of the data histories stored in the IS. The skills needed by the salespeople were much more than just a persuasive manner. They needed to be able to do data analysis and floor plan design, in addition to using the computer. The skills needed by the salespeople greatly changed with the introduction of IT.

The Internet has enabled changes in many jobs. For example, within minutes, financial analysts can download an annual report from a corporate website and check what others have said about the company's growth prospects. Librarians can check the holdings of other libraries online and request that particular volumes be routed to their own clients. Marketing professionals can research competitor's products and services on the Web without alerting these companies of their curiosity. Sales jobs are radically changing to complement online ordering systems. And technical support agents diagnose and resolve problems on client computers using the Internet and software from Motive Communications. The cost and time required to access information has plummeted, increasing personal productivity and giving workers new tools.

Work has become more team-oriented. Workers can more easily send documents over computer networks to others, and they can more easily ask questions using e-mail. The Internet has greatly enhanced collaboration. Other technologies such as e-mail, video teleconferencing, and publishing systems have provided collaborative applications. These systems accelerate information exchange in a cost-effective manner. But changes in the job design accompany this technology change. Managers have redesigned jobs to take advantage of the new group communications. For example, a consulting firm regularly uses Lotus Notes, a groupware program, as the basis for project management and task execution. Consultants use the groupware program to store and analyze data, to compose and edit documents, and to research and transfer knowledge between projects. In short, the entire work process is built around the use of a groupware system, whereas in the past, work would have been done independently of the information system.

The above examples are offered to show how IS are a key component in the design of the work done by workers. IT can greatly change the day-to-day tasks, which in turn change the skills needed by workers. The examples show that adding IS to a work environment changes the work done.

Creating New Types of Work

IT has led to the creation of new or redefined jobs. The entire high tech field has emerged in its entirety over the past 30 years. In 1960, computers were only used in research organizations, and most of those were in universities. Since then, particularly since the early 1980s and the explosion of the personal computer industry, dozens of new types of jobs have been created for those who design and build computers. And consulting firms have sprouted that specialize in doing whatever is needed to keep a customer's IS working, ranging from IS strategy setting (a task not even well defined as few as 15 years ago) to designing and implementing systems.

Even within traditional organizations, IS usage has created new types of jobs, such as knowledge managers who manage firms' knowledge systems (see Chapter 9 for more on knowledge management). And the IS departments have jobs for individuals who help create and manage the technologies, such as systems analysts and database and network administrators. The Internet has given rise to many other types of jobs, such as webmasters and site designers. And virtually every department in every business has someone who "knows the computer" as part of their job.

One source estimates that in 1998, over 3.8 million people around the world were employed in positions directly in the IT sector, such as programmers, analysts, IT managers, hardware assemblers, website designers, software sales personnel, and IT consultants. Many of these jobs simply did not exist a few years ago.

New Challenges in the Work of Managers

New working arrangements have created new challenges in how work is supervised, evaluated, and compensated. When most work was performed individually in a central location, supervision and evaluation were relatively easy. A manager could directly observe the salesperson who spent much of his day in an office. It was fairly simple to ascertain whether the employee was present and productive.

Modern organizations often face the challenge of managing a work force that is spread across the world, working in isolation from direct supervision, and in which each employee works more as a member of a team than as an individual. For example, rather than report to a central office, many salespeople rely on portable computers, cellular phones, and pagers to link them to customers. The technical complexity of certain products, such as enterprise software, necessitates a team-based sales approach combining the expertise of many individuals; it can be difficult to say which individual closed a sale, making it difficult to apportion rewards.

One technological solution, electronic employee monitoring, replaces direct supervision by automatically tracking certain activities, such as the number of calls processed, e-mail messages sent, or time spent surfing the Web. Direct employee evaluation can be replaced, in part, by pay-for-performance compensation strategies that reward employees for deliverables produced or targets met, as opposed to subjective factors such as "attitude" or "teamwork." These changes are summarized in Figure 3.2.

Drawbacks to these methods do exist, however. Employee monitoring systems may be intrusive and can hurt morale. Also, tracking job performance in terms of discrete, measurable tasks can serve to disconnect the worker from the larger business process in which he or she is involved, giving him or her less opportunity

	Supervision	Evaluation
Traditional Approach	Personal. Manager is usually present or relied on others to ensure employee is present and productive.	Focus is on process through direct observation. Manager sees how employee performed at work. Subjective (personal) factors are very important.
Newer Approach	Electronic, or assessed by deliverable. As long as the employee is producing value, he does not need formal supervision.	Focus is on output by deliverable (produce a report by a certain date) or by target (meet a sales quota). As long as deliverables are produced and/or targets achieved, the employee is meeting performance expectations adequately. Subjective factors may be less important and are harder to gage.

FIGURE 3.2 Changes in employee supervision and evaluation.

to broaden his or her skills and advance in the organization.[3] Breaking down jobs into simple tasks counters an organizational philosophy that seeks to empower individuals to make significant contributions to the company as a whole.

Compensation tends to follow from performance evaluation, which can be a problem when performance is evaluated in terms of discrete tasks. Metrics for performance must be meaningful in terms of the organization's broader goals, but these metrics are harder to define when work is decentralized and monitored electronically.

For example, operators of large call centers are finding it less expensive to have agents work at home using sophisticated voice and data communications equipment than to gather them into a large facility, adding substantial overhead to operating costs. Tracking metrics, such as "average time per call" and "number of calls answered," allow the manager to monitor agents' performance. This quantitative data makes for useful comparisons, but it cannot account for qualitative variables: for example, agents who spend more time handling calls may be providing better customer service. Agents who know they will be evaluated by the volume of calls they process may rush callers and provide poorer service in order to maximize their performance according to the narrow metric. Agents providing the poorest service could in fact be compensated best if the firm's performance evaluation and compensation strategy is linked only to such metrics.

New IT also challenge employee skills. Employees who cannot keep pace are increasingly unemployable. As many lower-level service or clerical jobs become partially automated, only those workers able to learn new technologies and adapt to changing work practices can anticipate stability in their long-term employment. Firms have had to institute extensive training programs to ensure their workers possess the skills to use IT effectively.

As summarized in Figure 3.3, IT has drastically changed the landscape of work today. In the next section, we examine how IT can change where work is done.

Work	IT creates millions of new jobs, some in entirely new industries.
Working Arrangements	More work is team-oriented, enabled by communications and collaboration technologies. Geographic constraints of some professions are eliminated, enabling telecommuting.
Human Resources	New strategies are needed to supervise, evaluate, and compensate remotely performed, team-oriented work. IT requires new skillsets that many workers lack.

FIGURE 3.3 Summary of IT's effects on employee life.

---

[3] Ibid., p. 211.

▶ HOW INFORMATION TECHNOLOGY IS CHANGING WHERE WORK IS DONE

This section examines another important effect of IT on work: the ability of some workers to work anywhere, at any time. The terms "telecommuting" and "mobile worker" are often used to describe these types of work arrangements. Workers who telecommute have arrangements with their employers so they can work from home instead of coming into the corporate office. The term telecommute is derived from combining "telecommunications" with "commuting," hence these workers use telecommunications instead of commuting to the office. Mobile workers are those who work from where ever they are. They have been outfitted with the technology necessary for access to coworkers, company computers, intranets, and other information sources. They have the ability to be "mobile" and still conduct work.

Telecommuting has been around since the 1970s, but in the late 1990s it gained popularity. Companies have found that building telecommuting capabilities can be an important tool for attracting and retaining employees, for increasing productivity of workers, and for providing flexibility to otherwise overworked individuals. For example, at Cisco Systems, two-thirds of the company's employees occasionally work from home. Since this change in policy, productivity has jumped 25 percent and the company has saved $1 million in overhead expenses. Cisco's employees report that "they love setting their own schedules, skipping rush hour, spending more time with their kids, and working at least part-time in comfortable surroundings."[4] And this result goes beyond just Cisco. Nearly 75 percent of telecommuters responding to an AT&T survey said they were more satisfied with their personal and family lives than before they started working at home.[5]

IT now allows employees to work from home, at a customer's site, or while traveling. In 1998, over 20 million Americans telecommuted, and this number continues to increase. Some experts predict that in 10 to 15 years, 50 percent of all work will be performed from remote locations. Several factors that drive this trend are shown in Figure 3.4.

First, work is increasingly knowledge-based. The U.S. economy continues to shift from manufacturing to service industries. Equipped with the right IT, an employee can create, assimilate, and distribute knowledge as effectively at home as he or she can at an office. The shift to knowledge-based work thus tends to minimize the need for a particular locus of activity.

Second, the new technologies that make work in remote locations viable are becoming better and cheaper. For example, prices of personal computers have held constant or dropped slightly, but processing power has roughly doubled every 18 months.[6] The capabilities of portable technologies have increased drastically,

---

[4] Anne Tergesen, "Making Stay-at-Homes Feel Welcome." *Business Week*, October 12, 1998, p. 155.

[5] Amy Dunkin, "Saying Adios to the Office." *Business Week*, October 12, 1998, p. 152.

[6] Gordon Moore, head of Intel, observed that the capacity of microprocessors doubled roughly every 12–18 months. While this observation was made in 1965, it still holds true. Eventually, it became known in the industry as Moore's Law.

Driver	Effect
Shift to knowledge-based work	Eliminates requirement that certain work be performed in a specific place.
New technologies	Makes remotely performed work practical and cost-effective.
Changing demographics and lifestyle preferences	Provides workers with geographic and time-shifting flexibility.

FIGURE 3.4 Driving factors of telecommuting.

making mobile work more effective and productive. Telecommunication speeds through conventional computer modems or more sophisticated technologies such as ADSL have increased exponentially while costs have plummeted. The Web offers an easy-to-use "front-end" to sophisticated "back-office" applications used by major corporations, such as those that run on mainframe computers.

New softwares are changing the way certain work is performed. For instance, Hewlett-Packard salespeople use laptops equipped with sales force automation software from Trilogy. This software allows them to configure and quote customer orders at the point of sale, ensuring accuracy. This innovation has dramatically improved customer satisfaction levels, reduced sales cycle time and cut costs. The technology has rendered the sales force more productive and more mobile. Armed with Trilogy's software, the sales representatives no longer have to coordinate the sales process with others who control updated configuration and pricing information.

The product that has most enabled the mobile work revolution is the laptop computer. The laptop effectively lets workers carry their offices with them. Any work traditionally performed on a desktop computer can now be performed on the road. Recent drops in price and jumps in performance have made laptops a realistic alternative for the masses. Earlier laptops lacked processing power, hard drive space, and multimedia capabilities. Users suffered with small screens and poor resolution, which made extended work difficult, and lugged heavy or bulky units. Today's small, lightweight laptops offer screens approaching the size of desktop monitors, powerful microprocessors, ample memory, large hard drives, and extensive multimedia capabilities, all for prices competitive with similarly capable desktop computers. These advances have enabled the laptop to become a virtual work's primary tool.

Laptops have become indispensable in certain professional fields, such as consulting, where employees frequently travel and need immediate access to their files and means for electronic communication. For example, consultants with PeopleSoft, a vendor of enterprise resource planning software, can plug in their laptops at any company office worldwide and get immediate access to the corporate network without any reconfiguration. The technical constraints of interoffice travel are eliminated.

Laptop computing has revolutionized work in nonprofessional settings, as well. For example, university students frequently carry laptops from dormitory to classroom to library. Students can send and receive e-mail, work on group projects, and even take tests from home.

A new breed of portable computer, the Personal Digital Assistant (PDA), offers a cost-effective alternative for certain functions. PDAs, such as the popular PalmPilot, offer contact management, scheduling, note taking, and e-mail. Because the PalmPilot can be programmed with a simple but robust language, custom applications can be written for it. A PDA typically costs only 10 to 40 percent of the price of a laptop, it fits in a shirt pocket or purse, and is faster and easier to use for certain functions.

Another class of portable computer, the hand-held terminal, is typically designed for a single, specific function. While its limited use makes it relatively costly, it can be programmed to be optimal for a given task. Hand-held terminals are most commonly carried by delivery personnel and repair technicians. For example, United Parcel Service (UPS) delivery personnel carry them to record when and where a package was delivered, whether the intended recipient directly received the merchandise, and how payment was made on COD orders. The units also store recipients' signatures. Additionally, the devices serve as communication tools, sending information between the delivery person and UPS offices via a two-way radio installed in the delivery truck. The terminals put important information at the fingertips of UPS drivers, empowering them to manage their own deliveries by bypassing dispatchers and alleviating the need for check-ins.

Repair mechanics for Otis Elevator use the small, lightweight Keyed-Data Terminal (KDT) to send text messages via radio to individuals and groups. Previously, mechanics were notified of service calls by pager. Because the pagers did not permit two-way communication, and because the mechanics lacked portable phones, they returned service calls to a central dispatch system, often by pay phone. Mechanics lost time finding pay phones—and, more particularly, pay phones that would allow them to accept return calls from central dispatch. In contrast, the KDT sends and receives messages anywhere—even to other mechanics in the field who can help diagnose and resolve mechanical problems. The terminal empowers the mechanic to manage his own work more effectively, as well as to access the knowledge of other mechanics.

For a work force in which employees are completely mobile and can work anywhere in the world, a new level of communications technology is needed. To this end, Motorola initiated Project Iridium, an ambitious project to launch 66 satellites into orbit to provide communications coverage for the entire planet. Equipped with a portable satellite phone, anyone, anywhere, can be reached with a high degree of clarity. It is too early to tell how this innovation may change the way work is performed. But we can imagine, for example, how it might affect an engineer for a Texas-based oil drilling equipment manufacturer at work with a client in the middle of the Arabian desert. If he or she needed to ask another engineer in the company a technical question, he or she could simply dial the satellite phone. That other engineer could be anywhere—on a ship, in a plane, on an oil rig, in another desert, or back in Texas. Key technologies such as portable phones are listed in Figure 3.5.

Technology	Used By	Impacts
Laptop computers	Professionals, particularly consultants and salespeople	Eliminate constraints of travel. Enable workers to be productive anywhere.
PDAs	Mostly professionals, but devices are gaining in mass acceptance	Provides a low-cost, simple way of organizing information and communicating data.
Handheld terminals	Service professionals, particularly delivery, technical support, and service and repair technicians	Enhances productivity and adds capabilities and real-time communication.
Portable phones	Any worker who travels during his or her work routine	Allows immediate voice (and sometimes data) communication.

FIGURE 3.5 Key technologies in redesigning work.

The third driving factor of telecommuting is that it enables workers to time-shift their work to accommodate their lifestyles. For instance, parents can modify their work schedules to allow time to take their children to school and extracurricular activities. Telecommuting provides an attractive alternative for parents who might otherwise decide to take leaves of absence from work for childrearing. Telecommuting also can enable persons housebound by illness, disability, or the lack of access to transportation to join the work force.

Telecommuting provides employees with enormous geographic flexibility. The freedom to live where one wishes, even at a remove from one's corporate office, can boost employee morale and job satisfaction; as a workplace policy, it may also lead to improved employee retention. Many employees can be more productive at home, and they actually work more hours than if they had to commute to an office. Furthermore, such impediments to productivity as traffic delays, canceled flights, bad weather, and mild illnesses become less significant.

Telecommuting has disadvantages, as well. Remote work challenges managers in addressing performance evaluation and compensation. Managers of telecommuters often evaluate employee performance in terms of results or deliverables rather than by the processes used to create those assets. Virtual offices make it more difficult for managers to understand the skills of the people reporting to them, which in turn makes performance evaluation more difficult. Managers may feel they are losing control over their employees, and some telecommuting employees will, in fact, abuse their privileges. Managers accustomed to traditional work models may strongly resist telecommuting.

Working remotely can disconnect an employee from his or her company's culture. The casual, face-to-face encounters that take place in offices transmit extensive cultural, political, and other organizational information. These encounters are lost to an employee who seldom, if ever, works at the office.

Virtual work also raises the specter of "electronic immigration." Once a company establishes an infrastructure for remote work, the work often can be performed abroad as easily as domestically. While U.S. immigration laws limit the number of foreigners that may work in the United States, no such limitations exist on work performed outside this country by workers who then transmit their work to the United States electronically. Because such work is not subject to minimum wage controls, companies may have a strong economic incentive to outsource work abroad. Companies find it particularly easy to outsource clerical work related to electronic production, such as data processing and computer programming. For instance, the Russian firm ArgusSof, employs 120 programmers contracted to Western firms through the Internet.

The ability to tap human resources where they are least expensive and expertise where it is most available can create a critical strategic asset. Not surprisingly, some labor unions, immigration experts and politicians, among others, worry that this form of "immigration" may replace U.S. jobs. Firms based in less-developed nations also find economic advantage in retaining employees abroad, rather then competing with U.S. demand and salaries for IT professionals.

Business and support tasks must be redesigned to support mobile and remote workers. Everyday business tasks such as submitting employee expense reports in person (as is common when an original signature is needed on the form) and attending daily progress meetings are not appropriate if most of the workers are remote. And support tasks such as fixing computers by dispatching someone from the central IS department may not be feasible if the worker is in a hotel in a remote city. Basic business and support processes must be designed with the remote worker in mind.

Telecommuting and mobile workers are an innovation in job design that has impacts on both the employee and the manager. The employee must be responsible for completing work tasks without being in the corporate office. And managers must find new ways to evaluate and supervise those employees without seeing them every day in the office. Organizations must adapt too, building business processes to support mobile and remote workers. And support processes must be redesigned to be of use to workers who are geographically distant. Benefits and drawbacks of telecommuting appear in Figure 3.6.

Employee Advantages of Telecommuting	Potential Problems
Reduced stress, heightened morale, and lower absenteeism	Harder to evaluate performance
Geographic flexibility	Employee may become disconnected from company culture
Higher personal productivity	Telecommuters are more easily replaced by electronic immigrants
Housebound individuals can join the workforce	High level of self-discipline required

FIGURE 3.6   Advantages and disadvantages of telecommuting.

▶ INFORMATION SYSTEMS ENABLES MORE GROUP WORK

Collaboration is a key task in many work processes, and IS has greatly changed how collaboration is done. Groupware tools, such as Lotus Notes and Microsoft Outlook, and technologies, such as video teleconferencing, have made it simple and cost-effective for people around the world to create, edit, and share documents and processes in electronic formats. And collaboration is central to many types of tasks, particularly those that benefit from exchange of ideas and criticism, such as product design, medicine, and story development.

Product design tasks have seen tremendous change with the use of IS. Consider the case of the appliance manufacturer, Whirlpool. The company's product data management (PDM) system unites design teams electronically through a central data repository that stores every element of the design process, from creating CAD drawings to filing change orders.[7] Engineers at Whirlpool facilities in Europe, Brazil, India, Mexico, and the United States collaborate online to create several basic designs for an appliance. Each geographic region then customizes the boilerplate design with the options that its local market demands. PDM cuts the time it takes to design an appliance in half and results in significant cost savings for Whirlpool. Collaboration technologies also have revolutionized product design in the automotive industry. Ford Motor Company now develops cars for world markets by electronically bridging design and engineering centers in the United States and Europe using video teleconferencing and corporate intranets. This faster, more efficient communication allows Ford to move cars from design to production in less time.

Advanced video teleconferencing technologies gave birth to the field known as "telemedicine." Telemedicine enables doctors to confer with distant colleagues, share data, and examine patients in remote locations, without losing time and money to travel. For example, one manufacturer of electronic imaging equipment helps employees seek medical expertise 2500 miles away. They are able to transmit employee X-rays, CAT-scans, and other radiological records for analysis by specialists at the UCLA Medical Center. Company executives predict that the program will save $2 million a year in health-care costs over seven years while offering employees access to specialty care that is not available locally.[8]

Collaborative technologies have had an impact on creativity tasks. At *CIO Magazine*, writers brainstorm topics for articles in a Lotus Notes discussion database. Writers enter their story ideas, then others comment on and debate them and suggest sources. Stories are developed faster because writers do not have to wait for face-to-face meetings to get feedback.

▶ FOOD FOR THOUGHT: THE PRODUCTIVITY PARADOX

Have IS made workers more productive? Many researchers argue that worker productivity has not actually increased as a result of IS despite enormous spending on IS products and services. Others suggest that the evidence says that employee pro-

---

[7] Hildebrand, Carol, "Forging a Global Appliance." *CIO Magazine*, May 1, 1995.

[8] Stuart, Anne, "Telecomputing: Going the Distance." *CIO Magazine*, January 1, 1996.

ductivity is finally rising as a result of IS. This issue is debated openly and publicly as the "productivity paradox."

Why might IT not improve, or even decrease, worker productivity? Some argue that while IS appear to make workers more productive, the cost of those computers more than offsets any gains in productivity. Others suggest that it is the continual need to upgrade that makes IS less valuable. One researcher compared PCs to the telephone. "PCs may be the telephones of the '90s-standard issue to every information and knowledge worker—but we don't replace our telephones every couple of years. After the first big bite of computerization, the subsequent upgrades, new releases, and added functions are just icing on the economic cake."[9] And still others believe that most of the IT spending has been for general infrastructure, rather than high-value added applications.

Still, there are those that argue for increased productivity. They claim that returns on computers investments have been about the same as those investments in non-IT equipment. One study of 367 large companies from 1988 to 1992 found that IT investments yielded over a 45 percent return on average, after depreciation in both the manufacturing and nonmanufacturing sectors.[10] Some argue that the way productivity is calculated is flawed. Economists measure productivity as physical output per unit of input. But statistics on productivity are not available for 58 percent of all service workers. Among the remaining 42 percent, for a significant number of industries—notably banking, financial services, education, health care, and government—output is imputed solely on the basis of input.[11]

Some argue that the redesign of jobs to incorporate the use of IS is really about extending the work day, and that means more work per worker, but not more work per worker per unit time. Stephan Roach, economist at Morgan Stanley, suggests that while we are seeing more work done, it's still not increased productivity.

> What is really happening for the high value added knowledge worker is, there has been an interminable lengthening of unmeasured work time that's going into the knowledge worker task. People are online now, not only in their homes but in cars, trains, boats, and planes, working work schedules that are not even close to being captured by the official data. So what we're really seeing here is not so much our inability to measure the output of the knowledge worker that is distorting our productivity results, but we're seeing an increasing distortion from our inability to really fully cost out the labor input that is going into the output of the knowledge worker. That's a really serious problem. Productivity is not about working longer. It's about getting more out of each unit of work time. For the cerebral function or task of the knowledge worker, that value added really comes from what's between the ears rather than by stretching work days in this invasive element of taking leisure and family time away from knowledge workers.[12]

---

[9] Stuart, Anne, "Telecomputing: Going the Distance." *CIO Magazine*, January 1, 1996.

[10] Davenport, Tom, "Cheap is Beautiful." *CIO Magazine*, March 1, 1998.

[11] See, for example, work done by Erik Brynjolfsson, from MIT Sloan School of Management or Paul Strassmann, author of *The Squandered Computer*.

[12] B., E. Baatz, "Altered Stats." *CIO Magazine*, October 15, 1994.

Some suggest that new metrics are needed. "Getting payoff from technology is just not a passive exercise. People aren't yet aware of the navigation measures, because they still view technology as self-harvesting. The next generation of measures will enable organizations to take control of the rate of return."[13] Others say that traditional economic measures of productivity showed an increase from .8 to 1.6 for the first half of the 1990s. And that increase is in part credited to the use of IS.

▶ SUMMARY

This chapter has explored how IT affects the work of employees by creating new work and new working arrangements, and by presenting new challenges in employee supervision, evaluation, compensation, and training. IT affects clerical and professional workers differently, and can result in deskilling. In addition, this chapter examined how IT can either informate or automate work, or both, and looked at why some workers would resist IT implementations. While it is outside the scope of this chapter to discuss the current research on job design, the topic has been a subject of great interest to academic researchers for decades. The reader is referred to the literature for models and studies of job design in general. This chapter also looked at how new technologies and trends are driving group work, telecommuting, and mobile work environments. It also explored new technologies and collaboration tools, and how these enable new types of work and working arrangements. Finally, the role of the Internet in the changing nature of work was discussed.

▶ DISCUSSION QUESTIONS

1. Why might a worker resist the implementation of a new technology? What are some of the possible consequences of asking a worker to use a computer or similar device in his or her job?

2. How can IT alter an individual's work? How can a manager insure that the impact is positive rather than negative?

3. What current technologies do you predict will have the most impact on the way work is done? Why?

4. Given the growth in telecommuting and other mobile work arrangements, how might offices physically change in the coming years? Will offices as we think of them today exist by 2010? Why or why not?

5. How is working at an online retailer different than at a brick-and-mortar retailer? What types of jobs are necessary at each? What skills are important?

---

[13] Ibid.

► *CASE STUDY 3-1*

BASEBALL IN THE UNITED STATES°

While many cultures have some sort of sport involving a stick and a ball, none holds the attention of the fans in the United States like baseball. Since the mid-1800s when the first recorded baseball game was played, the game has evolved from a contest between amateurs to a professional business. It is no wonder that IS have begun to change the playing field.

There is a moment, just before the pitch, when the pitcher and batter lock eyes, and each tries to figure out what the other is going to do. Fans revel in it, but baseball managers and players spend careers trying to reduce the uncertainty contained in that moment through an obsession with information to know as much about the opponent as possible. Until 1999, the information was mostly contained in the collective memory of the team players and managers, and decisions were made based on hunches and instincts gleaned from scraps of information compiled through discussions with those who had the information. But with the use of IS, the old game of intuition is quickly becoming one of research and analysis both on and off the field.

For example, between innings of the 1998 World Series, the championship game which would determine the first place team that year, the New York Yankees catcher spent much of his time in the dugout thumbing through computerized "spray charts" that show where the San Diego Padres' hitters hit the ball. He also studied graphics highlighting the weak spots in the strike zone so that he could call appropriate pitches the next inning. And New York won the series that year, 4 games to 0.

IS are also used to store and sort information about players from the time they appear in their high school teams through their professional careers. Scouts gather information on performance during each game played. They also compile information on contract histories, injuries, psychological makeup, athletic strengths and weaknesses. Some even gather information like personal presence on the field and testimony from their Little League (pre-high school) coach about a player whom no other team is looking for. And players are tracked through all three tiers of the system, from amateur high school and college ball, through professional minor league play, to advanced major league time. Since teams typically have five to six minor league clubs in their network, it can be expensive to gather complete information on each player. But since players spend at least two years in the minor league before hitting for the major league, keeping tabs on everyone helps the team reduce cycle time and expense. Every team considers its scouting applications as their "crown jewels," and their leaders refuse to share specifics with anyone outside the organization.

The player's job on the field is still hitting the ball and running the bases. But the jobs off the field are changing rapidly as IS are used to assist in scouting new players, tracking statistics of teams and their competition, and assisting in decision making at all levels of the business.

Discussion Questions

1. How is the job of the catcher different as a result of the use of IS?
2. Using the scouting information has changed the job of the managers from one of intuition to one of information. Team managers run the team and are responsible for activities

° Adapted from: Koch, Christopher, "A Whole New Ballgame." *CIO Magazine*, April 15, 1999. pp. 38–47.

such as negotiating deals with new players, trading players with other teams, and pulling together the roster for each game. Describe how you think the managers' job has changed with the use of IS for scouting.

3. How has Information Systems for scouting changed *where* work is done for the baseball team?

4. What new jobs must a team have in order to successfully use IS?

CHAPTER 4

STRATEGIC USE OF INFORMATION RESOURCES*

In 1994, Dell Computer Corporation formally stopped selling personal computers (PCs) in retail stores since reaching customers in this way was expensive, time consuming, and did not fit with Michael Dell's vision of the Direct Business Model. Information technology (IT) enabled this vision. The Internet combined with their well-designed information systems (IS) infrastructure allowed customers to electronically contact Dell and design a PC for their specific needs. Dell's ordering system is integrated with their production system and shares information automatically with each supplier of PC components. This IS enables the assembly of the most current computers without the expense of storing large inventories. The cost savings is passed on to the customer, and this business model allows Dell to focus its production capacity on building only the most current products. Since profit margins are small and new products arrive quickly to replace existing products, this creative use of IS is critical to Dell's strategic leadership. The ultimate result of this strategic use of IS is a cost savings reflected in the price of systems. But, in addition, Dell executives achieved a strategic advantage in reducing response time, building custom computers for reasonable costs and eliminating inventories that could become obsolete before they are sold.

Dell used its information resources to achieve high volumes without the high costs of the industry's traditional distribution channels. This led to continued profitable results and a competitive advantage. As with most strategic advantages, other companies have followed suit and adopted Dell's direct-to-the-customer model, but antiquated IS make this a difficult, if not an impossible, task. As the competitive landscape of the PC industry changed, Dell continued to innovate using information resources and now offers customized order configuring, sales inventory management, and technical support directly from the Internet.

* The author wishes to acknowledge and thank W. Thomas Cannon, MBA '99 for his help in reasearching and writing early drafts of this chapter.

As the Dell example illustrates, innovative use of a firm's information resources can provide companies with substantial advantages over competitors. This chapter uses the business strategy foundation from Chapter 1 to help general managers visualize how to use information resources for competitive advantage. This chapter briefly recounts how strategic use of information resources has evolved and highlights the difference between simply using IS and using IS strategically. Then, this chapter looks at how information resources can be used to support the strategic goals of an organization.

The material in this chapter enables a general manager to understand the link between business strategy and information strategy on the Information Systems Strategy Triangle. General managers want to find answers to questions such as, Does using information resources provide a sustainable competitive advantage? And, What tools are available to help shape their strategic use?

▶ EVOLUTION OF INFORMATION RESOURCES

The Eras model shows how organizations have used IS over the past decades. Figure 4.1 summarizes this view and provides a road map for a general manager to use in thinking strategically about the current use of information resources within the firm.

	Era I 1960s	Era II 1970s	Era III 1980s	Era IV 2000
Primary role of IT	Efficiency	Effectiveness	Strategic	Value creation
	Automate existing paper-based processes	Increase individual and group effectiveness	Industry/ organization transformation	Collaborative partnerships
Justify IT expenditures	ROI	Increasing productivity and better decision quality	Competitive position	Adding value
Target of systems	Organization	Individual manager/group	Business processes	Customer, supplier, ecosystem
Information model	Application specific	Data-driven	Business-driven	Knowledge-driven
Dominate technology	Mainframe "centralized intelligence"	Microcomputer "decentralized intelligence"	Client Server "distribution intelligence"	Internet "ubiquitous intelligence"

FIGURE 4.1 Eras of information usage in organizations.

IS strategy from the 1960s to the 1990s was driven by internal organizational needs: first came the need to lower existing transaction costs; second, to provide support for managers by collecting and distributing information; and third, to redesign business processes. As competitors built similar systems, organizations lost any advantages they had held from their IS, and competition within a given industry was once again driven by forces that had existed prior to the new technology. As each era begins, organizations adopt a strategic role for IS to address not only the firm's internal circumstances but its external circumstances as well. Thus, in the ubiquitous era, companies seek those applications that again provide them with advantage over competition. But further, they seek applications that keep them from being outgunned by new start-ups with innovative business models or traditional companies entering new markets. For example, a plethora of "dot coms" have challenged all industries and traditional businesses by entering the marketplace armed with Internet-based innovative systems. Traditional firms have found it difficult to keep up.

The Information System Strategy Triangle introduced in Chapter 1 reflects the link between IS strategy and organizational strategy and the internal requirements of the firm. The link between IS strategy and business strategy reflects the firm's external requirements. Maximizing the effectiveness of the firm's business strategy requires that the general manager be able both to identify and use information resources. This chapter looks at how information resources can be used strategically by general managers.

▶ INFORMATION RESOURCES AS STRATEGIC TOOLS

Crafting a strategic advantage requires the general manager to cleverly combine all of the firms resources, including financial resources, production resources, human resources, and information resources. Information resources are more than just the infrastructures. This generic term, *information resources,* includes data, as well as a combination of technology, people, and processes. Seen in this way, an IS infrastructure (a concept that is discussed in detail in Chapter 6) is an information resource, as is each of its constituent components. The relationship between a firm's IS managers and its business managers is another type of information resource. This relationship can create a unique advantage for a firm. The following list highlights some of the information resources available to a firm:

- IS infrastructure (hardware, software, network, and data components)
- Information and knowledge
- Proprietary technology
- Technical skills of the IT staff
- End users of the IS
- Relationship between IT and business managers
- Business processes

Committing and developing information resources require substantial financial resources. Therefore, a general manager evaluating an information resource might consider the following questions to better understand the type of advantage the information resource might create:[1]

- **What makes the information resource valuable?** The market forces of supply and demand determine the answer to this question. Scarce information resources are likely to be either hard to copy or to substitute. Also, a demand must exist for the resource: Scarcity does not add value unless there is need. Need is driven by the competitive position of the company within its industry. A company that is exiting a market will have different needs from a company that is entering a market. For example, a firm exiting a market does not require customer acquisition information, whereas, this is critical information for a firm just entering a market.

- **Who appropriates the value created by the information resource?** The value chain model can help determine where a resource's value lies and how the appropriation can be improved in a firm's favor.

- **Is the information resource equally distributed across firms?** A general manager is unlikely to possess a resource that is completely unique. However, by surveying the firms within an industry, he or she may establish that such a resource is distributed unequally. The value of a resource that is unequally distributed tends to be higher because it can create strategic advantage.

- **Is the information resource highly mobile?** A reliance on the individual skills of IT professionals exposes a firm to the risk that key individuals will leave the firm, taking the resource with them. Developing unique knowledge-sharing processes can help reduce the impact of the loss of a mobile employee. Recording the lessons learned from all team members after the completion of each project is one attempt at lowering this risk.

- **How quickly does the information resource depreciate?** No technological advantage remains of equal value over its life. Like other assets, information resources lose value over time. A general manager should understand the rate of this decline, as well as what factors may speed or slow it. For example, consider a database of customer information. How long, on average, is the current address of each customer valid? What events in the customers' lives might change their purchasing pattern and reduce the forecasting capability of your current information?

Information resources exist in a company alongside other resources. The general manager is responsible for organizing all resources so that business goals are met. Understanding the nature of the resources at hand is a prerequisite to using them effectively. By aligning the organization's IS strategy with its business strategy, the general manager maximizes its profit potential. Meanwhile, the firm's competitors are working to do the same. In this competitive environment, how should

[1] Adapted from: Collis, David J., and Montgomery, Cynthia A., "Competing on Resources: Strategy in the 1990s." *Harvard Business Review*, July–Aug 1995, reprint no. 95403.

the information resources be organized and applied to enable the organization to compete most effectively?

► HOW CAN INFORMATION RESOURCES BE USED STRATEGICALLY?

The general manager confronts many elements that influence the competitive environment of his enterprise. Overlooking a single element can have disastrous results for the firm. This slim tolerance for error requires the manager to take multiple views of the strategic landscape. We will discuss three such views that can help a general manager align IS strategy with business strategy. The first view uses Michael Porter's five forces model to look at the major influences on a firm's competitive environment. Information resources should be directed strategically to alter the competitive forces to benefit the firm's position in the industry. The second view uses Porter's value chain model to assess the internal operations of the organization. Information resources should be directed at altering the value-creating or value-supporting activities of the firm. This chapter will explore this view further to consider the value chain of an entire industry in order to identify opportunities for the organization to gain competitive advantage. The third view uses Charles Wiseman's theory of strategic thrusts to understand how organizations choose to compete in their selected markets. Wiseman offers a strategic option generator as a tool for selecting ways to align information resources with business strategy. These three views provide a general manager with varied perspectives from which to identify strategic opportunities to apply the firm's information resources.

Using Information Resources to Influence Competitive Forces

Porter provides the general manager with a classic view of the major forces that shape the competitive environment of a firm. These five forces are shown in Figure 4.2 along with some examples of how information resources can be applied to influence each force. This view reminds the general manager that competitive forces do not derive only from the actions of direct competitors. Each force now will be explored in more detail from an IS perspective.

Potential Threat of New Entrants

Existing firms within an industry often try to reduce the threat of new entrants to the marketplace by erecting barriers to entry. Such barriers include controlled access to limited distribution channels, public image of a firm, and government regulations of an industry. Information resources also can be used to build barriers that discourage competitors from entering the industry. For example, Massachusetts Mutual Life Insurance Company has created an IS infrastructure that connects the local sales agent with comprehensive information about products and customers. An insurance company newly entering the marketplace would have to spend millions of dollars to build the telecommunication and IS required to provide its sales force with the same competitive advantage. Therefore, the system at Mass Mutual may be a barrier to entry for new companies.

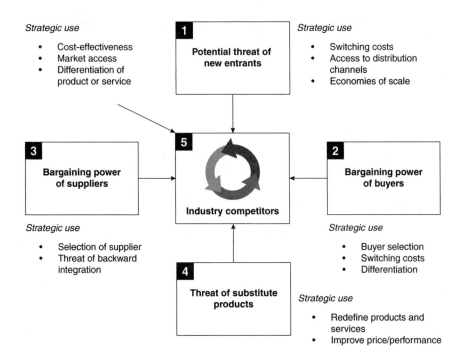

FIGURE 4.2 Porter's competitive forces with potential strategic use of information resources.

Adapted from Michael Porter, *Competitive Strategy*, 1980 and from Applegate, McFarlan and McKenney, *Corporate Information Systems Management: The Issues Facing Senior Executives*, 1996.

Bargaining Power of Buyers

Customers often have substantial power to affect the competitive environment. This can take the form of easy consumer access to several retail outlets to purchase the same product or the opportunity to purchase in large volumes at superstores like Wal-Mart. Information resources can be used to build switching costs that make it less attractive for customers to purchase from competitors. Switching costs can be any aspect of a buyer's purchasing decision that decreases the likelihood of "switching" his or her purchase to a competitor. This requires a deep understanding of how a customer obtains the product or service. For example, American Hospital Supply linked its customers' purchasing personnel directly to its own order-entry system, reducing the customers' ordering costs and providing them with access to inventory and delivery information that had not been previously available. This system reduced buyers' bargaining power in exchange for things they valued more: lower costs and useful information. American Hospital Supply created a switching cost with its information resources that discouraged its customers from using another vendor to purchase the same supplies.

Bargaining Power of Suppliers

Suppliers' bargaining power can reduce a firm's profitability. This force is strongest when there are few suppliers to choose from, the quality of their inputs is crucial to the finished product, or the volume of purchases is insignificant to the supplier.

For example, steel firms have lost some of their power over the automobile indus-try since car manufacturers have developed technologically advanced quality-control systems. Manufacturer's can now reject steel from suppliers when it does not meet the required quality levels. And through the Internet, firms continue to provide information for free as they attempt to increase their share of visitors to their websites. This decision reduces the power of information suppliers and neces-sitates finding new ways for content providers to develop and distribute informa-tion. Many Internet firms are backwardly integrating within the industry by creating their own information supply and reselling it to other Internet sites. Well-funded firms simply acquire these content providers, which is often quicker than building the capability from scratch.

Threat of Substitute Products

The potential of a substitute product in the marketplace depends on the buyers' willingness to substitute, the relative price-to-performance of the substitute, and the level of switching costs a buyer faces. Information resources can create advan-tages by reducing the threat of substitution. In the financial services industry, Merrill Lynch used innovative IS to create a product called the Cash Management Account. This account combined the benefits of a brokerage account, a money mar-ket account, a Visa credit card, and a checking account into a single product. Other firms lacking Merrill Lynch's IS were unable to provide all these services in a sin-gle account. The Cash Management Account helped attract 450,000 new broker-age accounts and allowed Merrill Lynch to build customer relationships that helped retain each account. Other brokerage firms took years to develop similar products; thus, customers could not easily find substitutes. Once substitutes became avail-able, Merrill Lynch still enjoyed an advantage since competitors had to overcome the cost to the customer of switching accounts. For a competitor to be successful, they had to offer not just a substitute, but a better product. So far none has.

Industry Competitors

Rivalry among the firms competing within an industry is high when it is expensive for a firm to leave the industry, the growth rate of the industry is declining, or prod-ucts have lost differentiation. Under these circumstances, the firm must focus on the competitive actions of a rival in order to protect market share. Intense rivalry in an industry assures that a competitor will respond quickly to your strategic actions. The banking industry illustrates this point. When a large Philadelphia-based bank developed an ATM network, several smaller competitors joined forces and shared information resources to create a competing network. The large bank was unable to create a significant advantage from its system and had to carry the full costs of developing the network by itself. Information resources were committed quickly to achieve neutralizing results due to the high rivalry that existed between the local bank competitors in Philadelphia.

As firms within an industry begin to implement standard business processes and technologies—often using enterprise-wide systems such as those of SAP and PeopleSoft—the industry becomes more attractive to consolidation through acqui-sition. Standardizing IS lowers the coordination costs of merging two enterprises and can result in a less competitive environment in the industry.

One way competitors differentiate themselves with an otherwise undifferentiated product is through creative use of IS. Information provides advantages in such competition when added to an existing product. For example, FedEx adds information to their delivery service helping them differentiate their offerings from those of other delivery services. A FedEx customer is able to track their packages, know exactly where their package is in-transit, see who signed for the package, and know exactly when it was delivered. Competitors offer some of the same information, but FedEx was able to take an early lead by using information to differentiate their services.

While many firms focus on gaining more power in relation to the five forces presented here, it is also possible to create competitive advantage by giving power in the form of information to other organizations or groups. This so-called "coopetition" model was discussed in Chapter 1. For example, Dell Computer's business strategy relies on storing information about individual customers and their orders rather than storing inventories of parts to fill potential orders. Sharing information about customers and orders with suppliers creates competitive advantages for Dell and the suppliers. The cooperative use of information allows the entire supply chain to more accurately predict inventory levels and to reduce costs incurred by inventories of obsolete products. In turn, customers benefit through lower costs and added ability to customize products at the time of purchase.

General managers can use Porter's model to identify the key forces currently affecting competition, to identify uses of information resources to influence forces, and to consider likely changes in these forces over time. The changing forces drive both the business strategy and IS strategy, and this model provides a way to think about how information resources can create competitive advantage. The alternative perspectives presented in the next section provide the general manager with an opportunity to select the proper mix of information resources and to apply them to achieve strategic advantage.

Using Information Resources to Alter the Value Chain

The value chain model addresses the activities that create, deliver, and support a company's product or service. Porter has divided these activities into two broad categories, as shown in Figure 4.3: support and primary activities. Primary activities relate directly to the value created in a product or service, while support activities make it possible for the primary activities to exist and remain coordinated. Each activity may affect how other activities are performed, suggesting that information resources should not be applied in isolation. For example, more efficient IS for repairing a product may increase the possible number of repairs per week, but the customer does not receive any value unless his product is repaired. This requires that the spare parts be available. Changing the rate of repair also affects the rate of spare parts ordering. If information resources are focused too narrowly on a specific activity then the expected value increase may not be realized, as other parts of the chain are not adjusted.

The value chain framework suggests that competition stems from two sources: lowering the cost to perform activities and adding value to a product or service so that buyers will pay more. To achieve true competitive advantage, a firm requires

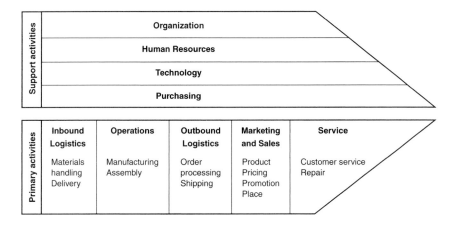

FIGURE 4.3   Value chain of the firm.
Adapted from Michael Porter and Victor Millar, "How Information Gives You Competitive Advantage." *Harvard Business Review,* July–Aug. 1985, reprint no. 85415.

accurate information on elements outside itself. Lowering activity costs only achieves advantage if the firm possesses information on its competitors' cost structures. While reducing isolated costs can improve profits temporarily, it does not provide a clear competitive advantage unless a firm can lower its costs below a competitor's. Doing so enables the firm to lower its prices so as to grow its market share.

Adding value is a strategic advantage only if a firm possesses accurate information regarding its customer. Which product attributes are valued, and where can improvements be made? Improving customer service when its product fails is a goal behind Otis Elevator's Otisline system. The customer's service call is automatically routed to the field technician with the skill and knowledge to complete the repair. Otis Elevator knows that customers value a fast response to minimize the down time of the elevator. This goal is achieved by using information resources to move the necessary information between activities. When a customer calls for service, their request is automatically and accurately entered and stored in the customer service database and communicated to the technician linked to that account. This technician is then contacted immediately over the wireless handheld computer network and told of the problem. That way the service technician can make sure he or she has both the parts and knowledge to make repairs. This provides Otis with an advantage since no time is wasted and the technician arrives at the job properly prepared to fix the problem.

While the value chain framework emphasizes the activities of the individual firm, it can be extended, as in Figure 4.4, to include the firm in a larger value system. This value system is a collection of firm value chains connected through a business relationship. From this perspective a variety of strategic opportunities exist to use information resources to gain a competitive advantage. Understanding how information is used within each value chain of the system can lead to the formation of entire new businesses designed to change the information component of value-added activities. Much of the advantage of supply chain management comes from this approach.

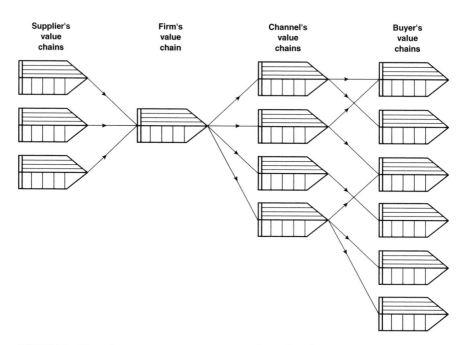

FIGURE 4.4 The value system: interconnecting relationships between organizations.

Opportunity also exists in the transfer of information across value chains. Amazon.com began by selling books directly to customers over the Internet and bypassing the traditional industry channels. Customers that valued the time saved by shopping from home rather than driving to physical retail outlets flocked to Amazon.com's website to buy books. Industry competitors Barnes and Noble and Borders Books were forced to develop their own websites—thus driving up their cost of doing business. And the new paradigm for Barnes and Noble and Borders means rethinking how their value chain works with the value proposition offered to their customers through their traditional business.

Many industries are experiencing the growth of strategic alliances that are directly linked to sharing information resources across existing value systems. An alliance between American Airlines, Marriott, and Budget Rent-A-Car called AMRIS created electronic access to provide the traveler with a single point of contact. Pooling the individual services of each company into one location saves the customer time in organizing and purchasing common travel services. Therefore, it creates strategic advantage.

Using Information Resources to Support the Strategic Thrusts of the Firm

Charles Wiseman's theory of strategic thrusts provides a comprehensive framework general managers can use to identify opportunities to use a firm's information resources competitively. Built from the concepts of Alfred Chandler and Michael Porter, it identifies five major efforts that organizations undertake to gain competitive advantages.

- *Differentiation thrusts* focus resources on product or service gaps not filled by competitors. Value can be created and offered to customers in a new form.

- *Cost thrusts* focus resources on reducing costs incurred by the firm, by suppliers, or by customers, or on increasing the costs of a competitor.

- *Innovation thrusts* focus resources on creating new products to sell or on creating new processes of creating, producing, or delivering a product.

- *Growth thrusts* focus resources on product expansion—width, depth, and length of product lines or on functional expansion—adding more of the value-adding activities in the value chain.

- *Alliance thrusts* focus resources on combining groups through acquisition, joint venture, or agreement. The purpose of an alliance is to create one or more of the following four generic advantages in the market: product integration, product distribution, product extension, and product development. Alliances require coordinating information resources of different organizations over extended periods of time.

These thrusts represent the strategic purposes that drive the use of the firm's resources. Wiseman asks three questions to refine this purpose and frame the search for specific opportunities: What is the mode of the thrust? What is the direction of the thrust? And what is the strategic target of the thrust? This chapter briefly discusses each question and then applies the overall framework to strategic information resources.

What Is the Mode?

The firm has two choices when applying a strategic thrust. Either the thrust acts offensively to improve the competitive advantage of the firm or defensively to reduce the opportunities available to competitors. For example, a firm can innovate offensively to gain product leadership in a market while others use innovation defensively to imitate the product leader, shorten product life cycles and thereby lower the profits available from new products. Each mode requires a different perspective on collecting, organizing, and using information in the organization based on the purpose of the thrust.

What Is the Direction?

A firm has two choices for direction—use the information system itself or provide the system to the chosen target. Many examples exist where firms began using a system and then gained further advantages by providing the system to a new target. FedEx originally developed its Powership system for use internally, but was able to build in customer switching costs by providing an enhanced version (Powership Plus) to its best customers. Customers were able to contact FedEx for a pickup, to track the progress of the package as it was delivered, and to handle invoicing direct from a desktop computer provided by FedEx. By changing the direction of their strategic thrust, FedEx was able to strengthen their position as innovators and make it difficult for competitors to match their level of service.

What Is the Strategic Target?

Wiseman presents three targets on which the firm can focus its strategic thrusts: supplier, customer, and competitor (see Figure 4.5). Each choice concerning a target has ramifications for the use of information resources. FedEx wanted to differentiate itself by offering a unique service in the shipping industry and selected the customer as its target. When UPS responded by providing a similar tracking service, it was targeting its competitor—FedEx—with the thrust. FedEx only had to develop a unique service for the customer; while UPS had to not only match a competitor's service but also surpass it to regain lost market share.

Wiseman has combined these questions into a strategic options generator (see Figure 4.6) to help structure decision making around the use of information

Suppliers	Customers	Competitors
Raw materials	Channel distributors	Direct
Information	Consumers	Potential
Labor	Industrial	Substitute
Capital	Reseller	
Insurance	Government	
Utilities	International	
Transportation		

FIGURE 4.5 Example of strategic targets.

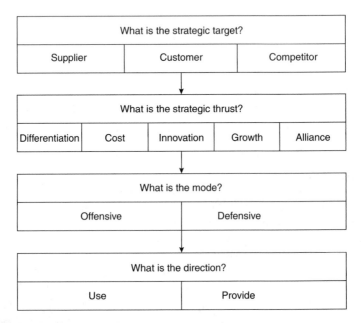

FIGURE 4.6 Strategic option generator.

From Charles M. Wiseman, *Strategy and Computers: Information Systems as Competitive Weapons,* 1985.

resources for competitive advantage. Consider the case of Dell Computer to demonstrate how this tool is used. The strategic target was the customer since the business model sought to eliminate the traditional retail channel and sell direct. This was an innovative thrust for the industry and was taken as an offensive move to lead the way in establishing a direct customer relationship. Dell employees used the IS to collect the customer's computer configuration information and send it to the manufacturing group. Dell's initial success allowed it to launch a second thrust, of the alliance type, which targeted suppliers by providing customer information down the supply chain. Recently a third thrust, of the innovation type, was targeted at customers and provided them with direct access to the computer configuration IS via the Internet. Customers could configure and place their orders without talking with a Dell employee.

▶ FOOD FOR THOUGHT: TIME-BASED COMPETITIVE ADVANTAGE

In the Internet economy, the pace of technological change continues to accelerate. Classical strategic advantages are created and destroyed based on which actions competitors take, how soon they take them and how long each action takes. But classic strategies take time to develop and implement. The 21st century will see organizations increasingly seeking to use technology to neutralize the competition as quickly as possible. Reaching individual customers and meeting their needs as close to instantaneously as possible will leave no time for competitive actions to change the customer's mind. The moment the need is expressed the product or service offer and exchange takes place. This focus on time-based competition has already begun. Consider the role that Dell Computers has played in compressing the time between the customer wanting a specific computer system and receiving that exact system on the doorstep. Dell's process can be executed in as little as 5 days from the time the customer places their order until they receive their custom-built system.

At the strategic level, the organization is confronted with increasing flows of information between itself, its stakeholders, its environment and its competitors. The combination of technology and information enables each of these information "partners" to quickly change its expectations of the future. This results in changing from one set of activities to another set that aligns more closely with the new expectations. Each of these re-alignments from an information partner requires a response from the organization. Typical planning cycles are thrown out the window, as the organization needs to respond quickly to customer, competitor, and environmental changes. The speed at which an organization can adapt its business processes to these changes will dictate the true competitive advantage that it holds in the market.

Information resources are the key to achieving a time-based advantage. Understanding how to use them is critical to the strategic success of business today. For example, every organization has been forced to build Web-based applications. Some have embraced this opportunity as a chance to reinvent themselves to create a new business strategy—one that responds instantly. Others simply post a basic Web page with no thought of the lost window of opportunity. The latter group have missed the point—time is of the essence and customers no longer accept slow, unresponsive service.

▶ SUMMARY

Each of the frameworks discussed in this chapter is interrelated. Using IS for strategic advantage requires an awareness of the many relationships that affect both competitive business and information strategies. The general manager who uses multiple tools for competitive analysis gets a clearer picture of the business situation and is more likely to organize information resources to effectively support business needs.

The value chain is useful in highlighting how the activities of the organization affect the customer. It illustrates the direct relationship between what the firm does and what the customers purchase. The competitive forces model reminds us that more than just the local competitors influence the reality of the business situation. Analyzing the five forces from both a business view and an information view will help general managers use information resources to minimize the effect of these forces on the organization. Finally, the strategic options generator offers specific questions whose answers can help guide the strategic use of the firm's information resources. Focusing on strategic thrusts helps ensure that information resources are used with the same intent as the rest of the firm's resources.

▶ DISCUSSION QUESTIONS

1. How can information itself provide a competitive advantage to an organization? Give 2–3 examples.

2. Consider Porter's five forces as described in this chapter. Pick one of them and describe how information technology might be used to provide a winning position for each of these businesses:

   a. A global airline

   b. A local dry cleaner

   c. A supermarket chain

   d. An appliance service firm (provides services to fix and maintain appliances)

   e. A bank

3. How might Wiseman's 5 strategic thrusts influence the way an organization uses information systems for competitive advantage? For each of these thrusts, suggest an example of how information systems can help an organization gain a competitive advantage.

4. It has been said that there are no sustainable competitive advantages gained from IT other than the capability of the IT organization itself. Do you agree or disagree? Defend your position.

▶ CASE STUDY 4-1

K-MART CORPORATION*

K-Mart Corporation operated one of the more successful retail operations in the discount industry. Competing with companies like Wal-Mart, Target Stores, and many others, K-Mart continued to grow and provide substantial returns to investors. The company has over 2,150

* Adapted from Megan Santosus, "Kmart Corp.: A Seasoned Performer." *CIO Magazine*, January 15, 1995; *CIO Magazine* website, www.cio.com/archive/011595_mart_print.html; and K-Mart press releases, October 14, 1999.

K-Mart, Big K-Mart and Super K-Mart stores in all 50 states in the U.S., and in Puerto Rico, Guam, and the U.S. Virgin Islands. To support operations, K-Mart developed sophisticated database marketing capabilities to track 2 billion transactions annually from more than 85 million households, in order to reach customers using targeted direct mail and eventually e-mail.

The company started as a five-and-dime store in downtown Detroit in 1899. Everything in the original store cost either 5 or 10 cents, and low prices appealed to customers. Founder S. S. Kresge's success fueled expansion to 85 stores by 1912. In 1953, a new era of retailing began expanding the variety offered by Kresge stores to other goods, such as wrapping papers, ribbons, and housedresses also at discount prices. Success continued, and in 1976 the S. S. Kresge Company opened 271 K-Mart stores. In 1977, K-Mart Corporation became the official company name, and by 1987 the company had sold all the remaining Kresge stores to concentrate only on discount merchandising. During the 1980s and 1990s, K-Mart acquired several companies including Walden Book Company, Builders Square (a home improvement retailer), Pay Less Drugstores, PACE Membership Warehouse, The Sports Authority (a sporting goods retailer), Borders (a bookstore chain), and 22 percent interest in Office Max (an office supply superstore chain). By the mid-1990s, management refocused on the core discount store business and by 1997 all of these acquisitions had been sold or divested.

An aggressive expansion plan, followed by declining profitability, resulted in a full restructuring in the mid-1990s. Every task of the turnaround was based on the mission statement:

> Kmart will become the discount store of choice for middle-income families with children by satisfying their routine and seasonal shopping needs as well as or better than the competition.

The stores have been redesigned to offer large assortments, big floor plans, and significantly improved shopping experiences. The new stores focused on selling name brand consumables, children's clothes, and home fashions. Organizational systems were also realigned with the mission statement. Associates are taught to put the customer first, including doing whatever is necessary to provide customer satisfaction. One element is the K-Mart Price Guarantee, empowering employees to match competitors price. Another was the redesign of return and exchange policies make it easy for customers to bring unwanted merchandise back. And the company also focused on enhancing the company website to not only include company information and press releases, but to support secure online shopping and specialty sites such as wellness tips from a certified fitness professional.

A key initiative for K-Mart is to continually improve the in-stock position. As recently as late 1994, Kmart stores were in stock less than 90 percent of the time, creating significant customer dissatisfaction. The target, and benchmark for all competitors in the industry, was an in-stock position of at least 98%. One avenue to achieve this objective was the Seasonal Merchandise Management System (SMMS). Holiday merchandise can exceed $2 billion. Running out of an item at that time of year severely impacts not only the immediate bottom line, but the company's reputation and the customer satisfaction in general. Customers who experience a stock-out on a item for a Christmas gift typically go to a competitor.

SMMS provides buyers and planners at headquarters with daily sales and inventory data. That means seasonal goods can be managed differently. Inventory and pricing decisions can be based on sales performance at the individual stores, rather than on projected trends system wide. Managers can maximize profits by keeping tabs on stores where items are selling well, and can build specific strategies for stores who need to move inventories before the season ends. Before SMMS, seasonal merchandise was managed at the corporate level, mandating chainwide markdowns when sales failed to meet projections. There was no consideration of local demand, and therefore no ability to customize sales plans for each store. Often stores where items were selling well ran out of merchandise when prices were discounted, leading to significant stock-out situations at peak season.

The system uploads sales and inventory data from each store overnight. In the morning, buyers and planners at corporate headquarters, and regional merchandising coordinators, can quickly assess the status of seasonal merchandise. Buyers and planners can view sales performance at a variety of levels such as item, department, and store or region. In addition, the system lets managers take action to meet sales targets. Items are managed end-to-end, from the decision to buy it to the stock in the store, until it is sold. That means customers experience better shopping experiences and managers can insure that their individual stores are able to meet demand at their local level.

Discussion Questions

1. What is the strategic advantage afforded K-Mart from the SMMS system? How does that system help it compete against its competition?
2. How long is the window of opportunity for K-Mart for an advantage such as that given by SMMS? That is, when do you think competitors will follow suit and implement their own SMMS?
3. SMMS is not an Internet application. Why not? Is there any significant advantage to be gained from putting it on the Web?
4. What other types of competitive advantages might K-Mart executives look for from IS in general?

CHAPTER 5

INFORMATION TECHNOLOGY AND CHANGING BUSINESS PROCESSES*

In 1988, executives at CIGNA Corporation faced a challenge: They had to radically improve operating efficiency. The company's income had fallen nearly 11 percent from the previous year. Benchmarks with other insurance industry leaders suggested that its operating costs had come to exceed what the market would bear, and, moreover, that productivity lagged significantly in some crucial areas. A review of the systems organization revealed that, not only were investments in information technology (IT) failing to support the strategic direction of the company, but, in effect, sophisticated new applications were being layered on top of existing organizations and processes, without a full understanding of how they might complement them, let alone improve them.

Accordingly, CIGNA's new chairman initiated a program to radically redesign the company's operating processes in key areas. Beginning with a relatively small volunteer unit—the reinsurance division—CIGNA concentrated on developing an in-house cadre of managers who could become expert in the processes of business transformation and begin to create an experience base that could be useful in successive redesign efforts. The successful efforts of this team in the reinsurance division were subsequently replicated in the information systems (IS) unit, adapted for various overseas groups, and then applied with tremendous success to a core unit that required substantial redirection: the property and casualty group, an 8,000 person business unit that had lost $1 billion. In all, between 1989 and 1993, CIGNA completed more than 20 reengineering initiatives, saving more than $100 million. Individual units experienced operating expenses that were cut by 42 percent, cycle

* The author wishes to acknowledge and thank Jeff Greer, MBA '99, for his help researching and writing early drafts of this paper.

times that improved 100 percent, customer satisfaction that improved 50 percent, and quality improvements of 75 percent.[1]

IT can enable or impede business change. The right design coupled with the right technology can result in changes such as CIGNA experienced. But the wrong business process design or the wrong technology can force a company into oblivion. This chapter outlines how managers can develop the perspective on business processes to effectively manage these types of change. This chapter describes key management tools used for transforming businesses: total quality management and radical process redesign. This chapter also describes an IT-based solution known as enterprise IS.

To a manager in the information age, an understanding of how IT enables business change is essential. The terms "management" and "change management" have become almost synonymous: To manage effectively means to manage change effectively. As IT becomes ever more prevalent and more powerful, the speed and magnitude of the changes that organizations must address to remain competitive will continue to increase. To be a successful manager, one must understand how IT enables change in a business, one must gain a process perspective of business, and one must understand how to transform business processes effectively. This chapter will provide the manager with a view of business process change. It will provide tools for analyzing how a company currently does business and for thinking about how to effectively manage the inevitable changes that result from competition and the availability of IT.

A brief word to the reader is needed. The term "process" is used extensively in this chapter. In some instances, it is used to refer to the steps taken to change aspects of the business. At other times, it is used to refer to the part of the business to be changed: the business process. The reader should be sensitive to the potentially confusing use of the term "process."

► BUSINESS PROCESS PERSPECTIVE

> At the heart of reengineering is the notion of discontinuous thinking—of recognizing and breaking away from the outdated rules and fundamental assumptions that underlie operations. Unless we change these rules, we are merely rearranging the deck chairs on the Titanic. We cannot achieve breakthroughs in performance by cutting fat or automating existing processes. Rather, we must challenge old assumptions and shed the old rules that made the business underperform in the first place.[2]

When effectively linked with improvements to business processes, advances in IT can enable changes that make a business more competitive. IT enables change when it makes it possible to do business in a new way that is better than before. But IT can also inhibit change, as when managers fail to adapt business processes

---

[1] Caron, J. R., Jarvenpaa, S., and Stoddard, D. "Business Reengineering at CIGNA Corporation: Lesson from the First Five Years." *Management Information Systems Quarterly* 18, no. 3, September 1994.

[2] Hammer, Michael, "Reengineering Work: Don't Automate, Obliterate." *Harvard Business Review*, July–August 1990, p. 4.

because they rely on inflexible systems to support those processes. When information technologies so inhere in a business environment that a company must adopt new technologies to survive in the marketplace, IT can also drive change—for better or for worse. Examples abound of industries that were fundamentally changed by advances in IT, and the success or failure of the enterprise has depended on the ability of its managers to adapt. This chapter considers IT as an *enabler* of business transformation: i.e., as a partner in transforming business processes to achieve competitive advantages.

Two popular concepts have been embraced in order to transform business: reengineering, or radical process improvement, and incremental, continuous process improvement, sometimes discussed in the context of total quality management (TQM). While some believe these concepts are passé, most companies either are involved with one or both of these methods of improvement. In the late 1990s, some said that reengineering is dead. But that is not the case for many businesses. In fact, some businesses are making radical process reconfiguration a core competency, in order to better serve customers whose demands are constantly changing. Both concepts are important because they continue to be two different tools a manager can use to effect change in the way his or her organization does business. The basis of both of these approaches is viewing the business as a set of business processes, rather than a set of hierarchical functions.

Many think of business by imagining a hierarchical structure organized around a set of functions. Looking at a traditional organization chart allows an understanding of what the business does in order to achieve its goals. A typical hierarchical structure, organized by function, might look like that shown in Figure 5.1.

Each group has a core competency, and each concentrates almost entirely on what it does best. The operations department focuses on operations, the marketing department focuses on marketing, and so on. Each major function within the organization gets its own department to ensure that work is done by groups of experts in that function. Even when companies use the perspective of the value chain model (as discussed in Chapter 1), there is still a focus on functions delivering their portion of the process and "throwing it over the wall" to the next group on the value chain. These "silos" are detrimental to achieving the optimal efficiency and effectiveness, since the handoffs are often a source of resistance in the business process.

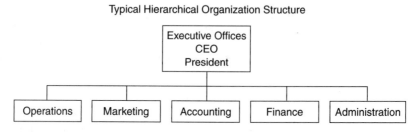

Typical Hierarchical Organization Structure

FIGURE 5.1 Hierarchical structure.

However, such organizations can experience significant suboptimization. First, individual departments often recreate information maintained by other departments. Second, communication gaps among departments are often wide. Third, as time passes, the structure and culture of a functionally organized business can become ingrained, creating a complex and frustrating bureaucracy.

The work that firms do changes over time. In a functionally organized business, each group is primarily concerned with its own set of objectives. While the executive officers typically work to ensure that these functions work together to create value, the task of providing the "big picture" to so many functionally oriented personnel can prove impossible. As time passes and business circumstances change, new work is created that relies on more than one of the old functional departments. Departments that have taken very different directions must now work together. They negotiate the terms of any new work processes with their own functional interests in mind, and the "big picture" optimum gets scrapped in favor of suboptimal compromises among the groups. These compromises then become repeated processes; they become standard operating procedures.

Losing the big picture means losing business effectiveness. After all, a business' main objective is to create as much value as possible for its shareholders and other stakeholders by satisfying its customers to the greatest extent possible. When functional groups duplicate work, when they fail to communicate with one another, when they lose the big picture and establish suboptimal processes, the customers and stakeholders are not being well served.

A manager can avoid such bureaucracy—or begin to "heal" it—by managing from a process perspective. A process perspective keeps the big picture in view and allows the manager to concentrate on the work that must be done to ensure the optimal creation of value. A process perspective helps the manager avoid or reduce duplicate work, facilitate cross-functional communication, optimize business processes, and, ultimately, best serve the customers and stakeholders.

In business, a process includes the following:

- A beginning and an end
- Inputs and outputs
- A set of tasks ("subprocesses") that turn the inputs into outputs
- A set of metrics for measuring effectiveness

This may seem like a simplistic model of a process, but the truth is that a business process is simply a set of tasks that are done to effect a transformation of inputs to outputs. Added to that are metrics to ensure critical dimensions of the process are managed. Metrics for a business process are things like *throughput*, which is how many outputs can be produced per unit time, or *cycle time*, which is how long it takes for the entire process to execute. Some use measures, such as number of handoffs in the process or actual work versus total cycle time. Other metrics may be based on the outputs themselves, such as customer satisfaction, revenue per output, profit per output, and quality of the output.

Examples of business processes include customer order fulfillment, manufacturing planning and execution, payroll, financial reporting, and procurement. A typical procurement process might look Figure 5.2. The process has a beginning and an end, inputs (requirements for goods or services) and outputs (receipt of goods, vendor payment), and subprocesses (filling out a purchase order, verifying the invoice). Metrics of the success of the process might include turnaround time and the number of paperwork errors.

The procurement process in Figure 5.2 cuts across the functional lines of a traditionally structured business. For example, the requirements for goods might originate in the operations department based on guidelines from the finance department. Paperwork would likely flow through the administration department, and the accounting department would be responsible for making payment to the vendor.

Focus on the process by its very nature ensures focus on the business' goals (the "big picture"). A process perspective recognizes that processes are often cross-functional. In the diagram in Figure 5.3, the vertical bars represent functional departments within a business. The horizontal bars represent processes that flow across those functional departments. A process perspective requires an understanding that processes properly exist to serve the larger goals of the business, and that functional departments must work together to optimize processes in light of the these goals.

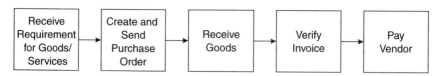

FIGURE 5.2 Sample business process.

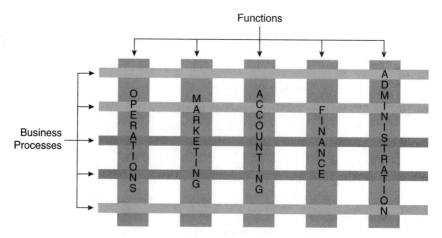

FIGURE 5.3 Cross-functional nature of business processes.

This is not to say that managers should focus strictly on processes or fail to consider functional areas or IT strategy. Just as processes exist to serve the larger goals of the business, so too do organizational and IT strategies. The Information Systems Strategy Triangle from Chapter 1 (see Figure 5.4) illustrates that both organizational strategy and information strategy should support overall business strategy. Focusing on process illuminates instances in which organizational strategy and information strategy are suboptimized and thus fail to support overall business strategy as they should.

For example, Nokia Telecommunications, the telecommunications manufacturing division of Finnish company Nokia, built their order fulfillment process to include tendering, order delivery, implementation, and after sales service tasks.[3] The company built cellular systems, switching systems, and transmission systems worldwide to companies offering mobile and fixed telecommunications services. Their order fulfillment process crossed division and product group boundaries, making it a cross-functional business process.

When managers gain process perspective, they begin to lead their organizations to change to optimize the value that customers and stakeholders receive. These managers begin to question the status quo. They do not accept "because we have always done it that way" as an answer to why business is conducted in a certain way. They concentrate instead on specific objectives and results. They begin to manage processes by:

- Identifying the customers of processes
- Identifying these customers' requirements
- Clarifying the value that each process adds to the overall goals of the organization

Finally, such managers begin to change the culture of the organization itself. By actively managing processes, managers share their perspective with other members of the organization until the organization itself becomes more process focused.

FIGURE 5.4 The Information Systems Strategy Triangle.

---

[3] For more details on Nokia's efforts see Jarvenpaa, S., and Tuomi, Ilkka, "Nokia Telecommunications: Redesign of International Logistics." Harvard Business School case study 9-996-006, September 1995.

To summarize, a process perspective recognizes that businesses operate as a set of processes that flow across functional departments. It enables a manger to analyze the business' processes in light of its larger goals. Finally, it provides a manager with insights into how those processes might better serve these goals.

▶ THE TOOLS FOR CHANGE

Once a manager gains a process perspective, he or she can learn to recognize when an organization will benefit from improving some of its processes. This section provides a discussion of ways in which managers can change processes.

One way managers can improve processes is with small, incremental changes. TQM is the process by which managers make such changes to improve business processes over time. This improvement process generally involves the following:

- Choosing a business process to improve
- Choosing a metric by which to measure the business process
- Enabling personnel involved with the process to find ways to improve it according to the metric

Personnel often react favorably to TQM because it gives them control and ownership of improvements and, therefore, renders change less threatening.

TQM approaches work well for tweaking existing processes, but more radical changes require more direct management. Radical redesign enables the organization to attain more aggressive improvement goals (again, as defined by a set of metrics). Industry terms for radical redesign include *business process redesign* (BPR) and *reengineering*. The goal of BPR or reengineering is to make a breakthrough impact on key metrics.

The difference in the TQM and BPR approaches over time is illustrated by the graph in Figure 5.5. The vertical axis measures in one sense, how well a business process meets its goals. Improvements are made either incrementally or radically. The horizontal axis measures time.

Not surprisingly, BPR typically faces greater internal resistance than will TQM. For this reason, managers should use BPR instead of TQM only when they require radical change: for instance, when the company is in trouble, when it imminently faces a major change in the operating environment, or when it must change significantly in order to outpace its competition.

Industry experts Hammer and Champy define business reengineering as "[t]he fundamental rethinking and radical redesign of a business process to achieve dramatic improvements in performance."[4] Petrozzo and Stepper define the same term as "[t]he concurrent redesign of processes, organizations, and their supporting information systems to achieve radical improvement in time, cost, quality, and customers'

---

[4] Hammer, M., "Reengineering Work: Don't Automate, Obliterate." *Harvard Business Review*, July–August 1990.

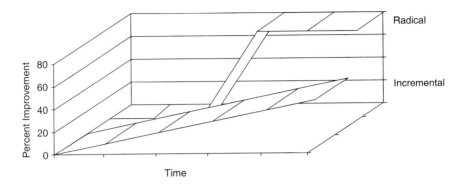

FIGURE 5.5 Comparison of radical and incremental improvement.

regard for the company's products and services."[5] Both of these definitions require that business processes improve against carefully determined metrics of success. Key aspects of both BPR and reengineering include:

- The need for radical change
- Thinking from a cross-functional process perspective (or, as consultants like to say, "thinking outside the box")
- Challenging old assumptions
- Networked (cross-functional) organizing
- Empowerment of individuals in the process
- Measurement of success via metrics tied directly to business goals

Radically Redesigning Processes

There are many different and effective approaches to radical process change. Each consultant or academic has a pet method. The methods have three elements in common:

- They begin with a vision of which performance metrics best reflect the success of overall business strategy.
- They make changes to the existing process.
- They measure the results using the predetermined metrics.

The diagram in Figure 5.6 illustrates a general view of how radical redesign methods work. A new process is envisioned, the change is designed and implemented and the impact is measured. A more specific method for changing a business process is illustrated in Figure 5.7. In this process, feedback from each step can affect any of the previous steps.

[5] Petrozzo, Daniel, and Stepper, John, *Successful Reengineering.* Princeton, NJ: Van Nostrand Reinhold, 1994.

FIGURE 5.6 Conceptual flow of process redesign.

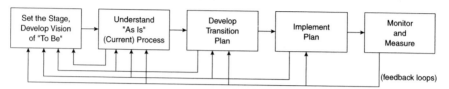

FIGURE 5.7 Method for redesigning a business process.

A notable difference between specific BPR methods is that some methods analyze the current business process before designing a new business process while others, such as reengineering, set a vision of how the process should be before analyzing the current process. The method illustrated in Figure 5.7 begins with a vision how the process should be, but some managers prefer to map the current process to completely understand how it exists in the status quo before considering redesign options. Both approaches are valid; a manager should choose based on which approach seems most appropriate to the task at hand. For example, a manager may decide that mapping the current process is unnecessary because a cursory understanding of the process coupled with a clear idea of the overriding business strategy is sufficient for an effective redesign.

Whichever approach a manager takes, he or she will follow more or less the same general methodology. He or she must begin by stating a case for action. This means that the manager must understand what it is about current conditions that makes them unfavorable and, in general terms, how business processes must change to address them. Next, the manager must assess the readiness of the organization to undertake change. Only after stating a compelling case for action and addressing organizational readiness should the manager identify those business processes that he or she believes should change to better support the overall business strategy and build a redesign team.

If the manager chooses to try to fully understand the business process as it currently exists, he or she should map it. The objective of process mapping is to understand and communicate the dimensions of the current process. Typically, process engineers will begin the process mapping procedure by defining the scope, mission, and boundaries of the business process. Next, the engineer will develop a high-level overview flowchart of the process. After that, he or she will develop a detailed flow diagram of everything that happens in the process. The diagram will use active verbs to describe activities and will identify all actors, inputs, and outputs of the process. After developing the detailed diagram, the engineer will verify it for accuracy with the actors in the process and adjust the diagram accordingly.

Another key task at this stage is to identify metrics of business success that clearly reflect both problems and opportunities in the status quo and that can measure the effectiveness of any new processes. It is vitally important that the metrics chosen relate to the key business drivers in any given situation. Examples include cost of production, cycle time, scrap and rework rates, customer satisfaction, revenues, and quality.

The manager's next step is to develop a transition plan. The plan should state the vision that the manager has for the new process as clearly and concretely as possible. The plan should include an initial design of the new process that directly addresses the metrics that, in turn, address the goals of the business. Finally, the transition plan should include the contents of an implementation plan. The implementation plan should include the following:

- An overview of the existing business process
- The names of the members of the improvement team
- Symptoms, known problems, and known opportunities to be addressed by the change
- The vision, objectives, and case for action for the new process
- An overview of the redesign methodology
- The new process design
- An analysis detailing the risks of transition
- A schedule and a list of deliverables
- Resources that the transition will require
- Resources that are available for the transition
- Signatures of personnel who own the transition

Consider CIGNA and how they managed this process. The company began by building a core reengineering team of 10 specialists, high performing individuals with 5–10 years experience in CIGNA. This core team had five specialists with strong systems experience, and the rest had operations, business, or business analysis experience. In fact, CIGNA used this group to train future leaders. Each of these managers had 12–18 months experience in the reengineering group to help build a culture of acceptance. The demand for project was so high that they brought on extra help using outside consultants and had a cadre of consultants waiting in the wings to assist when needed.

The CIGNA Reinsurance division (CIGNA-RE) was the pilot project for the company. Benchmarks set by the reengineering group suggested that CIGNA-RE could be magnitudes more effective with the same number of employees, the CIGNA-RE business portfolio needed to change, and the cost structure of CIGNA-RE was too high for their market. The group was ready to make radical change. The president of the division was even more enthused when she heard that she would get a new information system as part of the process.

The core reengineering team worked with CIGNA-RE managers to build a plan for reengineering its business. The president devoted significant time to this program—50–75 percent of her time during the design phase and 30–50 percent during the implementation phase. She built an executive committee consisting of her senior staff, which met regularly with the reengineering team.

The redesigned processes meant that new client-server IS, new individual skills, and new managerial skills would be needed. The IS change was particularly difficult because the new client-server platform meant that many of the IS people had to be replaced in order to acquire the right skills in a short amount of time. The administrative and systems staffs were reorganized into teams. Everyone in CIGNA-RE had to apply for a job in this new organization, since none of the original jobs were left. This had the much desired effect of breaking old habits and signaling major change. Much management effort was spent forging a new culture that focused on customer satisfaction and accountability. CIGNA-RE was able to achieve results within about 18 months, while reducing complexity. They reported a 40 percent reduction in operating costs, and magnitudes of improvement in process cycle times. The number of different IS applications they used was reduced from 17 applications to 5. And 27 job descriptions were reduced to 5.

CIGNA-RE's president suggested that the improvement program at CIGNA will never be done. She wants to promote a climate of adaptability within her division to make sure that better ways to do business are continually embraced by her organization. Further, CIGNA managers saw many similar improvements in their divisions from subsequent reengineering efforts.

By 1993, interest in reengineering had died down at CIGNA, so the CIO took direct measures to resurrect it. He hired a new head of the reengineering team, and he sought a large, significant area in which to apply the tools. The property and casualty area had seen significant losses over the years, and they were ready to examine how to turn themselves around. The effort was significantly bigger than any attempted at CIGNA before. But the results were achieved in 24 months, during which time 4 of 8 senior managers were replaced in order to assure the new culture could thrive. Today the CIGNA culture includes acceptance for IS-based transformation of business processes.

The implementation of a radically redesigned process presents any business with a highly complex set of challenges. Strong project management skills are critical (see Chapter 10). Before turning to these matters, however, this chapter discusses a recent development in IS that is currently supporting—and in some cases shaping—large-scale changes in business processes: enterprise information systems (EIS).

Enterprise Information Systems

Over the past few years many managers turned to vendors offering systems known as enterprise information systems, or simply enterprise systems, as a tool to support or in some cases drive changes in business processes. An enterprise system is a comprehensive software package that incorporates all modules needed to run the operations of a business. Specifically, an enterprise system would include modules to support the following:

- Manufacturing (materials management, inventory, plant maintenance, production planning, routing, shipping, purchasing, etc.)
- Accounting (general ledger, accounts payable, accounts receivable, cash management, forecasting, cost-accounting, profitability analysis, etc.)
- Human resources (employee data, position management, skills inventory, time accounting, payroll, travel expenses, etc.)
- Sales (order entry, order management, delivery support, sales planning, pricing, etc.)

The popularity of enterprise systems was based on the fact that most organizations needed a way to manage the jungle of IS in their company. Enterprise systems were designed to help large companies manage the fragmentation of information stored in hundreds of individual desktop, department, and business unit computers across the organization. In many organizations, the Management Information System (MIS) department was not able to keep up with the changing business demands of their operational counterparts. General managers routinely complained that the MIS department could not complete the design and installation of new modules needed to run the business in a timely manner. Further, the IS that were installed had grown, and many were underperforming. Systems that should be able to interconnect were not able to do so, errors increasingly occurred in systems that were critical to the business, and there was tremendous redundancy of information stored in each application. The threat of the Year 2000 problem (Y2K, a problem where computers used two digits instead of 4 digits to represent the year, making it impossible to distinguish between the years such as 2000 and 1900) pushed many senior managers to outside vendors who offered Y2K compliant enterprise systems as the solution for their companies. And finally, in some cases, business processes were so untamed that managers thought installing an enterprise system would be a way to standardize processes across their businesses. These managers wanted to transform their business processes by forcing all to conform to a software package.

By far the most widely used enterprise system was offered by a German company, SAP. Their product, R/3, was installed or being implemented in virtually every large, global corporation. But there were many other competitors, including PeopleSoft, Baan, and Oracle. And many other vendors offered a selection of software systems that, when integrated, formed an enterprise system.

The benefit of an enterprise system is that all modules of the information system easily communicate with each other, offering enormous efficiencies over stand-alone systems. In business, information from one functional area is often needed by another area. For example, an inventory system stores information about vendors who supply specific parts. This same information is required by the accounts payable system, which pays vendors for their goods. It makes sense for these two systems to be integrated in order to have accurate and current records of vendors.

The obvious benefits notwithstanding, implementing an enterprise system represents an enormous amount of work. Using the same simple example above, if an organization has allowed both the manufacturing and the accounting departments to keep their own records of vendors, then most likely these records are kept in somewhat different forms (one department may keep the vendor name as "IBM," the other as "International Business Machines" or even "IBM Corp," all of which make it difficult to integrate the databases together). Such data inconsistencies must be addressed in order for the enterprise system to provide optimal advantage.

Moreover, while enterprise system systems are flexible and customizable to a point, most also require business processes to be redesigned in order to achieve optimal performance of the integrated modules. The flexibility in the EIS comes from being able to change parameters in a process, such as the type of part number the company will use. However, all systems make assumptions about how the business processes work, and at some level, customization is not possible. For example, one major Fortune 500 company refused to implement a vendor's enterprise system because the company manufactured products in lots of "one" and the vendor's system would not handle the volume of lots of "one" the company experienced. For companies whose competitive advantage is their business processes, enterprise systems may not be the appropriate answer. Implementing enterprise systems requires organizations to make changes in their organization structure, and often in the individual tasks done by workers. Recall in Chapter 1, the Information Systems Strategy Triangle suggests that implementing an information system must be accompanied with appropriate organizational changes to be effective. Implementing an enterprise system is no different. For example, who will now be responsible for entering the vendor information that was formerly kept in two locations? How will that information be entered into the enterprise system? The answer to such simple operational questions often require managers at a minimum to modify business processes, and more likely to redesign them completely to accommodate the information system. A *Harvard Business Review* article from 1998 described the horrors for some companies.[6]

> FoxMeyer Drug argues that its system helped drive it into bankruptcy. Mobile Europe spent hundreds of millions of dollars on its system only to abandon it when its merger partner objected. Dell Computer found that its system would not fit its new, decentralized management model. Applied Materials gave up on its system when it found itself overwhelmed by the organizational changes involved. Dow Chemical spent seven years and close to a half a billion dollars implementing a mainframe-based enterprise system; now it has decided to start over on a client-server version.

Managers considering the implementation of an enterprise system must consider many issues that are outside the scope of this chapter. Some of those questions include clarifying how much integration is needed between disparate business

---

[6] Davenport, Thomas H., "Putting the Enterprise into the Enterprise System." *Harvard Business Review*, July–August 1998, pp. 121–135.

units, and what generic processes are in the best interest of the firm. Other questions relate to setting business strategy and operational competitiveness.

The relevant issue for this chapter, then, becomes how to optimize the design of the business process and the enterprise system. When is it appropriate to use the enterprise system to drive business process redesign, and when is it appropriate to redesign the process first, then implement an enterprise system?

There are several instances when it is appropriate to let the enterprise system drive business process redesign. First, when an organization is just starting out and processes do not yet exist, it is appropriate to begin with an enterprise system as a way to structure operational business processes. After all, most of the processes embedded in the "vanilla" enterprise system from a top vendor are based on the best practices of corporations who have been in business for years. Second, when an organization does not rely on its operational business processes as a source of competitive advantage, then using an enterprise system to redesign these processes is appropriate. For example, a major computer manufacturer relies on its ability to process orders faster than its competitors. It would not be to that organization's benefit to use an enterprise system to drive the redesign of the process because doing so would force the manufacturer to restrict its process to that which is available from enterprise system vendors. And, more importantly, any other manufacturer could then copy the process, neutralizing any advantages. Third, it is reasonable for an organization to let the enterprise system drive business process change when the current systems are in crisis and there is not enough time, resources, or knowledge in the firm to fix them. While this is not an optimal situation, managers must make tough decisions about how to fix the problems. A business must have working operational processes, and using an enterprise system as the basis for process design may be the only workable plan. That was the situation for many companies faced with Y2K.

Likewise, it is sometimes inappropriate to let an enterprise system drive business process change. As previously alluded, when an organization derives a strategic advantage through its operational business processes, it is usually not advisable to buy a vendor's enterprise system. Using a standard, publicly available information system that both the company and its competitors can buy from a vendor may mean that any competitive advantage is lost. The manufacturer described earlier decided not to use a standard integrated enterprise system because doing so would have meant redesigning its order fulfillment process, which had become the cornerstone of its success. Furthermore, the manufacturer believed that relying on a third party as the provider of such a strategic system would be a mistake in the long run. Should the system have had a bug or have needed to be redesigned to accommodate unique aspects of the business, the manufacturer would have been forced to negotiate with the enterprise system vendor to get it to modify the enterprise system. With a system designed in-house, the manufacturer was able to ensure complete control over the IS that drive its critical processes.

Compaq Computer Corporation found a middle ground when considering implementing an enterprise system. As described in *Harvard Business Review,*[7]

[7] Davenport, Ibid.

Compaq was changing their business strategy from a build-to-inventory to a build-to-order company. In an effort to quickly transform the company, managers agreed that a new enterprise system would make sense. However, they realized that the key to become a build-to-order company was to have a unique order and fulfillment system. Compaq managers decided to build their own module for this business process. To insure compatibility with the vendor's enterprise system, the module was written in the same language as the enterprise system and was designed to be integrated into the other modules. Compaq's installation took longer than a standard enterprise system installation and cost more, but it was able to provide Compaq with the advantages of enterprise systems without costing the company the advantages it sought in its new business strategy.

A manager must therefore make several critical decisions when considering business process redesign and enterprise system. First, a manager should decide whether there is strategic advantage to the company from the operational processes under consideration for redesign. If not, then an enterprise system might be appropriate. If so, then the manager should assess whether implementing an enterprise system could significantly hurt the company. If not, then again an enterprise system might be appropriate. If so, then the manager should analyze the source of this risk. If the risk stems from asking people to change, a change management program may make the enterprise system a reasonable choice. If the risk is that changing the process would hurt the business strategically, then most likely an enterprise system would be an inappropriate decision for the organization.

▶ FOOD FOR THOUGHT: REVOLUTIONARY DESIGN BUT EVOLUTIONARY IMPLEMENTATION

This chapter has described a business as a set of processes and has outlined methods for changing these processes. But while all processes can be improved in some way, there is a school of thought that believes reengineering or revolutionary change is not always the right tool to use, even when substantial change is required. This section addresses the concept of *revolutionary design* of change coupled with *evolutionary implementation* of change.

The original concept of reengineering described a theory of radical change through process design. The article by Michael Hammer that is cited in the opening of this chapter—by far the best-known publication on reengineering—describes the concept of process design as one of starting with a "clean sheet of paper." The idea was not to let the existing process, nor any of the potential constraints in the environment, get in the way of the redesign. Starting with a greenfields approach, in theory, allowed the process designers to create the best possible design. But the implementation of these new processes proved more difficult than most organizations were willing to tolerate.

There have been dozens of stories of companies who have attempted reengineering, only to fail to realize the advantages they sought. Radically changing a business is not an easy task. Research has been done to determine why companies failed to reach their goals. Some of the more common reasons are summarized in Figure 5.8.

Lack of senior management support at the right times and the right places. Some estimates suggest that 50 percent or more of a senior manager's time is necessary to make radical change successful.

Lack of a coherent communications program. Radical change can scare many employees who are unsure if they will have a job when the changes are completed. Companies who fail to communicate regularly, clearly, and honestly have an increased risk of failure.

Introducing unnecessary complexity into the new process design. For example, some companies try to introduce new IS that are unproven or need extensive customization and training. That adds a level of complexity to a reengineering project that is often difficult to manage.

Underestimating the amount of effort needed to redesign and implement the new processes. Companies, of course, do not stop operation while they reengineer, and therefore, many companies find themselves spread too thin when trying to reengineer and continue operations. Some have compared it to "changing airplanes in midair"—not impossible, but definitely not easy.

Combining reengineering with downsizing. Many organizations really just want to downsize their operations and get rid of some of their labor costs. They call that initiative reengineering instead of downsizing, and think their employees will understand that the new business design just takes fewer people. Employees are smarter than that, and often make the implementation of the radical design impossible.

FIGURE 5.8   Reasons reengineering fails to meet objectives.

Instead, researchers have found that many reengineering projects employ a radical design, but an evolutionary implementation plan.[8] When companies face a crisis, they may have no choice but to implement radical redesign in a revolutionary way. But in many cases, the objectives of a reengineering project take a minimum of several months to complete. Companies find that too much change too quickly can do more harm than good to their short-term business objectives.

Thus, a more common approach is to use reengineering techniques to **design** a radical new process, but to **implement** it in smaller, more digestible steps. Evolutionary implementation can reduce the risk of failure, ease the adaptation of new processes, and allow individual employees to participate more fully. Of course, evolutionary implementation also means that it will take longer to realize benefits from the redesign. Individuals lose sight of the goal if it takes too long to get there. And some organizations face rapidly changing business environments that make the implementation goal a moving target; a longer implementation period risks reaching the goal too late.

The revolutionary implementation path will work for organizations under certain coinciding conditions: the change will occur in a small, self-contained unit; a

[8] Stoddard, D. and Jarvenpaa, S. "Reengineering Design is Radical, Reengineering Change is Not!" Harvard Business School case note number 196–037, July 1995.

real performance crisis exists; and the organization can devote extensive resources to the implementation.[9] A company lacking these conditions increases its risk of failure if it proceeds with a radical implementation plan.

Let us return for a moment to the business example discussed in this chapter: CIGNA's phased reengineering effort. CIGNA's implementation strategy for each phase was quite aggressive. Yet its CFO, Jim Stewart, remarked that only about 50 percent of the reengineering initiatives were successful the first time, even with senior managers' backing.[10] And while the designs were radical, in some cases the implementation took well over 12 months (considered a long time by traditional redesign consultants).

But CIGNA's effort to institutionalize redesign of business processes continues. The CFO commented,

> The institutionalization of reengineering requires constant reinforcement. You need trial after trial, project after project. After you have built a critical mass of believers, the management practice [of reengineering] begins to take on a life of its own.[11]

▶ SUMMARY

This chapter has explored the relationship between transformation of a business and information systems. IS can enable or impede business change. IS enables change by providing both the tools to implement the change, and the tools on which the change is based. But IS can impede change, particularly when the desired information is mismatched with the capabilities of the IS.

To understand the role IS plays in business transformation, one must take a business process, rather than a functional, perspective. Business processes are a well-defined, ordered set of tasks that have a beginning and an end, a set of associated metrics, and cross-functional boundaries. Most businesses operate business processes, even if their organization charts are structured by functions rather than by processes.

Making changes in business processes is typically done through either TQM or BPR techniques. TQM techniques tend to imply an evolutionary change, where processes are improved incrementally. BPR techniques, on the other hand, imply a more radical objective and improvement. Both techniques can be disruptive to the normal flow of the business, hence strong project management skills are needed.

Enterprise information systems are large information systems that provide the core functionality needed to run a business. These systems are typically implemented in order to help organizations share data between divisions. However, in some cases EIS are used to affect organizational transformation by imposing a set of assumptions on the business processes managed by the EIS.

[9] Ibid.

[10] Jarvenpaa, S. and Stoddard, D., "CIGNA Corporation Inc., Managing and Institutionalizing Business Reengineering." Harvard Business School case study 195-097, December 1994.

[11] Caron, J. R., Jarvenpaa, S., and Stoddard, D. "Business Reegineering at CIGNA Corporation: Lesson from the First Five Years." *Management Information Systems Quarterly* 18, no. 3, September 1994.

In summary, information systems are useful as tools to manage business transformation and as tools to enable business transformation. The general manager must take care to ensure that consequences of the tools themselves are well understood and well managed.

► DISCUSSION QUESTIONS

1. Why was radical design of business processes embraced so quickly and so deeply by senior managers of so many companies? In your opinion, and using hindsight, was this a benefit for businesses? Why or why not?

2. Off-the-shelf enterprise IS often force an organization to redesign their business processes. What are the critical success factors to make sure the implementation of an enterprise system is successful?

3. Have you been involved with a company doing a redesign of their business processes? If so, what were the key things that went right? What went wrong? What could have been done better to minimize the risk of failure?

► CASE STUDY 5-1

COCA-COLA VENDING MACHINES[*]

Vending machines are often out of their most popular items, waiting for service personnel to replenish them. Coca-Cola Amatil Ltd., the company that bottles Coca-Cola in Australia and several countries in the Asia-Pacific region, has equipped about 35,000 of their vending machines with microprocessors and cellular transmitters that transfer information daily to a database at company headquarters in Sydney, Australia. The system collects sales information and can be used to analyze performance of the vending machines. There is also a link to the sales and distribution transaction processing system. Sales data are collected and transmitted, enabling service personnel to refill the machines as needed, rather than at predetermined intervals.

The microprocessors also detect faulty machines so repair technicians can be dispatched to fix them more quickly. Each machine is polled every evening to determine usage. This enables the company to do more efficient delivery routing by knowing which machines need to be filled, what product they need, and how much is needed. The information is also useful to track sales and usage trends.

Questions

1. What was the business strategy of Coca-Cola Amitil, Ltd. when it made the decision to install this new technology? What would have been the major components of the cost/benefit analysis which justified this project?
2. How does the process of managing sales of sodas through vending machines change with the introduction of this system?
3. How might this system change the process of maintenance and repair of the machines?

---

[*] Adapted from Violino, Bob, "Extended Enterprise." *Information Week*, March 22, 1999, pp. 46–63.

CHAPTER 6

ARCHITECTURE AND INFRASTRUCTURE*

NTC, a division of Nokia, manufactures switches, base stations, network multiplexers, optical line equipment, and other hardware for fixed and mobile telecommunications networks. After the telecommunications industry was deregulated and new markets began to emerge, NTC expanded rapidly from its home territories in Scandinavia. It targeted new telecommunications operators such as cable and cellular companies. By 1994, it had developed or acquired sales and service units in 28 countries. From 1993 to 1994, revenues grew by more than 50 percent, with 80 percent of total revenues coming from outside the home territories.

As NTC rapidly grew and globalized, its sales focus shifted from components to systems. This switch required its account managers to serve as contacts for all of the various product divisions, from cellular systems to switching systems and transmission systems. To fulfill these broader responsibilities, the account managers needed better support tools. They also needed to reduce paperwork, which often represented a duplication of effort. Thus, in February 1993, NTC launched an international project to provide integrated delivery of information technology (IT) support for sales and after-sales services. Specific project goals included providing a uniform customer interface, reducing order fulfillment time, and decreasing the cost of operations.

The architecture of the completed system comprised loosely coupled modules with standardized interfaces. The communication architecture used message switching with a well-defined interface standard. The infrastructure for the system was Windows NT and Oracle 7 databases.[1]

So far this text has explored the organizational, tactical, and strategic importance of IT. This chapter examines the mechanisms by which business strategy is transformed into tangible information systems (IS): IT architecture and infrastructure. The terms "architecture" and "infrastructure" are often used inter-

---

* The author wishes to acknowledge and thank Vince Cavasin, MBA '99 for his help in researching and writing early drafts of this chapter.

[1] S. Jarvenpaa and I. Touomi "Nokia Telecommunications: Redesign of International Logistics" Harvard Business School Publishing, case no. 996-006, September 1995.

changeably in the context of IT. This chapter discusses how the two differ, and the role each plays in realizing a business strategy.

▶ FROM VISION TO IMPLEMENTATION

As shown in Figure 6.1, architecture translates strategy into infrastructure. Building a house is similar: the owner has a vision of how the final product should look and function. The architect develops plans based on this vision. These plans provide a guide—unchangeable in some areas, but subject to interpretation in others—for the carpenters, plumbers, and electricians who actually construct the house. Guided by past experience and by industry standards, these builders select the materials and construction techniques best suited to the plan. When the process works, the completed house fulfills its owner's vision, even though he or she had very little to do with the actual construction.

An IT architecture, then, provides a blueprint, translating business strategy into a plan for IS. An IT infrastructure consists of physical components, chosen and assembled in a manner that best suits the plan—and therefore best enables the overarching business strategy.[2]

The Manager's Role

Even though he or she is not drawing up plans or pounding nails, the homeowner in the example needs to know what he or she can reasonably expect from the architect and builders. He or she must know enough about architecture, specifically about styling and layout, to work effectively with the architect as he or she draws up the plans. Similarly, the homeowner must know enough about construction details such as the benefits of various types of siding, windows, and insulation to set reasonable expectations for the builder.

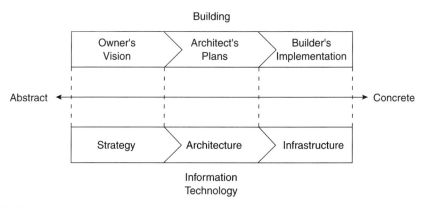

FIGURE 6.1   From the abstract to the concrete—building vs. IT.

[2] Hay, Gordon, and Rick Muñoz. "Establishing an IT Architecture Strategy." *Information Systems Management,* Summer 1997.

Like the homeowner, the manager must understand what he or she can expect from IT architecture and infrastructure if he or she is to make full and realistic use of them. The manager must effectively communicate his or her business vision to IT architects and implementers, and, if necessary, modify the plans if IT cannot realistically support them. For without the involvement of the manager, IT architects could inadvertently make decisions that limit the manager's business options in the future.

For example, a sales manager for a large distribution company did not want to partake in the discussions of providing sales force automation systems for his group. He felt that each individual salesperson could buy a laptop, if he or she wanted one, and the IT group would be able to provide support. No architecture was designed, and no long range thought was given to how IT might support or inhibit the sales group. Salespeople did buy laptops, and other personal organizing devices. Soon, the IT group was unable to support all the different systems the salespeople had, so they developed a set of standards for systems they would support, based on the infrastructure they used elsewhere in the company. Again, the manager just blindly accepted that decision. And salespeople with systems outside the standards bought new systems. Then the sales manager wanted to change the way his group managed sales leads. He approached the IT department for help, and in the discussions which ensued, he learned that earlier infrastructure decisions made by the IT group now made it very expensive to implement the new capability he wanted. If he had been involved with earlier decisions and had been able to convey his vision of what the sales group wanted to do, the interaction would have resulted in an IT infrastructure that provided a platform for the changes he now wanted to make. The IT group had built an infrastructure without an architecture that met the business objectives of the sales and marketing management.

▶ THE LEAP FROM STRATEGY TO ARCHITECTURE TO INFRASTRUCTURE

The huge number of IT choices available coupled with the incredible speed of technology advances may make the manager's task seem nearly impossible. This section considers the two steps of the process: first, translating strategy into architecture and, second, translating architecture into infrastructure. A simple framework will help managers sort IT issues. Although this framework may not encompass every possible issue, it comprehends the vast majority of those associated with effectively defining IT architecture and infrastructure.

From Strategy to Architecture

The manager must first set the business requirements for the desired IS, as shown in Figure 6.2.

By outlining the overarching business strategy and then fleshing out the business requirements associated with each goal, the manager can provide the architect with a clear picture of what the IS must accomplish. Of course, the manager's

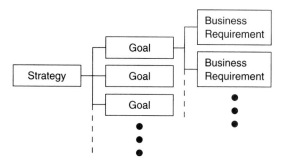

FIGURE 6.2 From strategy to business requirements.

job is not complete here. He or she must now work with the architect to translate these business requirements into a more detailed view of the systems requirements and processes that will shape an IT architecture. This process is depicted in Figure 6.3.

From Architecture to Infrastructure

The next step is to translate the architecture into infrastructure. This task entails adding yet more detail to the architectural plan that emerged in the previous phase. Now the detail comprises actual hardware and software. This phase is illustrated in Figure 6.4.

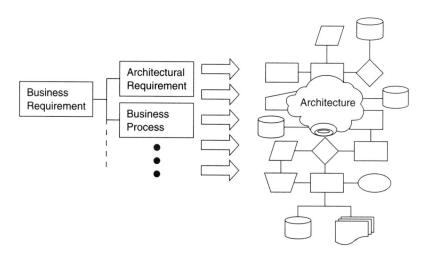

FIGURE 6.3 From business requirements to architecture.

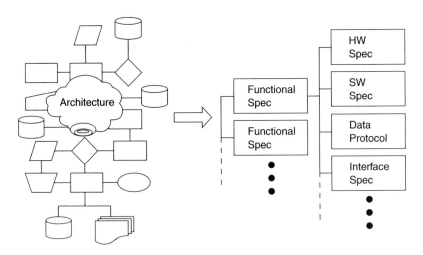

FIGURE 6.4   From architecture to infrastructure.

A Framework for the Translation

For purposes of developing a framework for transforming business strategy into IT architecture and infrastructure, one must describe the basic components of an information system. These components are:

- **Hardware**—the physical components that handle computation, storage, or transmission of data: e.g., personal computers, servers, mainframes, hard drives, RAM, fiber-optic cabling, modems, and telephone lines.

- **Software**—the programs that run on hardware to enable work to be performed: e.g., operating systems, databases, accounting packages, word processors, and enterprise resource planning systems. Some software, such as an operating system like Windows, Windows NT, or Linux, provide the platform on which other software, the applications, run. Applications, on the other hand, are software that automate tasks such as storing data, transferring files, creating documents, and calculating numbers. Applications include generic software like word processors and spreadsheets, and specific software like sales force automation systems, human resource management systems, payroll systems, and manufacturing management systems.

- **Network**—hardware and software components connected according to a common protocol to create a shared computing environment.

- **Data**—the electronic representation of the numbers and text upon which the IT infrastructure must perform work; here we are mainly concerned with the quantity and format of data, and how often it must be transferred from one piece of hardware to another or translated from one format to another.

The framework that will guide the analysis of these components is shown in Figure 6.5*a*. This framework is simplistic in order to make the point that initially understanding the information system in an organization is not difficult. Understanding the technology behind each component of the infrastructure and the technical requirements of the architecture is a very complex task. But the general manager must begin with an overview that is complete and that delivers a big picture of the IS.

This framework asks three types of questions that must be answered for each of the components of the information system: what, who, and where. The "what" questions are those that are most commonly asked. They are questions that identify the specific type of technology in the information system. The "who" questions are those that seek to understand what individuals, groups, and departments are involved. In most cases, the individual user is not the owner of the system, nor even the person who maintains it. And in many cases, the systems are leased, not owned, by the company, making the owner a party completely outside the organization. In understanding the overall information system, it is important to get a picture of the people involved. The third set of questions are about "where." With the proliferation of networks, many IS are designed and built with components in multiple locations, often even crossing oceans. Learning about an information system means understanding where everything is located.

This framework is most useful when applied to both the architecture and the infrastructure. To illustrate the connections between strategy and systems, the table in Figure 6.5*b* has been populated with questions that typify those asked in addressing architecture and infrastructure issues associated with each component.

The questions shown in Figure 6.5*b* are only representative of those to be asked; the specific questions managers would ask about their organizations depend on the business strategy the organization is following. However, this framework can help managers raise appropriate questions as they seek to translate business strategy into infrastructure in their organizations. The answers derived with IT architects and implementers should provide a robust product.

Component	What	Who	Where
Hardware	What hardware does the organization have?	Who manages it? Who uses it? Who owns it?	Where is it located? Where is it used?
Software	What software does the organization have?	Who manages it? Who uses it? Who owns it?	Where is it located? Where is it used?
Network	What networking does the organization have?	Who manages it? Who uses it? Who owns it?	Where is it located? Where is it used?
Data	What data does the organization have?	Who manages it? Who uses it? Who owns it?	Where is it located? Where is it used?

FIGURE 6.5a Information systems analysis framework.

Component	What		Who		Where	
	Architecture	Infrastructure	Architecture	Infrastructure	Architecture	Infrastructure
Hardware	Does fulfillment of our strategy require thick or thin clients?	What size hard drives do we equip our thick clients with?	Who knows the most about servers in our organization?	Who will operate the server?	Does our architecture require centralized or distributed servers?	Must we hire a server administrator for the Tokyo office?
Software	Does fulfillment of our strategy require ERP software?	Shall we go with SAP or Oracle Applications?	Who is affected by a move to SAP?	Who will need SAP training?	Does our geographical organization require multiple database instances?	Does Oracle provide the multiple-database functionality we need?
Network	What kind of bandwidth do we need to fulfill our strategy?	Will 10baseT Ethernet suffice?	Who needs a connection to the network?	Who needs an ISDN line to his or her home?	Does our WAN need to span the Atlantic?	Shall we lease a cable or use satellite?
Data	Do our vendors all use the same EDI format?	Which VAN provides all the translation services we need?	Who needs access to sensitive data?	Who needs encryption software?	Will backups be stored on-site or off-site?	Which storage service shall we select?

FIGURE 6.5b Information systems analysis framework with sample questions.

An example of an architecture popular in many organization is a client/server architecture. Client/server architecture is one in which the hardware, software, networking, and data are arranged in a way that distributes the functionality between multiple small computers. This is in contrast to another architecture, commonly called a "mainframe architecture." A mainframe architecture has a central computer which handles all of the functionality of the system. There are trade-offs a manager must be aware of when considering architecture decisions. For example, client/server architectures are more module, since additional servers can be added with relative ease, and more flexible, since additional clients can be added with specific functionality for specific users. But mainframe architectures are easier to manage in some ways, because all functionality is centralized in the main computer, instead of distributed throughout all the clients and servers.

An example of a company making these trade-offs is Air Products and Chemicals.[3] The company had two major data centers, one in the UK and the other in Pennsylvania. When the business strategy of Air Products changed from man-

---

[3] Quotes in this section are all from Warren McFarlan, *Air Products and Chemicals: IT Organization and Architecture Considerations.* Harvard Business School case study, no. 196-017, August 22, 1995.

aging increasing growth to managing cost containment and productivity, the managers decided to transfer the processing of mainframe applications from the U.K. to the U.S. This move was done to cut costs and, at the same time, encourage sharing of applications to assist the business strategy of global consistency. To do this, the architecture was redesigned and included plans to use two large communication circuits under the ocean to continue to support the business needs in Europe. Client/server architecture was a very difficult choice for Air Products to implement. As one manager commented, "Running a global system with multiple national platforms and choosing technologies from around the world introduces more problems still. Our old methods of design and implementation for the mainframe just don't apply anymore."

▶ OTHER MANAGERIAL CONSIDERATIONS

The framework guides the manager toward the design and implementation of an appropriate information system. Next, this chapter will explore managerial issues that arise with regard to both architecture and infrastructure.

Understanding Existing Architecture

At the beginning of any project, the first step is to assess the current situation. Understanding existing IT architecture allows the manager to evaluate the IT requirements of an evolving business strategy against current IT capacity. The architecture, rather than the infrastructure, is the basis for this evaluation since the specific technologies used to build the infrastructure are chosen based on the overall plan, or architecture. As previously discussed, it is these architectural plans that supports the business strategy. Assuming some overlap is found, the manager can then evaluate the associated infrastructure and the degree to which it can be utilized going forward.

Relevant questions for managers to ask include:

- What IT architecture is already in place?
- Is the company developing the IT architecture from scratch?
- Is the company replacing an existing architecture?
- Does the company need to work within the confines of an existing architecture?
- Is the company expanding an existing architecture?

Starting from scratch allows the most flexibility in determining how IT architecture will enable a new business strategy, and a clean architectural slate generally translates into a clean infrastructure slate. However, it can be a challenge to plan effectively even in the situation of starting from scratch. For example, in a resource-starved start-up environment, it is far too easy to let effective IT planning fall by the wayside. Sometimes, the problem is less a shortcoming in IT management and more one of poorly devised business strategy. A strong business strategy is a prerequisite for IT architecture design, which is in turn a prerequisite for infrastructure design.

It is crucial that managers plan effectively. As the need for strategic IT planning inevitably becomes more widespread, this managerial skill will become ever more necessary to maintain competitiveness. Companies that miss the boat, especially in the crucial start-up phase, will be doomed to failure.

Of course, managers seldom have the relative luxury of starting with a clean IT slate. More often, they have to deal in some way with an existing architecture and infrastructure. In this case, they encounter both opportunity—to leverage the existing architecture and infrastructure and their attendant human resource experience pool—and challenge—to overcome or work within the old system's shortcomings. By implementing the following steps, managers can derive the most value and suffer the least pain when working with legacy architectures and infrastructures:

1. Objectively analyze the existing architecture and infrastructure. Remember, architecture and infrastructure are separate entities; managers must assess the capability, capacity, reliability, and expandability of each.

2. Objectively analyze the strategy served by the existing architecture. What were the strategic goals it was designed to attain? To what extent do those goals align with current strategic goals?

3. Objectively analyze the ability of the existing architecture and infrastructure to further the current strategic goals. In what areas is there alignment? What parts of the existing architecture or infrastructure must be modified? Replaced?

Whether managers are facing a fresh start or an existing architecture, they must ensure that the architecture will satisfy their strategic requirements, and that the associated infrastructure is modern and efficient. The following sections will help managers assess the capabilities most important to their system architectures.

Distinguishing Current versus Future Requirements

Defining an IT architecture that fulfills an organization's needs today is relatively simple; the problem is, by the time it is installed those needs will have changed. The primary reason to base an architecture on an organization's strategic goals is to allow for inevitable future changes—changes in the business environment, in the organization, in the IT requirements, and in the technology itself.

The following sections discuss longevity-related issues that should be considered in IT planning. Chapter 10 discusses more detailed project management issues such as systems design.

Strategic Time Frame

Understanding the life-span of an IT infrastructure and architecture is critical. How far into the future does the strategy extend? How long can the architecture and its associated infrastructure fulfill strategic goals? What issues could arise and change these assumptions?

Answers to these questions vary widely from industry to industry. Strategic time frames depend on industry-wide factors such as level of commitment to fixed resources, maturity of the industry, cyclicality, and barriers to entry. As discussed in Chapter 1, hypercompetition has increased the pace of change to the point where any strategic decision must be viewed as temporary. Architectural longevity depends not only on the strategic planning horizon, but on the nature of a manager's reliance on IT and on the specific rate of advances affecting the information technologies on which he or she depends. And hypercompetition implies that any architecture must be designed with maximum flexibility and scalability to insure it can handle the imminent business changes. Imagine the planning horizon for a dot-com company in an industry in which Internet technologies and applications are changing daily, if not more often.

While all industries must address the rapid progress of IT, those facing evolutionary change will have more predictable planning horizons than those facing the potential emergence of a "killer app."[4] The steel industry provides a good example of the former situation. A steel producer can safely design an IT architecture to improve such back-office functions as inventory management, logistics, human resource management, and even production control. The infrastructure components associated with such an architecture are relatively easy to expand over time as business needs change. However, because the product, in this case steel, requires a physical production and delivery infrastructure, it is highly unlikely that IT will radically change the face of competition in this industry over the next several years. The steel producer's strategic planning time frame for IT investments is therefore longer and more predictable than that for a business in a more information-intensive industry.

Publishers of reference books provide a good example of an information-intensive industry facing radical IT changes. Consider the case of *Encyclopaedia Britannica*. Until the early 1990s, Britannica's intellectual content, brand, and aggressive sales and marketing efforts yielded the best reputation in the industry and brisk sales. Its IT architecture and infrastructure supported these traditional strengths, but its strategy failed to recognize the threat posed by emerging technologies until Microsoft placed low-end competitor Funk & Wagnalls' product on a CD, added some public domain clip-art, called it "Encarta," and virtually started giving it away. Suddenly, a product viewed by Britannica management as more a toy than a serious reference tool began devastating *Encyclopaedia Britannica's* sales. Rather than rethink its business strategy, Britannica simply modified its IT infrastructure to facilitate the introduction of a CD version as a supplement to its printed volumes. The result was a continued decline in sales.[5] Britannica's experience is a

---

[4] Downes, Larry, and Chunka Mui. *Unleashing the Killer App*. Boston: Harvard Business School Press, 1998.

[5] Evans, Philip B., and Thomas S. Wurster. "Strategy and the New Economics of Information." *Harvard Business Review*, September–October, 1997.

lesson for managers in information-related businesses: set shorter planning horizons and prepare to adapt to unexpected changes.

Technological Advances

While a manager may think of technological advances as primarily affecting IT infrastructure, the architecture must be able to support any such advance. Can the architecture adapt to emerging technologies? Can a manager delay the implementation of certain components until he or she can evaluate the potential of new technologies?

At a minimum, the architecture should be able to handle expected technological advances, as by anticipating projected growth rates in storage capacity and computing power. An exceptional architecture will also have the capacity to absorb unexpected technological leaps.

The following are guidelines for planning adaptable IT architecture and infrastructure. At this point, these two terms are used together, since in most IT planning they are discussed together. These guidelines are derived from work by Meta Group.[6]

- Plan for applications and systems that are independent and loosely coupled rather than monolithic. This approach allows managers to modify or replace only those applications that are affected by a change in the state of technology.

- Boundaries between infrastructure components should be clear, so that if one component changes, others are minimally affected, or if effects are unavoidable, the impact is easily identifiable and quantifiable.

- When designing a network architecture, strive to provide access to all users when it makes sense to do so (i.e., when security concerns allow it). A robust and consistent network architecture simplifies training and knowledge sharing, and provides some resource redundancy. An example is an architecture that allows employees to use a different server or printer if their local one goes down.

Note that requirements concerning reliability may mitigate the need for technological adaptability under certain circumstances. If the architecture requires high reliability, a manager will seldom be tempted by cutting-edge technologies. For example, despite Microsoft's virtual monopoly in providing PC operating systems, its Web server runs on only 21 percent of sites; Red Hat's Linux-based Apache server dominates this reliability-sensitive market with 36 percent of websites.[7]

---

[6] DeBoever, Larry R., and Richard D. Buchanan. "Three Architectural Sins." *CIO Magazine,* May 1, 1997.

[7] SiteMetrics Corporation. "Internet Server Survey (February 1998)." Retrieved from the World Wide Web: http://www.sitemetrics.com/serversurvey/ss_98_q1/index.htm.

Growth Requirements

What's the company's projected growth? What does the architecture have to do to support it? How will it respond if the company greatly exceeds its growth goals? What if the projected growth never materializes?

Consider a case in which growth requirements were poorly anticipated: America Online (AOL).[8] In late 1996, AOL management decided to change its pricing scheme from pay-as-you-surf to a flat fee-an important strategic move in the marketplace. Although AOL thoroughly analyzed the financial reward the change might bring, it failed to consider adequately the impact it could have on its IT infrastructure.

The change vastly overloaded AOL's infrastructure, causing lengthy service interruptions for all customers. It is unlikely that AOL would have had to do any serious systems redesign to respond to the increase in demand; it simply needed to increase its infrastructure capacity. Ultimately, this planning failure cost AOL millions in IT investments and even more in defending its image when customers spoke badly of the service they received from AOL.

AOL's plight underscores the importance of analyzing the impact of strategic business decisions on IT architecture and infrastructure, and at least ensuring a contingency plan exists for potential unexpected effects of a strategy change.

Assessing Financial Issues

Like any business investment, IT infrastructure components should be evaluated based on their expected financial value. Unfortunately, payback from IT investments is often difficult to quantify; it can come in the form of increased productivity, increased interoperability with business partners, improved service for customers, or yet more abstract improvements. For this reason, the Gartner Group suggests focusing on how IT investments enable business objectives rather than on their quantitative returns.[9]

Still, some effort can and should be made to quantify the return on infrastructure investments. This effort can be simplified if a manager works through the following steps with the IT staff.

1. Quantify costs. The easy part is costing out the proposed infrastructure components and estimating the total investment necessary. Don't forget to include installation and training costs in the total.

2. Determine the anticipated life cycles of system components. Experienced IT staff or consultants can help establish life-cycle trends both for a company and an industry in order to estimate the useful life of various systems.

3. Quantify benefits. This is the hard part. Get input from all affected user groups, as well as the IT group—which presumably knows most about the equipment's capabilities. If possible, form a team with representatives from

[8] Koch, Christopher. "A Tough Sell." *CIO Magazine,* May 1, 1997.

[9] Rosser, B. "Key Issues in Strategic Planning and Architecture." Gartner Group research note: Key Issues, April 15, 1996.

each of these groups and work together to identify all potential areas in which the new IT system may bring value. Some starting points are mentioned in the introduction to this section, and each business will have additions best elicited during live-group brainstorming.

4. Quantify risks. Work with the IT staff to identify cost trends in the equipment the company proposes to acquire. Also, assess any risk that might be attributable to delaying acquisition, as opposed to paying more to get the latest technology now.

5. Consider ongoing dollar costs and benefits. Make sure to examine how the new equipment will affect maintenance costs, as well as upgrade costs associated with the current infrastructure.

Once this analysis is complete, the manager will have the information necessary to do the company's preferred discounted cash flow analysis (i.e., net present value or internal rate of return computation).

Since it is likely that the manager will not have succeeded in fully quantifying all the costs and benefits associated with new equipment, the results of this analysis should form only one component of the decision whether to invest. Though he or she may not be able to put a dollar value on it, significant qualitative weight should be given to an assessment of the company's ability to achieve its strategic goals *without* the proposed IT investment.

Differentiating between Architecture and Infrastructure

The concepts covered in the previous section tend to apply to both IT architecture and infrastructure. This section distinguished between current and future requirements, and the associated financial issues. Figure 6.6 shows the extent to which each of the criteria discussed can be used to evaluate architecture and infrastructure. The issues to be sorted out about architecture and the plans for the information system include all four criteria in this chapter. However, issues regarding the infrastructure, the components chosen to implement the architecture, are primarily about technological advances, growth requirements, and financial considerations. The strategic time frame is an issue that is decided before the infrastructure discussion begins.

▶ FROM STRATEGY TO INFRASTRUCTURE: AN EXAMPLE

This section considers a simple example to illustrate the application of concepts from preceding sections. The case discussed is BluntCo, a fictitious maker of cigar clippers.

Step 1: Defining the Strategic Goals

The managers at BluntCo recognize the increasing popularity of cigars; in fact, they can hardly keep up with demand for their clippers. At the same time, however, BluntCo's president, Tres Smokur, is concerned that cigar mania may end. Smokur

	Applicability	
Criteria	Architecture	Infrastructure
Strategic time frame	Very applicable	Not applicable
Technological advances	Very applicable	Somewhat applicable
Growth requirements	Very applicable	Very applicable
Assessing financial issues	Somewhat applicable	Very applicable

FIGURE 6.6 Applicability of evaluation criteria to discussion of architecture and infrastructure.

wants to ensure that BluntCo can respond to sudden changes in demand for clippers.

Along with the board of directors, Smokur sets BluntCo's strategy: To lower costs and improve responsiveness to market demand by outsourcing clipper manufacturing and distribution.

BluntCo's strategic goals, then, can be stated as follows:

- To lower costs by outsourcing clipper manufacturing

- To lower costs by outsourcing clipper distribution

- To improve market responsiveness by outsourcing clipper manufacturing

- To improve market responsiveness by outsourcing clipper distribution

Step 2: Define Related Architectural Goals

To keep things simple, consider more closely only one of BluntCo's strategic goals: To lower costs by outsourcing clipper manufacturing. How can BluntCo's architecture enable this goal? It must provide the following key interfaces to the new manufacturing partners:

- Sales to manufacturing partners: send forecasts, confirm orders received

- Manufacturing partner to sales: send capacity, confirm orders shipped

- Manufacturing partner to accounting: confirm orders shipped, electronic invoices, various inventory levels, returns

- Accounting to manufacturing partner: transfer funds for orders fulfilled

Step 3: Apply Strategy-to-Infrastructure Framework

With the architecture goals in hand apply the framework presented in the first section of this chapter. Figure 6.7 lists questions raised when applying the framework to BluntCo's architecture goals and related infrastructure. Note that not all questions apply in a given situation.

Only a few of the questions that the framework could lead BluntCo to ask are provided; a comprehensive treatment of this situation would require more information than we can contrive in a simple example.

Component	What		Who		Where	
	Architecture	Infrastructure	Architecture	Infrastructure	Architecture	Infrastructure
Hardware	What kind of supplemental server capacity will the new EDI transactions require?	Will BluntCo's current dual-CPU NT servers handle the capacity, or will the company have to add additional CPUs and/or disks?	NA	Who is responsible for setting up necessary hardware at partner site?	Where does responsibility for EDI owning and maintaining EDI hardware fall within BluntCo?	Which hardware components will need to be replaced or modified to connect to new EDI hardware?
Software	What parts of BluntCo's software architecture will the new architecture affect?	Will BluntCo's current Access database interface adequately with new EDI software?	Who knows the current software architecture well enough to manage the EDI enhancements?	Who will do any new SQL coding required to accommodate new software?	NA	Where will software patches be required to achieve compatibility with changes resulting from new software components?
Network	What is the anticipated volume of transactions between BluntCo and its manufacturing partners?	High volume may require leased lines to carry transaction data; dial-up connections may suffice for low volume.	Who is responsible for additional networking expense incurred by partners due to increased demands of EDI architecture?	NA	Where will security concerns arise in BluntCo's current network architecture?	Where will BluntCo house new networking hardware required for EDI?
Data	Will data formats supporting the new architecture be compatible with BluntCo's existing formats?	Which formats must BluntCo translate?	Who will be responsible for using sales data to project future volumes to report to manufacturing partner?	Who will be responsible for backing up additional data resulting from new architecture?	Where does the current architecture contain potential bottlenecks given changes anticipated in data flows?	Does the new architecture require BluntCo to switch from its current 10Base-T Ethernet to 100Base-T?

FIGURE 6.7   Framework application.

Step 4: Evaluate Additional Issues

The last task is to weigh the managerial considerations outlined in the second section of this chapter. Weigh them against the same architectural goals outlined in Step 2. Figure 6.8 shows how these considerations apply to BluntCo's situation.

Applicability

Criteria	Architecture	Infrastructure
Strategic time frame	Indefinite: Smokur's strategic goal is to be able to respond to fluctuations in market demand.	NA
Technological advances	EDI technology is fairly stable; the state-of-the-art should suffice for any foreseeable market growth.	NA
Reliability requirements	Reliability in the EDI links to partners is extremely important to BluntCo's business.	BluntCo will choose established vendors to supply new EDI hardware and software.
Growth requirements	Smokur anticipates continued growth in demand for BluntCo clippers in the next three to five years, and flat sales after that.	BluntCo will adopt EDI transaction capacity based on projected market size in three years but ensure that options exist for upgrading if growth surpasses expectations.
NPV of investment	NA—in this limited case, NPV analysis applies only to infrastructure.	BluntCo will analyze NPV of various hardware and software solutions before investing.
Infrastructure cost trends	NA	EDI component cost trends reflect industry averages, but are not compelling enough to cause BluntCo to postpone deployment.
Ongoing investment	NA—in this limited case, ongoing investment only applies to infrastructure.	Various options will be evaluated for their ongoing investment costs.
Payback horizon	BluntCo expects the new architecture to pay for itself within three years.	Various options will be evaluated using conservative sales growth projections to see how they match the three-year goal.
Incidental investments	The new architecture represents a radical shift in the way BluntCo does business and will require extensive training and work force adjustment.	Training costs for each option will be analyzed. Redeployment costs for employees displaced by the outsourcing also will be considered.
Source of financing	BluntCo is currently cash-rich, and an ample budget exists to go forward with the new architecture.	NA
Maintainability	The new architecture raises some maintenance issues, but also eliminates those associated with in-house manufacturing.	Various options will be evaluated for their maintenance costs.

FIGURE 6.8 BluntCo's managerial considerations. *(continues)*

Applicability

Criteria	Architecture	Infrastructure
Scalability	Outsourcing should provide more scalability than BluntCo's current manufacturing model, which is constrained by assembly-line capacity. Both primary and secondary vendors will be identified to provide scalability in the volume of clippers manufactured.	The scalability required of various new hardware and software components is not significant, but options will be evaluated based on their ability to meet scalability requirements.
Complexity	While the new architecture is a significant departure from the current in-house model and may be considered more technically complex, this is somewhat mitigated by removal of in-house manufacturing and its attendant complexity.	Various hardware and software options will be evaluated for their complexity.
Standardization	NA	BluntCo will adopt the ANSI X12 EDI standard, and make this a requirement of its manufacturing partners.
HR compatibility	The new model will displace some current human resources. BluntCo must analyze the costs and effect on morale associated with this change.	Current staff is not familiar with EDI and must be trained; some new staff will have to be hired. BluntCo must analyze the associated costs.

FIGURE 6.8 BluntCo's managerial considerations. *(continued)*

Again, note that not every issue in the evaluation criteria was addressed for BluntCo, but this example shows a broad sampling of the kinds of issues that will arise.

▶ FOOD FOR THOUGHT: TOTAL COST OF OWNERSHIP

This section looks at total cost of ownership (TCO), a technique to account for infrastructure costs that is fast becoming the industry standard. Gartner Group introduced TCO in the late 1980s when PC-based IT infrastructures began gaining popularity.[10] Other IT experts have since modified the concept and this section synthesizes the best thinking about TCO.

TCO attempts to comprehend all the costs associated with owning and operating an IT infrastructure. It looks beyond initial capital investments to include costs associated with technical support, administration, and training. This technique esti-

---

[10] Gartenberg, M. "Beyond the Numbers: Common TCO Myths Revealed." Gartner Group research note: Technology, March 2, 1998.

mates annual costs per user for each potential infrastructure choice; these costs are then totaled. Careful estimates of TCO provide the best investment numbers to compare with financial return numbers when analyzing the net returns on various IT options.

Figure 6.9 uses the hardware/software/network/data categories to organize the TCO components the manager should evaluate for each infrastructure option. This table allows the manager to evaluate infrastructure components at a medium level of detail, and categorically to allocate "softer" costs like administration and support. More or less detail can be used. It sometimes helps to separate soft costs into a separate category, since a single department often provides them. The manager can adapt this framework for use with varying IT infrastructures.

Category	Infrastructure component	Option 1 per end user cost	Option 2 per end user cost
Hardware	Desktops Servers Mobile platforms Printers Archival storage Technical support Administration Training Informal support Total Hardware Cost		
Software	OS Office Suite Database Proprietary Technical support Administration Training Informal support Total Software Cost		
Network	LAN WAN Dial-in lines/modems Technical support Administration Total Network Cost		
Data	Removable media Onsite backup storage Offsite backup storage Total Data Cost Total Cost of Ownership		

FIGURE 6.9 TCO component evaluation.

The Component Breakdown

In order to clarify how the TCO framework is used, this section will examine the hardware category in more detail. As used in Figure 6.9, hardware means computing platforms and peripherals. The components listed are somewhat arbitrary, and an organization in which every user possessed every component would be highly unusual. For shared components like servers and printers, TCO estimates should be computed per component and then divided among all users who access them.

For more complex situations, such as when only certain groups of users possess certain components, it is wise to segment the hardware analysis by platform. For example, in an organization where every employee possesses a desktop that accesses a server and half the employees also possess stand-alone laptops that do not access a server, one TCO table could be built for desktop and server hardware, and another for laptop hardware. Each table would include software, network, and data costs associated only with its specific platforms.

Soft costs, such as technical support, administration, and training are easier to estimate than they may first appear. To simplify, these calculations can be broken down further using a table such as Figure 6.10.

Category	Component	Responsible party	Annual hours	Cost/ hour	Total cost
Technical support	Hardware phone support	Call center			
	In-person hardware troubleshooting	IT operations			
	Hardware hot swaps	IT operations			
	Physical hardware repair	IT operations			
	Total cost of technical support				
Administration	Hardware setup	System administrator			
	Hardware upgrades/ modifications	System administrator			
	New hardware evaluation	IT operations			
	Total cost of administration				
Training	New employee training	IT operations			
	Ongoing administrator training	Hardware vendor			
	Total cost of training				
	Total soft costs for hardware				

FIGURE 6.10 Calculating soft costs.

The final soft cost, informal support, may be harder to pin down, but it is important nonetheless. Informal support comprises the sometimes highly complex networks that develop among coworkers through which many problems are fixed and much training takes place without the involvement of any official support staff. In many circumstances, these activities can prove more efficient and effective than working through official channels. Still, managers want to analyze the costs of informal support for two reasons:

1. The costs—both in salary and in opportunity—of a non-support employee providing informal support may prove significantly higher than analogous costs for a formal support employee. For example, it costs much more in both dollars per hour and foregone management activity for a mid-level manager to help a line employee troubleshoot an e-mail problem than it would for a formal support employee to provide the same service.

2. The quantity of informal support activity in an organization provides an indirect measure of the efficiency of its IT support organization. The formal support organization should respond with sufficient promptness and thoroughness to discourage all but the briefest informal support transactions.

Various IT infrastructure options will affect informal support activities differently. For example, a more user-friendly systems interface may alleviate the need for much informal support, justifying a slightly higher software expenditure. Similarly, an investment in support management software may be justified if it reduces the need for informal support.

Although putting dollar values on informal support may be a challenge, managers will want to make an effort to gauge the relative potential of each component option to affect the need for informal support.

TCO as a Management Tool

While this discussion has focused on TCO as a tool for evaluating which infrastructure components to choose, TCO also can help managers understand how infrastructure costs break down. Gartner Group research consistently shows that the labor costs associated with an IT infrastructure far outweigh the actual capital investment costs.[11] TCO provides the fullest picture of where managers spend their IT dollars. Like other benchmarks, TCO results can be evaluated over time against industry standards (much TCO target data for various IT infrastructure choices is available from industry research firms). Even without comparison data, the numbers that emerge from TCO studies assist in decisions about budgeting, resource allocation, and organizational structure.

---

[11] Kirwin, W. "TCO: The Emerging Manageable Desktop." Gartner Group Top VIEW, September 24, 1996.

▶ SUMMARY

This chapter has examined how managers can effectively translate business strategy into IT architecture and infrastructure. Following are a few of the key points covered: Strategy drives architecture, which drives infrastructure. Strategic business goals dictate IT architecture requirements. These requirements provide an extensible blueprint suggesting which infrastructure components will best facilitate the realization of the strategic goals. The manager's role is to understand how to plan IT in order to realize business goals. With this knowledge, he or she can facilitate the process of translating business goals to IT architecture and then modifying the selection of infrastructure components as necessary.

Use a logical framework to guide the translation from business strategy to IS design. This translation can be simplified by categorizing components into broad classes (hardware, software, network, data), which make up both IT architecture and infrastructure. Consider managerial issues. While translating strategy into infrastructure, it is important to know the state of any existing architecture and infrastructure, to weigh current against future architectural requirements, and to analyze the financial consequences of the various systems options under consideration. Monitor the performance of the systems on an ongoing basis. Consider using TCO to create appropriate benchmarks.

Making infrastructure and architecture decisions involves joint discussion with business managers and IS professionals. Decisions such as whether to buy a software package from a vendor or to build a system in-house often have wider implications than just solving the initial business need. Chapter 8 discusses the makeup and responsibilities of the IS professionals.

As IT becomes more crucial to creating and sustaining competitive advantage, so does the need for managers to effectively translate business strategy into IT infrastructure. The frameworks and examples presented in this chapter can help facilitate that translation.

▶ DISCUSSION QUESTIONS

1. Think about a company you know well. What is an example of the IT architecture at that company? What is an example of the IT infrastructure?

2. What, in your opinion, is the difference in a client/server architecture and a mainframe architecture? What is an example of a business decision that would be affected by the choice of the architecture?

3. How does the Internet affect an organization's architecture?

4. TCO is one way to account for costs associated with a specific infrastructure. But that method does not include additional costs such as disposal costs—the cost to get rid of the system when its no longer of use. What other additional costs might be of importance in making total cost calculations?

BUSH INTERCONTINENTAL AIRPORT IN HOUSTON°

Airplane travel is smooth when airports run smoothly, and for an airport to run smoothly, effective IS is critical. A successful operation of the network of IS at the airport is not only a source of personal pride for the airport personnel, but can become a key determining factor in airlines' decisions about where to expand their services. And that can directly affect both the bottom line of the airport budget as well as the entire economic success of the region in which the airport operates. The systems at the Houston Intercontinental Airport (IAH) illustrate this. Consider the following scenario:

> A Chicago businessperson returns from Mexico City. His plane touches down 20 minutes early for a layover in Houston and is able to taxi directly to a waiting gate. The businessperson deplanes, quickly passes through Immigration, retrieves baggage, and completes Customs with no problems. The passenger checks the video display in the airport to confirm connecting flight information, and learns there is 45 minutes until boarding time. That leaves time to make a call to the office, have a snack at the food court, visit the restroom, and get to the gate in time to upgrade his seat. The passenger then boards his flight, handing the gate attendant his electronic boarding pass, which is scanned through the computer at the door of the jetway, and confirms the passenger is cleared to board the plane for the next leg of his trip. In this case, various airport systems precleared passengers through Immigration, tracked the early arrival of the plane and made sure personnel were ready to unload the baggage and assist at the baggage carousel, gathered departure information from 20 separate airlines to display for easy viewing, and provided fast, reliable fiber-optic connections to let attendants check records on the spot.

Behind the scene at IAH, the ninth busiest international airport in the United States, is a large, complex information system. Standard airport business applications such as budgeting, records management, rates and charges, warehouse inventory, and purchasing are used by airport personnel. In addition, the airport requires automated systems for managing flight information, security access control, ground transportation, paging/information, airfield lighting, radio and facility maintenance, vehicle maintenance, parking, concession tracking, and a wide range of planning, design, and construction tasks. The parking business alone is a $22 million operation, and in 1999 was outsourced to Amoco Parking. The City of Houston owns and operates the airport through their Department of Aviation (DOA).

The airport consists of four terminals for passenger travel, called "A", "B", "C", and "IAB" (IAB stands for the Mickey Leland International Airlines Building). Terminals A and B were built in 1969, C in 1981, and IAB in 1990. That resulted in a mix of information technologies to be managed by the Aviation MIS department (AMIS). While IAB had the newest technology available, terminals A, B, and C handled the bulk of the traffic and revenue generated by the airport. Terminal C and most of terminal B are leased to Continental Airlines, Inc. and they handle 75 percent of all the traffic that passes through the airport. The infrastructure needed to manage this airport must include both old and new technologies. And while this mixture presents challenges, it also helps keep innovation in perspective since

---

° Source: Some of this material was adapted from "Airport '95." *CIO Magazine,* September 1, 1995. (website: www.cio.com/archive/rc_gv_air1_content.html). The rest is from conversations with chief resource officer for the Houston Airport System, Frank Haley, December 2, 1999.

the airport just needs to make sure things work, rather than be on the leading edge of innovations.

There are multiple stand alone systems in the airport, as well as a series of LANs and workstations. Four servers support more than 150 terminals or personal computers at IAH. The DOA itself manages 8 LANs supporting 455 personal computers and 12 servers. There are also four Stratus minicomputers to support airport operations. Two of the Stratus systems run IAH's most crucial safety and scheduling systems, and are therefore kept in a secure, air-conditioned room in one of the older terminals. A mainframe computer located in downtown Houston is connected to the DOA network. In addition, each individual airline that leases space from the DOA has installed its own terminals for its own business.

The network at the airport is primarily fiber optic, with T-1 lines connecting the Ethernet-based LANs at each airport to create a city-wide WAN. In 1999, a capital improvement program was initiated to install a non-collapsible fiber ring around the city of Houston to connect all the airports to the administration building. It is non-collapsible because the architecture of the network is such that if one link fails, the entire network itself does not collapse. This improvement program will install OC3 service, the equivalent of 100 T-1 lines, as the backbone of the network. And the network itself is leased from the local telephone company, Southwestern Bell Telephone.

Software on the PCs includes standard business applications as well as specialized applications like those previously described. The Microsoft Office suite, including Word, Excel, and Access, is used. All the computers run an e-mail, calendaring, and scheduling program in Microsoft Outlook, which runs on an Exchange server. The system works well for them because everyone throughout the organization uses it to schedule every meeting and appointment. And there are more than 220 custom programs developed by the Applications Development staff. Programming is primarily done in the FoxBase development language, which builds applications to run on the database management program. Applications have been built for such diverse situations as emergency preparedness, event tracking, monthly fuel delivery reports, and taxicab trip logs.

Managing flight data at the airport is an interesting task. Airlines provide their own flight information. All airlines, except Continental, use the airport provided terminals and data for flight arrivals and departures. Continental has its own systems for displaying that information to passengers. Therefore, terminals A and IAH display multiple airline schedules, while those in B and C only display Continental flights.

Discussion Questions

1. What are the key components of the IS architecture at IAH?
2. Consider the software applications in this architecture. Which do you think are running on the local PCs and which are running on the servers or mainframes in the network?
3. What are the advantages and disadvantages to the DOA of leasing the networking from Southwestern Bell?

CHAPTER 7

THE BUSINESS OF E-BUSINESS*

In 1995, a pair of entrepreneurs who had developed a paper-free check acceptance process decided to market their system, RediCheck, on the Internet. Up to that point, they had targeted their service mainly to telemarketing and mail-order companies. Their decision to take the company online and to reposition it as an Internet payment-acceptance company proved to be both astute and well timed. Since that change, the company, now called iTransact Corporation (www.itransact.com), has processed many millions of dollars in Internet payments and has assisted hundreds of established offline businesses and online-only start-ups. It is clear to iTransact and to many of the companies that use its electronic checking, credit card, and electronic funds transfer (EFT) services that the tide of business has turned toward e-business.

E-business occurs when buyers and sellers interact electronically. Engaging in e-business is more than just using a credit card to make purchases. When someone buys a gallon of milk and a box of cereal at the supermarket and pays with a five-dollar bill, they are engaging in commerce. If, instead, they pay by swiping their MasterCard through the credit card terminal, they are engaging in electronic commerce (e-commerce). Such a transaction represents e-commerce in its simplest form. There is still a considerable amount of paper involved: On the customer end alone, he manages a cash register receipt, a credit card receipt, a credit card statement, and a credit card payment (usually via check). At the other end of the e-commerce spectrum, a transaction such as EFT—wherein funds are transferred directly from the buyer's bank account to the seller's—can occur with no "paper trail" whatsoever. If the buyer makes his purchases over the Internet and pays for the items with the same credit card, that is considered e-business. In most environments today, e-business is more than e-commerce.

The Internet is the backbone for e-business marketplaces in which transactions occur instantly over the network and involve virtually no paper. Indeed, e-commerce

* The author wishes to acknowledge and thank Matthew Spafford Sumsion, MBA '99 for his help in researching and writing early drafts of this chapter.

129

is a term which frequently implies Internet-based transactions. The world of e-business in general, and the Internet and World Wide Web in particular, is changing so fast that information in a textbook is surely out of date before the text reaches the students' hands. But it is such an important topic that this chapter is provided to offer some foundation for managers who will be managing companies in the Internet age.

To that end, this chapter discusses how the Internet is changing business to business and business to consumer commerce. It covers business and professional uses of the Net, not personal and individual uses. This chapter has most likely left out many current Internet applications, and the authors apologize for that in advance. But this chapter provides a basic understanding and additional interesting ideas that can be used in discussions about current Internet activities.

▶ DEFINITIONS

Since the Internet plays such a great part in e-business, it may be valuable at this point to define "Internet," and the related terms "World Wide Web" and "Information Superhighway." These terms are often used interchangeably, but it is helpful to recognize the distinctions (see Figure 7.1 for a summary).

Internet

The *Internet* is a global, *inter*connected *net*work (hence the name) of millions of individual computers (called *hosts*). The history of the Internet begins with the United States Department of Defense's ARPANET, a network designed to support the communications between cities in the U.S. in the event of a major disaster. The idea was to build a network that would continue to work even if parts of it were destroyed. In 1985, the National Science Foundation built NSFNET using the ARPANET protocols. NSFNET was essentially the backbone network provided

Internet	*Inter*connected *net*work of millions of individual computers with no central control.
World Wide Web (WWW)	Popular method for accessing Internet information, utilizes hypertext to link documents.
Information Superhighway	High-speed, global communications network—arguably synonymous with "Internet."
Intranet	Internet-style information used exclusively within an organization, inaccessible by outsiders.
Extranet	A company's interorganizational information, unavailable to users of its intranet or to the wider Internet community.

FIGURE 7.1 A summary of key definitions.

free to universities and research centers. These organizations just had to build a connection. NSF eventually withdrew as the manager of the network as commercial telecommunications companies and private and public institutions built their own links into the network. Today, there is no single "owner" of the Internet. Instead, it is a collection of networks which all can link to each other, share the same protocols, and support the exchange of packets of information (see Chapter 6 for more information on network architecture in general).

Statistics are hard to acquire since there is no one well-defined way to measure usage. But one thing is clear—the number of business and individual users continues to grow rapidly. Users from over 100 countries can link to this computer network for exchanges of news, messages, data, and commerce. The Internet has no governing board or central control; all information available on the Net is simply provided by any individual or organization that chooses to make the information available to the Internet community. Available information can include anything from pictures of someone's cat to Anheuser Busch's current annual report to backwards recordings of Beatles records. This information is available to anyone with access to the Internet. This access is gained, usually by subscription, through an Internet service provider (ISP).

World Wide Web

The *World Wide Web* (or "web" or "WWW") is an increasingly popular system for accessing much of the information on the Internet, via the use of specially formatted documents. The documents can be formatted in a relatively simple computer language called hypertext markup language (HTML) or any one of a number of more sophisticated languages, such as JAVA or C++. HTML was created by a researcher in Switzerland in 1989 and is part of an Internet standard called the hypertext transport protocol (the "http" at the beginning of Internet addresses) which enables the access of information stored on other Internet computers. *Hypertext* is another name for the usually underlined links (or *hyperlinks*, *hot links*, or *hot spots*), which, by clicking on them, provide access to other documents, graphics, or files located anywhere in the world. *Web browsers*, such as Netscape's Navigator and Microsoft's Internet Explorer, are software programs that enable navigation of the World Wide Web.

Information Superhighway

When he was the U.S. Vice President, Al Gore coined the term *Information Superhighway* to describe the vision of a communications network that carries high-speed information all over the world. The Information Superhighway encompasses voice, data, telephony, cable television, satellite systems, and other conduits of information. It makes it possible for anyone to instantly access news, messages, research materials, and entertainment. Since the Internet already provides many of these features (and will doubtlessly be expanded to include more of them), the term "Internet" arguably can be used as a synonym for the bulkier "Information

Superhighway." Indeed, one Internet dictionary casually describes "Information Superhighway" as "a term often used by newbies [computer novices] and Al Gore to describe the Internet."[1]

More Nets: Intranets, Extranets, and E-Marketplaces

Many derivatives have developed based on the Internet, including intranets, extranets, and net markets.

An *intranet* looks and acts like the Internet, but it is comprised of information used exclusively within a company and unavailable to the Internet community as a whole. Employees of AT&T, for example, can use company computers to access an employee handbook (containing links to such things as employee data, benefit information, and procedures for dealing with irate callers) via the company's intranet. Companies build intranets to facilitate information sharing within their business. Since AT&T may not want its customers and competitors to have access to employee information—nor does it want its employees to spend all of their working time on the Internet at entertainment sites— it may build a security "firewall" between the Internet and the AT&T intranet.

So what is an *extranet*? Some sources would argue that it's just another redundant term for the Internet, or that "there is no such thing."[2] It is not quite that simple, however, since a company can utilize an extranet that is distinctly different from its intranet or from the Internet as a whole. Just as a company's intranet contains Internet-style information for exclusive use within the company, the company could also have an extranet containing information for use outside the company. For example, extranet information could be intended for use by a company's subcontractors or suppliers, or for private use by a specific external subsidiary with a need to know. Dell Computers, for example, created custom Web pages for their key customers which contain company information and links that are specifically tailored to the interest of that customer. As with intranets, extranets are not accessible by the Internet at large and are usually protected by a security firewall.

E-marketplaces are a special kind of network that bring together different companies. Sometimes called *net-markets*, these networks are typically built by a consortium of key businesses in the marketplace, or by a third-party e-business interested in providing the marketplace. Much like the New York Stock Exchange creates a physical marketplace for trading stocks, e-markets create a virtual marketplace for buying, selling, or trading goods and services. There are vertical e-marketplaces that operate in specific industries, like DirectAg.com, a virtual marketplace for agriculture goods. And there are horizontal e-marketplaces that operate across industries, typically targeting a specific business function or need that occurs in many types of businesses. TradeOut.com is an example of a horizontal e-marketplace site that provides a trading place for surplus equipment.

---

[1] Kadow's Internet Dictionary, http://www.msg.net/kadow/answers/h.html#highway. URL verified November 8, 1998.

[2] Fairdene New Media, http://www.fairdene.demon.co.uk/extranet.html. URL verified November 8, 1998.

Marketspace versus Marketplace

Some have come to regard transactions taking place over the Internet as significantly different from those taking place in a physical marketplace. The term "marketspace" was coined by Jeffery Rapport and John Sviokla in 1994.[3] A *marketspace* is a virtual market where the transactions taking place are all based on information exchange, rather than the exchange of goods and services. Take, for example, Internet-based auctions, such as those conducted on e-Bay or Amazon.com. At a traditional auction, the goods to be sold are shown to the potential buyers, who then compete in real-time to buy the items. The highest bidder gets the goods right then, and makes payment right then. But in a marketspace, like the online auctions, the goods are not physically available, rather *information* about the goods is available. Decisions are made about whether to buy an item based on information presented by the auction site and the seller. The interaction takes place over an electronic network involving a wide number of locations, rather than just one physical auction house.

Companies operating in a marketspace have a very different way of delivering value than those in a marketplace. Both types of businesses are involved in commerce, the selling of goods to customers. However, a marketspace company does not typically own or even hold the inventory it sells to customers. It acts more as a market-maker, connecting buyers with suppliers. For example, e-Bay holds no inventory, so valuing its inventory is not a useful metric. Likewise, many online retailers, such as Amazon.com and florist Calix and Corolla, hold little or no inventory, preferring to connect buyers with sellers. Rapport and Sviokla claim that managers must understand the differences in operating in a marketplace and a marketspace in order to manage their customers appropriately.

> Managers face two critical challenges: first, to recognize the full potential of the marketspace transactions in a coherent manner, and second, to choose the best means to make money in this new arena . . . Content, Context and Infrastructure are easily disaggregrated in marketspace, [and that means] . . . customer loyalty looks very different in marketspace.[4]

Success in a marketspace means identifying what adds value for the customer and then insuring that level of the transaction is managed appropriately. Sometimes the context of the transaction is what breeds customer loyalty. Customers regularly visit e-Bay because they are loyal to that medium. Sometimes content breeds loyalty. Customers look for Fisher-Price toys because they want that quality, regardless of where they purchase it. And sometimes the infrastructure breeds loyalty, as in the case of Time-Warner cable where customers who want cable TV then buy other Time-Warner services, such as cable modem high speed Internet access. Managers must think about all three layers of the customer interaction in a marketspace in order to successfully build their Internet strategy.

---

[3] Rapport, J. and J. Sviokla. "Managing in Marketspace," *Harvard Business Review*, reprint no. 94608, November–December 1994, pp. 141–153.

[4] Ibid.

▶ INTERNET BUSINESS MODELS

Businesses on the Internet are typically described by a short acronym indicating the basic business model of the organization. Commerce between businesses (B-to-B), and between businesses and their customers (B-to-C), are the basic models of e-business. The difference is in who is targeted as the customer. B-to-B companies primarily focus on selling and interacting with other businesses, usually as part of the overall value chain (see Chapter 4 for a discussion of the value chain model). Their customers are other businesses who, in turn, either sell goods and services to other businesses or to eventual end-customers. B-to-C businesses are those that sell directly to consumers. For example, Amazon.com is considered a B-to-C e-business, selling primarily to consumers. There are many derivatives of the B-to-B model. Figure 7.2 summarizes some of them.

Once a Web-based business has decided who the primary customers will be, a business model is then developed as to how commerce will take place. The standard model is based on traditional business interactions; customers visit a website to see the goods and services offered, then choose and buy what they want. But the features of the Internet, such as the immediate interaction, the global reach, and the ease of use, have spawned various more innovative models, such as auctions, reverse auctions, net markets, portals, application service providers, and bricks-and-clicks. Figure 7.3 summarizes these models.

Auctions, such as that seen on the popular site e-bay.com, allow sellers to place items on the network, and buyers to bid for those items using the website. A reverse-auction, on the other hand, lets the buyer put up a request for products and/or services, and has the suppliers bid for the business. An example is Priceline.com, where a customer can state the price he or she wants to pay for a particular airline ticket (or hotel room or other service) and the airlines (or other vendors) respond with a bid for that customer by offering a ticket at or below the customer's price. In some reverse auctions, the customer has a choice among bids, and in others the customer is locked in if any supplier presents a bid matching his or her basic criteria.

B-to-B	Business to Business—targets sales and services primarily to other businesses
B-to-C	Business to Consumer—targets sales and services primarily to consumers
B-to-E	Business to Employee—companies that provide services other companies can use to interface with employees (like retirement funds management, health care management, and other benefits management)
B-to-G	Business-to-Government—companies who sell the bulk of their goods and services to state, local, and national governments
C-to-C	Consumer to Consumer—sites that primarily offer goods and services to assist consumers to interact (auctions are an example)
Hybrid	A combination of B-to-B and B-to-C models

FIGURE 7.2   Basic business models for the Internet.

Model	Description
Auctions	Sellers place descriptions of items or services on the auction site and buyers bid for them. An example is e-bay.
Reverse auctions	Buyers state what they want to buy and sellers offer items or services to meet the request. An example is Priceline.com.
Net markets	Site offers a place for both buyers and sellers to find each other and locate services either or both may want in conjunction with the sale. An example is Autobytel.com.
Portals	Site offers a customized home page for the individual, offering information, services, and links to other sites customized based on user's stated preferences. An example is Yahoo!
Bricks and clicks	Hybrid business model combining a website with a traditional physical business model. An example is Toys 'R Us.
ASP	Site offers business process functionality to customers, who use this site as their own internal business process. An example is Agillion.

FIGURE 7.3 Business models mechanisms for Web-based businesses.

Net market sites provide a digital intermediary between buyers and sellers, typically offering services such as financing, insurance, research, and warranties. Autobytel.com, for example, offers buyers of automobiles the chance to do research and select the car they want. The site then assists the buyer in finding the model at an agreeable price either through a network of new car dealers who do business over this site, a network of used car dealers, or an auction. The site then offers options for financing the car, insuring the car, warranting the car, maintaining the car, and buying additional items for the car.

Portals, once thought of as the technology to provide a structure for information on the Web, have become a creative business model for some Web businesses. Portals are easy-to-use websites that provide access to critical information, research, applications, and processes that individuals on the Web want. They have taken on significant importance as the portal frames what the individual sees and the links to which he or she has access. Portals are offered within companies, as the interface to the company intranet, or publicly, where the site customizes the page for the individual customers. For example, Intranets.com has a service that allows individuals or groups to set up an intranet completely hosted on the Intranet.com computers but available to invited members from any Internet access point. Customers are encouraged to set up the home page of the intranet as their personal home page, and links are developed based on preferences given by the user when he or she signs up for the service. This home page is, in essence, a portal to the entire Web.

Application service providers (ASPs) offer a business model whereby the website becomes an outsourced information system for the customer. ASPs provide a site with complete functionality for specific needs of their clients. For example, Agillion.com offers a site for the small business person. The site has tools for managing customers, interacting with customers, and supporting the marketing, sales, and communications functions throughout the business. But when a customer uses Agillion.com, all of the information and processing are done at Agillion.com's computer center, not at the customer's computer. Agillion.com, in essence, offers to be the information systems (IS) team for its customers. There are a large number of ASPs; WebHarbor.com offers a search engine to help locate the ASP that offers exactly the services needed.

Another business model, called "bricks and clicks," is based on combining an e-business with a physical business. In this model, the website is coupled with a traditional, physical business to leverage the best of both the Internet world and the "brick and mortar" business. The Web business traditionally brings new thinking, new distribution possibilities, and new sales outlets to the table, while the physical business brings some sense of stability and possibly even customers, concepts, brand recognition, and other resources to the Web business. The resulting hybrid is a business model intended to be the best of both worlds.

Electronic Data Interchange

Electronic data interchange (EDI) provides the basic technology for e-commerce. The World Wide Web's hypertext transfer protocol (http) allows the transfer of documents and other information on the Internet using human interaction. In a similar way, EDI allows the transfer of business data on the Internet (such as quote requests, order forms, and invoices) with little or no human interaction. EDI utilizes an agreed standard (called ANSI X12) to allow a software program on one computer system to relay information back and forth to a software program on another computer system, thus allowing organizations to exchange data pertinent to business transactions.

An EDI transmission occurs between partners. Each transmission, or *transaction set*, comprises one or more *data segments* framed by header and trailer codes. One transaction set might contain information equivalent to that in a standard business document. Data segments, in turn, comprise strings of *data elements*, or facts—such as prices or product specifications—separated by delimiters.[5]

Step 1	Buyer's computer sends purchase order to seller's computer.
Step 2	Seller's computer sends purchase order confirmation to buyer's computer.
Step 3	Seller's computer sends booking request to transport company's computer.
Step 4	Transport company's computer sends booking confirmation to seller's computer.
Step 5	Seller's computer sends advance ship notice to buyer's computer.
Step 6	Transport company's computer sends status to seller's computer.
Step 7	Buyer's computer sends receipt advice to seller's computer.
Step 8	Seller's computer sends invoice to buyer's computer.
Step 9	Buyer's computer sends payment to seller's computer.

FIGURE 7.4 EDI transactions for purchase, shipment, and payment.

[5] Part of this description is based on information from Whatis.com, http://whatis.com/edi.htm. URL verified November 8, 1998.

In *Frontiers of Electronic Commerce,* Kalakota and Whinston demonstrate how EDI substantially automates the information flow and facilitates management of a business process. The steps are listed in Figure 7.4. Since it allows detailed information to be exchanged with little human interaction and expense, EDI is a crucial element of e-business.

▶ ADVANTAGES AND DISADVANTAGES OF E-BUSINESS

By increasing its reliance on e-commerce, an organization stands to improve its operations in numerous ways, including cost, speed, security, and competitiveness. The rapid growth of the Internet is both a cause and an effect of the increasing shift of commerce into electronic channels.

Cost

As with nearly all business elements, less human interaction means less expense. The savings in labor and training costs can be tremendously greater than the costs of installing and maintaining electronic systems. Companies dealing with thousands of suppliers and tens of thousands of purchase orders a year can find significant savings from EDI. For example, managers at RJR Nabisco calculated that purchase orders previously costing between $75 and $125 to process now cost 93 cents.[6]

Electronic search engines can save companies and individuals time and expenses. This technology understands what is needed, then electronically searches the Internet, automating the information search process. For example, popular search engines such as Yahoo! and Ask.com take simple questions and provide the user with links to various possible answers anywhere on the Web. Other sites take customer requests and selectively send them to potentially interested companies or individuals, aggregating the responses and cutting down on the research time. A third type of technology, called "bots," go out onto the Web with specific search instructions and electronically look for the information sought.

In addition to labor savings, cost savings come from reductions in inventory costs, storage costs, and rework costs. Companies doing business on the Internet can save considerably on inventory expenses if the business is set up for e-procurement and just-in-time manufacturing, or simply by using the Internet to ship customer orders directly from suppliers rather than through internal company processes. A site on the World Wide Web can offer a company's entire product line without the company having to keep anything physically in stock or even print catalogs. An organization can set up a website to handle functions that previously required human interaction—everything from providing product details to entering orders to obtaining payment information and providing customer service. Further, less human interaction means less human error—another cost reduction.

---

[6] Kalakota, R. and Whinster, A. Frontiers of Electronic Commerce. Reading, MA: Addison Wesley, 1996, pg. 314.

Speed

Not only can many organizations complete electronic transactions more cheaply than physical transactions, they can also complete them more quickly. Purchases can be made on a website in real-time, meaning that in the instant a customer decides to pay for an item, the sale can be made and the item can be shipped. For example, customer orders from BMG Music Service used to have a three- to five-week turnaround time. Once a title became available, the company had to print and mail catalogs and reply cards to each of its customers (via bulk mail), then wait for the cards to come back (again by mail), where the orders were separated from the rest of the mail and finally processed. Now, a customer can go to BMG's website (www.bmgmusicservice.com) and submit an online order the instant a title becomes available. The speed in purchasing is especially apparent in the case of digital products, such as software, audio, and video feeds; a customer can choose to buy these and then immediately download them from the Internet. In the music example the product can be instantly downloaded to the customer's personal computer or his or her MPEG player. This instant downloading completely eliminates the entire supply chain, reducing the lead time to nothing.

Security

Security used to be a major concern for doing business on the Internet. Customers wondered how safe their credit card numbers would be if they typed them into a Web-based order form. Technologies have come a long way to provide security. Innovative businesspeople have built tools that encrypt or otherwise disguise personal information, financial information, and business information. Websites, called *security validators,* have been created to validate the security level of other sites, and to provide a seal of approval when a particular website is protected. And businesses themselves have made the security measures more visible through explicit statements, icons, pop-up windows, and other means of communication.

Concerns remain about the safety of e-commerce transactions—what if, for example, someone were to steal all those credit card numbers as they are relayed over the Internet? Interception of e-commerce data may be possible, but it is rare and increasingly unlikely. And consider the risks of paper transactions: credit card receipts (and credit cards themselves) are stolen and the numbers are used fraudulently. Checkbooks are stolen and used fraudulently. Signatures can be forged. Transactions with a paper trail are hardly foolproof and may indeed be riskier than e-commerce transactions. Copy machines can make multiple copies of secure documents just as fast as e-mails can be sent with multiple copies. The difference is in the speed of the communication. A file with secure information can be sent anywhere in the world in a matter of seconds over the Net, whereas the paper-based file takes longer to reach a destination. The security of e-commerce continues to improve. Innovations such as secure servers, passwords, digital signatures, and encryption are already in place, and transactions need not be relayed via public forums like e-mail. Electronic commerce may well become the safest way to do business.

Competitiveness

The Internet has significantly lowered barriers to entry for upstart retailers. A new company on the Internet potentially can draw from the same base of customers that visits long-established organizations, allowing small and large companies to compete on an arguably level playing field. That gives small companies a new advantage, since they can look the same as a large company on their website. For example, Garden Escape (www.garden.com) was started by four Internet entrepreneurs in September 1995 and has since grown into one of the world's largest retailers of plants and garden supplies on or off the Internet. Similarly, Preview Travel (www.previewtravel.com), online since May 1996, has grown to become one of the largest travel agencies in the United States. The key to competitiveness is not necessarily what the website looks like, or even what services are offered. It is the delivery and responsiveness behind the Web page that differentiates the good companies from the bad. Image is less important on the Web than actions. Simply having a site on the Web does not mean that customers will visit, but the Internet allows for competition on an ever-widening playing field, and many companies have learned that they cannot afford *not* to have an Internet presence.

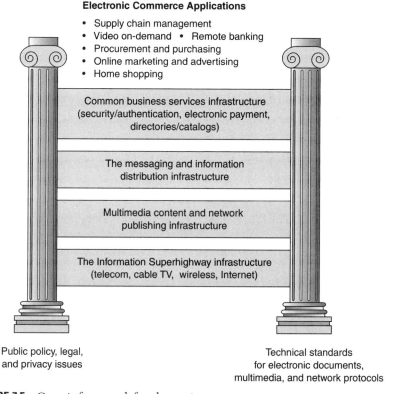

Electronic Commerce Applications
- Supply chain management
- Video on-demand • Remote banking
- Procurement and purchasing
- Online marketing and advertising
- Home shopping

Common business services infrastructure
(security/authentication, electronic payment,
directories/catalogs)

The messaging and information
distribution infrastructure

Multimedia content and network
publishing infrastructure

The Information Superhighway infrastructure
(telecom, cable TV, wireless, Internet)

Public policy, legal,
and privacy issues

Technical standards
for electronic documents,
multimedia, and network protocols

FIGURE 7.5 Generic framework for electronic commerce.

Figure from Kalakota, R. and Whinster, A. Frontiers of Electronic Commerce. Reading, MA: Addison Wesley, 1996, pg. 314

▶ FRAMEWORK OF ELECTRONIC COMMERCE

Kalakota and Whinston offer a generic framework for e-commerce, shown in Figure 7.5. The framework assumes that new applications will continue to be built on existing technology infrastructure—the computers, communications networks, and communication software that comprise the Internet. It uses four key building blocks:

- Common business services, for facilitating the buying and selling process
- Messaging and information distribution, as a means of sending and retrieving information
- Multimedia content and network publishing, for creating a product and a means to communicate about it
- The Internet, for providing the highway system along which all e-commerce travels

Two pillars supporting all e-commerce are integral to the framework:[7]

- Public policy, to govern such issues as universal access, privacy, and information pricing
- Technical standards, to dictate the nature of information publishing, user interfaces, and transport in the interest of compatibility across the entire network

Common Business Services Infrastructure

The first of the four building blocks is the common business services infrastructure. This building block consists of three main elements: security, electronic payments, and directory services and search engines.

Security

Authentication is a security process whereby proof is obtained that the users are truly who they say they are: i.e., that their identity is verified as authentic. Authentication can be as simple as verifying the name and password of a user prior to allowing him or her access to an account. Additionally, it can include the use of a digital signature. Authentication can also be used to ensure that data transmissions are delivered to the appropriate receiver, to verify the source (or sender) of the data, and to ensure that the data has not been tampered with en route to its destination.

Much like a handwritten signature is used to guarantee that the signer of a paper document is truly the person who composed it, a *digital signature* can be used to prove that the sender of a message (e.g., a file or e-mail message) is truly who he or she claims to be. A digital code is applied to an electronically transmitted message. The recipient of the message can compare this code upon receipt of the message with the sender's digital signature. If the two do not match, either the message originated somewhere other than with the stated sender, or the message

---

[7] Kalakota, R. and Whinster, A. *Frontiers of Electronic Commerce. Reading*, MA: Addison-Wesley, 1996, p. 314.

has been intercepted and altered. Different forms of encryption can be used to ensure that digital signatures cannot be forged.

One simple way to provide authentication is through the use of a *password*. A password is a string of arbitrary characters that is known only to a select person or group. A computer or software program can be programmed to respond to commands or open messages only after the correct password has been entered; in this way, the system authenticates the identity of the user and prevents unauthorized access. When typed, passwords typically appear on the screen as a series of asterisks (*****) to prevent others from seeing them. Passwords are most effective when users select characters that would be difficult for others to guess; in practice, however, most people select simple passwords such as birth dates and nicknames, weakening the efficacy of the authentication process.

Encryption is the translation of data into a secret code: i.e., into a form that can only be read by the intended receiver. Here's how it works (Figure 7.6 includes a diagram of the process): the sender composes a message for the recipient in *plain text*, then uses an *encryption key* to encode it. The recipient has a *decryption key*, which he uses to decode the sender's message and read it, once again, as plain text. If an intruder were to observe the sender's message to the recipient, it would be incomprehensible, or *cipher text*.

If both the sender and recipient use the same key, this is called *symmetric encryption*. Another common type of encryption, *asymmetric encryption*, uses differentiated keys, called *public keys* and *private keys*. The sender, for example, has access to the recipient's public key, but so do others. Any of them can compose a message to the recipient and encrypt it with his public key. The message, however, must be decrypted with a private key, and only the recipient has access to it. Two of the most widely used public key encryption types are DES (data encryption standard) and PGP (pretty good privacy).

Many companies doing business on the Web utilize what are called *secure servers* in order to protect the privacy of the data they send and receive. Normally, text transferred from a browser to a Web server is sent as plain text; if anyone were to intercept the transmission, it would be legible. To prevent the interception of plain text, secure servers utilize encryption technology to convert plain text into encrypted text before it is transmitted. Internet merchants that do not have their own secure servers can partner with an e-commerce provider that will allow the merchant's sensitive transactions to occur on the provider's secure site.

Firewalls are a different type of security measure. Firewalls block out undesirable requests for entrance into a website, and keep those on the inside from

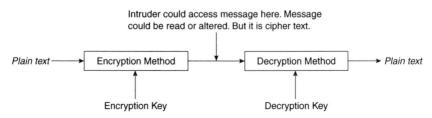

FIGURE 7.6 Encryption.

reaching outside. For example, a hacker trying to reach a corporate website in order to plant a bug or virus could encounter a firewall, making it much more difficult to get access to the servers. Likewise, an employee trying to access a restricted website outside the corporate intranet may be blocked from doing so by a firewall.

Electronic Payments

There are a number of payment vehicles that businesses can use to make and receive payments on the Internet. These include credit cards, electronic checks, EFT, smart cards, and e-cash. Perceptually, these methods are simply the electronic equivalents of everyday, offline payment methods: e.g., credit cards, checks, and cash.

Since credit card information has been relayed electronically for years, making the switch from current credit card payments to Internet credit card payments does not require a great cognitive or technological leap. Offline credit card transactions work according to the process outlined in Figure 7.7.

Internet credit card transactions utilize a similar process, but they can eliminate much of the offline equipment and merchant interface. "Virtual terminals" allow merchants to use the Internet in place of a swipe machine, and "transaction processors" allow merchants to stay out of the transaction entirely.

A *virtual terminal* is the Internet equivalent of the credit card swipe machine. Internet businesses typically cannot obtain actual cards to swipe, so they require a different method for relaying the card information to the processor. They can do this via a virtual terminal—an Internet interface that acts in place of a credit card swipe machine (or "terminal"). Figure 7.8 outlines the process.

Virtual terminal providers generally assess a per-transaction fee. The virtual terminal offers the advantage of allowing a business to accept credit card payments without having to buy or lease more expensive credit card terminals (or "black

Step 1	Merchant obtains a customer's credit card number and expiration date, either manually (via transcription or a card imprint) or electronically (via a swipe machine).
Step 2	Merchant relays this information and the payment amount to credit card processor, either manually (e.g., mail) or electronically (via a phone line).
Step 3	Processor deposits purchase amounts into merchant's bank account.

FIGURE 7.7 Traditional credit card transactions.

Step 1	Customer visits merchant's website, selects a product or service to purchase, and enters credit card information.
Step 2	This information is relayed to the merchant.
Step 3	When convenient, merchant accesses virtual terminal and inputs or uploads the collected credit card information; this information is relayed to credit card processor.

FIGURE 7.8 Virtual terminals.

boxes"). The disadvantage is that the merchant must still manually enter each transaction.

Transaction processors provide the Internet convenience of virtual terminals, but go a step further: they allow the merchant to stay out of the transaction entirely. This service is ideal for merchants who wish to sell products on the Internet and do not want to worry about handling any of the credit card information themselves. Figure 7.9 summarizes the process. Transaction processors such as iTransact (www.itransact.com) generally charge a per-transaction fee. Advantages for a business include not having to obtain credit card equipment and not having to assist in or be present for the actual transactions.

Since many Internet customers do not have credit cards or choose not to use them, *Internet checking* services provide merchants with the ability to accept checks over the Internet. Figure 7.10 summarizes how this process works.

The merchant has a couple of options as to where the checks will be printed. Some Internet checking providers will sell or lease the merchant check-printing software and/or hardware. In this case, the customers' check information is relayed to the merchant, who prints the checks in-house. Other providers (e.g., RediCheck, www.redicheck.com) offer a hands-off method, fulfilling a role similar to that of the credit card transaction processor. In this case, the provider/processor obtains the customers' information and also handles check printing responsibilities. Internet checking allows businesses to accept real-time payments from customers who prefer using checks to credit cards. A drawback is that there is still paper involved: i.e., an actual check must be printed and deposited in the merchant's bank.

Electronic funds transfer (EFT) is similar to Internet checking, but with one distinct difference: there is no paper check involved. Funds are simply transferred

| Step 1 | Customer visits merchant's website, selects a product or service to purchase, and enters credit card information. |
| Step 2 | This information is automatically collected by the transaction processor and relayed to the credit card processor. |

FIGURE 7.9 Transaction processors.

Step 1	Customer visits merchant's website, selects a product or service to purchase, and enters check information (specifically, the ABA number printed at the bottom of the check).
Step 2	This information is used to generate an actual paper check, printed with the same information as the other checks in the customer's checkbook. The customer's name is printed on the signature line with a note that the customer has authorized the transaction.
Step 3	The check is then processed exactly like any other check.

FIGURE 7.10 Internet checking.

from the customer's bank account to the merchant's bank account. Figure 7.11 contains a summary of the process. Since no check draft is printed with EFT, a business can potentially receive funds more quickly than with electronic checking. Funds transfers, however, are typically more expensive on a per-transaction basis than electronic checks.

Digital cash is the nearest equivalent to cash transactions on the Internet. It was designed specifically for small-ticket transactions (i.e., several dollars or less), where transaction fees and expenses would make credit card or check purchases impractical. In practice, however, it is used for purchases of any size as yet another payment alternative. Figure 7.12 describes the process. Digital cash providers (e.g., DigiCash, www.digicash.com) generally keep a percentage of each transaction.

Digital cash can also be stored on a *smart card*. A smart card, explains Whatis.com, "is a plastic card with an embedded microchip that can be loaded with data, used for telephone calling, electronic cash payments, and other applications, and then periodically 'recharged' for additional use."[8] Smart cards currently can be used for such small-ticket items as vending machines, toll booths, bus fares, and phone calls. Keyboards are being designed with smart card swipe capabilities in order to effectuate similar transactions on the Internet.

In deciding on a payment acceptance scheme or schemes, managers must take into account factors such as efficiency, security, price, and ease of customer use.

Step 1	Customer visits merchant's website, selects a product or service to purchase, and enters check information: specifically, the ABA number printed at the bottom of the check. (Some EFT providers will also allow funds to be transferred from savings accounts.)
Step 2	Merchant relays this information to an EFT provider.
Step 3	EFT provider verifies customer account information against an Automated Clearing House (ACH) database; funds are debited from customer's bank account and credited to merchant's bank account.

FIGURE 7.11   Electronic funds transfer (EFT).

Step 1	Customer signs up with a digital cash provider and purchases a software "purse" of a given amount, which is stored on customer's computer.
Step 2	Customer visits website of merchant who accepts digital cash and agrees to pay via this method.
Step 3	Payment amount is deducted from customer's "purse" and deposited into merchant's account.

FIGURE 7.12   Digital cash.

[8] Whatis.com, http://whatis.com/smartcar.htm. URL verified November 8, 1998.

Directory Services and Search Engines

Additional components of the common business services infrastructure include services used to index the contents of the Internet: e.g., directory services and search engines. Managers should pay attention to these services for two reasons: first, they provide useful and extensive information about the Internet, and second, they can provide visibility since becoming listed with them gives potential customers a route of access.

Inter@ctive Week describes a directory service as "a collection of industrial-strength databases that store information about the applications, equipment, and users on a network."[9] It provides users with an interface with the applications and equipment on the network in accordance with scripted policies and terms of service.

As briefly mentioned above, a *search engine* is a program that searches the Internet (or an intranet or individual site) for specified keywords. A search engine typically contains an interface, allowing a user to enter these keywords. The search engine then sends out a "crawler" or "spider" to collect documents that contain the keywords. It then indexes the collected documents for easy review. Popular search engines on the Internet include Yahoo!, Infoseek, Excite, AskJeeves, and Alta Vista.

Messaging and Information Distribution Infrastructure

The second building block in the generic framework for electronic commerce is the messaging and information distribution infrastructure. Messaging software effectuates the movement of information through the channels of the Internet. It takes such forms as e-mail, newsgroups, point-to-point file transfers, and groupware.

One of the first uses of the Internet, *e-mail* still constitutes a good portion of Internet traffic. Most e-mail messages consist strictly of text, but e-mail can also be used to transfer images, video clips, sound clips, and other types of computer files.

Many e-mail services (e.g., Eudora, Outlook Express) require the user to have an account with an ISP. Incoming and outgoing e-mail is routed through the ISP's mail server, and all e-mail a user receives is stored on his or her own computer. However, a growing number of Web-based e-mail providers allow a user to send and receive e-mail from any computer by accessing the provider's website and entering a user name and password. Web-based e-mail allows a user to keep the same e-mail address long term (i.e., as long as the provider stays in business), whereas e-mail routed through an ISP usually contains the name of the ISP as part of the e-mail address, and a user must therefore change e-mail addresses each time he or she changes ISPs. Disadvantages of Web-based services include limits on the number of messages that can be stored and on the size of files that can be sent and received. Web-based e-mail is typically offered free; service providers display advertisements on users' pages and collect demographics and other marketing data from users upon enrollment.

[9] Inter@ctive Week, June 16, 1997. http://www.zdnet.com/intweek/print/970616/inwk0028.html. Copyright © 1997 Interactive Enterprises, LLC. URL verified November 8, 1998.

Another permutation of e-mail is the mailing *list server*. Users subscribe to a mailing list; when any user sends a message to the server, a copy of the message is sent to everyone on the list. This allows for restricted-access discussion groups; only subscribed members can participate in or view the discussions since they are transmitted via e-mail. Popular mailing list providers include ListServ and Majordomo.

Newsgroup discussions are similar to those carried on in mailing list servers with the important distinction being that the text of the discussions typically is viewable on an Internet or intranet web page; unless this page is shielded with a firewall or password, outsiders are able to view and/or participate in the discussion. Some newsgroups are moderated: i.e., a group leader can decide to remove entries from the discussion. The Internet's "Usenet" offers access to literally thousands of newsgroups. Commercial messages are unwelcome in most Internet newsgroups, unless the group or moderator has explicitly stated otherwise. A business can create a newsgroup specifically for use by its employees.

File transferring consists simply of transferring a copy of a file from one computer to another on the Internet. The most common procedure, File Transfer Protocol (FTP), allows entire files—even large ones—to be transferred within an office or across the globe more quickly and securely than with e-mail.

Groupware is, as its name implies, group software: i.e., software that enables a group to work together on a project, even from remote locations, by allowing them simultaneous access to the same file. Calendars, written documents, e-mail messages, and databases can be shared through such software products as Lotus Notes and Microsoft Exchange. CU-SeeMe and Microsoft NetMeeting actually make electronic "face-to-face" meetings possible.[10] Public groupware sites are increasingly popular, such as e-groups.com and intranets.com. These sites provide services of interest to geographically dispersed work teams who would like to use the Web, but do not have a server of their own.

Multimedia Content

Multimedia content comprises the third building block in the generic framework for electronic commerce. Very different kinds of vehicles must travel the Information Superhighway, and not all vehicles can traverse the same routes. Commerce involving the transmission of movies or electronic books, for example, requires routing them according to the technical specifications of their individual components. If movies comprise video and audio components, and electronic books include text, graphics, and photographs, then each may be transmitted quite differently on the Internet.[11]

After such multimedia content is created, it is stored as electronic documents on servers, which in turn are linked to each other via networks. Customers access them via software and hardware clients.

---

[10] Whatis.com, http://whatis.com/groupwar.htm. URL verified November 8, 1998.

[11] Kalakota, 5–6.

Internet Infrastructure

The fourth and final building block in the generic framework for electronic commerce is the infrastructure of the Internet. How does the Internet actually work? What does it consist of? To answer these questions, a manager must first understand that information transmitted via the Web is first broken into data "packets." These packets travel independently of each other across the Web, sometimes following entirely different routes. Once the packets arrive at their destination, they are reassembled into a complete message. Rus Shuler of the Revere Group maps the journey of these packets in Figure 7.13 (note that CSU/DSU is Channel Service Unit/Data Service Unit).

An Internet Service Provider maintains a pool of modems for customers who dial in. A computer manages this pool and controls the flow of data from each modem to a backbone or dedicated line router. The computer usually collects billing and usage information as well.

Packets from a customer's computer traverse the phone network and the ISP's local equipment and are routed onto the ISP's backbone. From there the packets may pass through several other routers and backbones, dedicated lines, and other networks until they find their destination, a single computer with a specified address.[12]

As the Internet becomes more sophisticated and complex, telephone lines are becoming only one method by which information is transmitted. Cole, Raywid, and Braverman cite in particular wireless access technologies, cable systems, and digital subscriber lines (DSLs).[13]

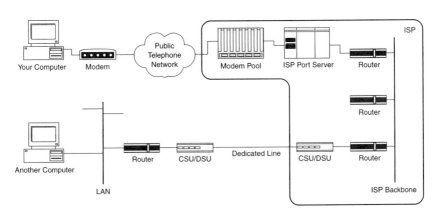

FIGURE 7.13 A sample journey of information from one Internet computer to another.
Source: Rus Shuler, Ballantyne Consulting Group. Used with permission.

---

[12] Source: http://rus1.home.mindspring.com/whitepapers/internet_whitepaper.html © 1998 Rus Shuler/The Revere Group. URL verified December 13, 1998.

[13] Source: http://www.crblaw.com/faqwork.htm © 1998 Cole, Raywid & Braverman, LLP. URL verified November 8, 1998.

Public Policy

This chapter has discussed the four building blocks in the generic framework. Just as important are two pillars supporting it: public policy and technical standards.

In the rapidly developing world of e-commerce, very basic policy and legal questions are emerging. These issues include the cost of accessing information, regulation to protect consumers from fraud and to protect their right to privacy, and the policing of information traffic to detect pirating or pornography.[14]

In April 1998, the U.S. Department of Commerce released "The Emerging Digital Economy," a detailed report about the evolution of e-commerce. Privacy issues figured prominently. The report quoted a recent *Business Week/Harris* poll, whose respondents most often cited privacy concerns as a reason for not using the Internet. More than three-quarters of current users said they would use the Web more if privacy were guaranteed.

The report cited three common e-commerce practices as causing privacy concerns: requesting personal information from new visitors to a site, creating customer profiles based on personal information gathered in order to deliver purchased goods, and leaving electronic "footprints" of visits to different Web sites and of purchases made, without the knowledge of the customer. The report argued that consumers should be given the opportunity to block the gathering of information or, when they freely give it, to indicate how they would like it to be used.[15]

For the time being, at least, the government will rely on industry self-regulation to address these issues. The report encouraged the private sector to establish rules of conduct, which would be disclosed to consumers, as well as mechanisms for tracking compliance and offering recourse to consumers in situations of noncompliance. It said consumers should know the identity of any collector of personal information and the intended uses of the information; in addition, they should have the right to access information about themselves that a company holds, and to correct or amend it as necessary.[16]

Technical Standards

The second pillar upon which the e-commerce framework rests is technical standards for electronic documents, multimedia, and network protocols. Such standards are essential to e-commerce because they ensure seamless integration across the data transportation network, as well as access for consumers on any device they choose—laser disc, PC, hand-held device, etc.—and on all operating systems.[17]

The key Internet standard is TCP/IP, which stands for *transmission control protocol* and *Internet protocol*. In the article "How the Internet Works," Richard Wiggins explains that protocols "are the specifications for the interface between two computers, and they set standards to define how computers communicate with

---

[14] Kalakota, 6.

[15] Source: http://www.ecommerce.gov/emerging.htm, Chapter 5. URL verified November 8, 1998.

[16] Ibid.

[17] Kalakota, 7.

each other to accomplish specific tasks." TCP is a *connection-oriented* protocol—one which establishes a connection between processes on different host computers before data is transmitted—while IP "defines a *connectionless* service through which data is delivered from computer to computer."[18]

In other words, all Internet-connected computers, regardless of manufacturer or operating system, must speak the TCP/IP language in order to communicate with each other. Therefore, before investing in computers and networking systems, managers should ascertain that the systems will conform to these standards.

▶ OTHER USES OF THE INTERNET

Society has only begun to explore the capacity of the Internet. It has already sparked an information revolution; as it continues its explosive growth, it can also affect the nature of human interactions. The Web is used for a variety of interesting and diverse applications, some of which are discussed in this section.

Interpersonal Communication

Though e-mail is a relatively new method of communication, it has already become widely used and commonplace. The Internet, however, is also used for other forms of communication and will increasingly be used for more. Figure 7.14 summarizes some current uses.

Sample Usage	Description	Example
Telephony	Using the Internet for communications usually done over facilities from the telephone company	Making voice-telephone calls is possible, but not popular. Net companies are beginning to challenge the long distance market by offering no long-distance charges.
Webcams	Using video cameras to feed images directly to websites	Sites like JenniCam (www.jennicam.org), which features a young woman who lives nearly every minute of her life in front of a camera connected to the Internet.
Videoconferencing	Combining audio telephony with webcams resulting in long-distance meetings	Companies holding virtual meetings with most members at their own desk are used frequently. Applications like geographically dispersed families holding virtual reunions, and clubs gathering virtually are available, but not common.

FIGURE 7.14 A summary of interpersonal communication applications on the Internet.

[18] Wiggins, Richard. "How the Internet Works." *Internet World*, October 1996, pp. 59–60

News Media

Just as the Gulf War solidified cable TV's (especially CNN's) position as the break-through news medium of the 1980s, the Clinton sex scandal made the Internet the news provider of the 1990s. In 1998, the Starr Report was first made available to the public via the Internet; those interested could go online and read the report, or they could watch TV, where they were treated to the spectacle of news reporters reading the report from the Internet. Delivering news in general on the Net is not much different from watching TV. Figure 7.15 summarizes some popular media on the Web.

Reference

Constantly changing information makes many reference materials outdated even before their printing is complete. The Internet provides an ideal alternative, since information on the Net can be updated as frequently as necessary. Figure 7.16 summarizes examples of reference sources on the Internet.

Sample Usage	Description	Example
Television	Using the Internet to deliver to the desktop the same content delivered by television stations	Real-time news, traffic conditions, and weather updates are available from all the networks (for example, www.cbs.com), but using live video and audio news feeds on the website is not done.
Radio	Using digital audio technology to deliver the same content as radio stations, making local radio broadcasts available live around the world	Larger radio stations, and even individual shows, have websites with printed, rather than live audio content. A few have live audio news, talk shows, and music broadcasts on the net (for example, www.jbandsandy.com).
Newspapers	Using the Internet to deliver the content of local newspapers, but with additional features such as the use of audio and video	Most newspapers have a website that allows searching back articles and reading current articles (for example, www.latimes.com). A few add audio or video to that content.
Magazines	Like newspapers, using the Internet to deliver the same content as paper-based magazines	Most magazines have a website with the same content as their newsstand equivalents. Some, like *Fast Company* (www.fastcompany.com), deliver additional content on the Web. But few add video and audio features.

FIGURE 7.15 A summary of media Internet applications.

Sample Usage	Description	Example
Dictionaries	Using the search power of the Internet to deliver the content of dictionaries	Numerous dictionaries and thesauruses exist, offering definitions, pronunciations, etymologies, and anagrams of words, phrases, and abbreviations (for example, www.dictionary.com). Foreign language translation dictionaries are also available. Most use flat text files, not audio, to deliver content.
Encyclopedias	Using the Internet to deliver the content of encyclopedias	The Internet, by itself, is considered by some to be a giant electronic encyclopedia with search engines serving as the index (for example, www.encyclopedia.com). But traditional encyclopedia companies (for example, www.eb.com) are updating format and content using the Web.
Telephone Directories	Local and global directories are put on the Internet making it possible to find the telephone number and address of anyone in the world	Internet telephone directories (for example, www.infobel.be) cover entire countries and are updated constantly. Most do not yet link with telephony to make the call, but that might be the next application.
Atlases	Using the Internet to deliver maps of countries, states, regions, even local areas, sometimes with directions	A traveler can download maps with detailed directions from source to destination (for example, maps.yahoo.com). Some automobiles come equipped with systems which can access this detail in real-time making it possible to get directions without stopping the car.
Libraries	Locating books, references, and having questions answered on the Web	The Web is one giant electronic library and search engines are the electronic librarians (for example, www.ask.com). Just about any question can be answered by finding a website with content on that topic. Some libraries also have put up websites in an effort to provide a portal to the information they store.

FIGURE 7.16 A summary of reference resources on the Internet.

Services

Companies providing strictly information-based services may soon discover that they must either provide these services over the Internet or face extinction. Figure 7.17 summarizes some popular services and their status on the Internet.

Sample Usage	Description	Example
Travel agencies	Online reservations for ticketing, car rental, hotels, and other services offered by travel agencies	Many sites will compile all the information a traveler needs to make a trip. Major hotels, car rental companies, and airlines have their own Web pages (for example, www.continentalair. com) on which reservations can be made. Smaller bed and breakfast type hotels sometimes have websites, but finding them is not always easy.
Medical diagnosis	Using the Internet to diagnose and suggest treatment for common, and sometimes uncommon, medical conditions	Sites facilitate looking up medical terms and conditions, understanding medication and side effects, and identifying holistic health alternatives (for example, www.drkoop.com). Some sites point to local resources for personal attention.
Employment	Job posting, resume routing, and other tasks associated with finding a job are done online	Some sites list jobs locally, whereas others list nationally. Many companies use their web sites as a way to list job openings so current and future employees can search electronically.
Classified advertising	Using the Web to place personal and business classified ads	Classified ads are common on the Internet, but have not yet replaced trade papers such as Auto Trader or Thrifty Nickel. Online shoppers can access ads on the Net, usually with more information, such as pictures, than printed ads allow. Auctions are also a Web-based alternative to classified ads.
Automobile problem diagnosis	Owners enter information about make, model, and year of car, and interactively diagnose its problems	A growing number of databases about car problems are available. Sites suggest repairs for common problems, and help diagnose and suggest solutions for rarer problems (for example, www.autosite.com).

FIGURE 7.17 Sample services on the Internet.

Entertainment

The Internet is the home for many types of entertainment, including games, gambling, and movies. Music and film are increasingly prevalent on the Internet. Anything in a digital format can also be relayed over the Internet, and movies and records are already available in digital form: e.g., on compact discs or digital video discs. Currently, music and video are commonly found on the Web. Figure 7.18 summarizes these and other types of entertainment.

Education

Much of education is based on the acquisition of information. With the Internet, teachers and students do not always require physical proximity for purposes of

Sample Usage	Description	Example
Movies	Movies are made available on the Internet	Digital versions of popular movies, such as the 187-minute film *Titanic*, are being relayed over the Internet months before the video stores have them. Some expect the Web to replace video rental and sales, delivering any movie at any time to any place.
Music	Using the Internet to deliver tracks and even entire albums	Technologies like MP3 enable listeners to download songs directly from the Web into a portable listening device. The entertainment industry is trying to figure out how to compete with free distribution of copyrighted songs (and other sounds).
Concerts	Using Internet technologies to broadcast real-time concerts, ballets, and operas	Some concerts are staged for pay-per-view TV, and the Internet is an alternative delivery vehicle. Some performers are trying out the Web to link performers around the world and to stage an Internet-based concert.
Books	Using the Web to host books	Thousands of books are already available in digital form, but the screens on most computers make it difficult to read them electronically. But most people prefer to have a book in paper format. Sites like www.amazon.com are changing the distribution of physical books, and may someday deliver digital books to individuals.

FIGURE 7.18 Sample entertainment applications on the Internet. *(continues)*

Sample Usage	Description	Example
Sports	Broadcasting live sporting events over the Internet	Most major sporting events are broadcast in audio format over the Internet. Local events, like little league and soccer, are expected as the number of individuals with portable webcams increases.
Games	Games that traditionally required everyone in the same room are played over the Internet, engaging players from all over the world	Games is a big business. Traditional games, such as scrabble, monopoly, and chess, are available in e-mail forms (for example, email.games.com). New types of games have emerged that are played only on the Web through gamesites, sites that host the game (for example, www.bezerk.com).
Gambling	Using the Internet to place bets on just about any event or game imaginable	Internet gambling is a multi-billion dollar industry, attracting players to virtual sites located in countries where gambling is legal even if a player is in a city where it is illegal (U.S. regulators are trying to figure out how to enforce laws). The whole range of casino games are available, as are horse racing and even betting on sports events.
Special events	Making special events such as speeches, gala premiers, and races viewable and sometimes interactive on the Internet	Some events are staged specifically for the Web, and individuals can engage in chats to interact with those at the event in person. Sophisticated home entertainment systems are increasingly making the virtual experience a legitimate option to the in-person experience.

FIGURE 7.18 Sample entertainment applications on the Internet. (*continued*)

instruction. Some classes can be taught online, and students may soon be able to select courses from the best teachers, anywhere in the world. The Internet is greatly transforming education, as Figure 7.19 suggests.

These tables list the products and services which either are becoming, or could easily become, primarily Internet-based. These lists, however, only begin to scratch the surface of possibilities. Business managers must realize that in the near future, virtually any product, service, or piece of information that *can* be relayed digitally *will* be relayed digitally: i.e., via the Internet. And that thought has great implications for just about every business.

Sample Usage	Description	Example
Universities	Providing education and degrees to individuals using the Internet as the network for interaction	Many traditional universities use the Internet not only to support research, but to deliver course supporting materials such as syllabi, chat rooms, and readings. Some new forms of virtual universities are emerging that have no physical buildings at all, and only operate over the Internet (for example, www.vu.org).
Research	Using the Internet to support research activities	The Internet began as a research network, and continues to be used extensively to link university researchers, private industry researchers, and government agencies. Researchers also use it extensively as a source to locate current projects because the traditional outlet for disseminating findings, journal publishing, takes months if not years and makes it difficult to keep abreast of the most current work.
Special education	Using the Internet to support initiatives in educating slow learners and disabled individuals	Sites offer suggestions for resources to help special education. Some predict that video and audio capabilities will enable special education students to learn at their own pace, but few sites offer that type of learning.
K–12	Using the Internet to support educational activities in primary and secondary schools	President Clinton's 1999 State of the Union address announced his vision for giving every school child access to the Internet by 2000. This vision resulted in every K–12 teacher and administrator evaluating how and what students should do with the Internet. Many schools have some access, and children do everything from research to chatting with peers in foreign lands.

FIGURE 7.19   A summary of sample educational applications of the Internet.

▶ FOOD FOR THOUGHT: E-LEARNING

E-learning is using the Internet to enable learning. The Internet has provided a basis for radically changing the way learning is done. Traditional learning takes place in a classroom, typically with an instructor and a room full of students. Regardless of whether the students are graduates, undergraduates, executives, or even those attending a corporate training session, the traditional model is the default model for most learning situations. But the Internet is beginning to change that.

Today, businesses do not want their employees to ever stop learning. In the fast paced environment of today's business world, having current knowledge is a strategic advantage. Further, relatively little within an organization is static. That was not the case a short while ago. In the past, someone wanting to go to work received training by apprenticing with an expert whom the student modeled, studied, and imitated in order to learn a trade. When the apprenticeship ended, the worker was considered fully trained and ready to earn a living practicing the trade. But that is not the case any longer. A business that does not encourage employees to continually learn and adapt, and that does not build in the ability to learn and adapt, is setting itself up for failure.

Consider Cisco, the maker of routers and other devices used to create networks that become roadways for the Internet. John Chambers, CEO, believes e-learning is a critical success factor for Cisco. "There are two fundamental equalizers in life— the Internet and education. E-learning eliminates the barriers of time and distance creating universal, learning-on-demand opportunities for people, companies, and countries."[19] Cisco managers believe that e-learning helps them increase productivity as well as build loyalty. How do they and others investing in e-learning participate?

There are many different types of e-learning. Figure 7.20 summarizes some of them, including computer-based training, distance learning, online learning, and on-demand learning. In today's environment, the terms are often used inter-

Type of e-learning	Definition
Computer-based training	Any course or lesson presented on a computer, typically not connected to a network.
Distance learning	Any type of educational situation in which the instructor and students are separated by location.
Online learning	Courses presented on a computer that is hooked up to a network.
Technology-based instruction	Training through media other than the classroom. That includes computers, but also refers to television, audiotape, videotape, and print.
Web-based instruction	Courses available on the Internet which typically have embedded links to other Web-based resources.
On-demand learning	Learning broken up into knowledge chunks and delivered as demanded within a business process.

FIGURE 7.20   Types of e-learning.

Adapted from Carliner, S. "An Overview of Online Learning," a white paper published by Lakewood conferences, on website http://www.lakewoodconferences.com/wp, May 25, 2000.

[19] John Chambers as quoted on the Cisco Website, www.cisco.com, May 25, 2000.

changeably, but there are several distinct concepts embedded within the alternatives. Distance learning, for example, is when students are geographically spread out, but use technology to engage in a collective learning session such as a class. This is a different learning experience from online learning, where the learner uses a computer as the primary teaching vehicle. And that is somewhat different from on-demand learning, where information is broken up into small chunks, or nuggets, and pushed out to the learner within the context of their work processes.

If learning can be embedded within the business processes executed by workers, then organizations can make major changes in their business strategy and their organization strategy. Embedding learning within a business process means that when the individual executing the process requires assistance, the process is smart enough to detect it and push information out to the learner to assist him or her in completing the task. It might operate somewhat like an electronic "on the job training" opportunity. The advantage is that if it is done right, the skills needed to complete the job change. And that may mean hiring different types of individuals for the job. Further, if the information pushed out to the learner must be updated, the computer system can do that instantly. That is quite an advantage over traditional courses, where materials must be prepared weeks in advance in order to be ready for the classroom.

E-learning is a relatively new concept. The features of the Internet are enabling innovative organizations to rethink how they disseminate knowledge, information, and training to their employees. And the effects this technology will have on universities and traditional schools is one of the most debated topics of e-business.

▶ SUMMARY

The Internet has the distinction of being an entirely new marketplace, a previously nonexistent place to conduct business. The Internet is a revolutionary innovation in shopping because it connects buyers and sellers from all over the world. It is also the most revolutionary advertising medium since television, and may quickly prove to be more effective than TV since it offers better segmentation and the added feature of interactivity. Internet-based e-commerce is becoming less mysterious and more commonplace; soon it will be second nature to consumers. Quite simply, the Internet is on its way to becoming the single most popular method for conducting business, whether it is B-to-B transactions or B-to-C transactions. Its rules, however, are still in the formative stages, so innovative and forward-thinking business people have the potential to shape them in lucrative and otherwise rewarding ways.

In order for managers to use e-commerce for maximum effectiveness and efficiency, they must understand the elements that comprise it. Kalakota and Whinston place the key elements in a generic framework for electronic commerce, which consists of four building blocks and two pillars. (The framework is depicted in Figure 7.5.)

The first building block is the common business services infrastructure. This includes security and authentication (various methods a manager can use to protect electronic information), electronic payment (manners in which a business can accept payments via the Internet), and directory services and search engines (services a manager can use both to locate important business information and to increase market awareness of his or her business offering). The second building block is the messaging and information distribution infrastructure, which includes electronic methods whereby a business can increase the efficiency of its internal and external communications. The third building block is multimedia content. Determining the various media elements of a business offering helps a manager to determine what sort of vehicle to use to disseminate that offering. The final building block is the Information Superhighway infrastructure, which a manager should understand in order to know how information gets from point A to point B on the Internet.

The first pillar is composed of public policy and legal and privacy issues. Managers must stay abreast of these issues because they are still being formulated and fundamentally affect how business is conducted on the Internet. The second pillar consists of technical standards and protocols. Managers must ascertain that their systems, as well as their electronic products and services, speak the Internet's language.

Business managers can expect a future in which the Internet becomes larger, faster, more powerful, and more commonplace. In the near future, Internet connections may even become portable. Consideration of the Internet and its role in the exploding world of e-commerce, therefore, should figure into all important business decisions. Managers must ask themselves these questions: Which elements of our business can be made available online? If there are elements of our business that can be electronically automated but are not yet, how long can we afford to perform them manually? If we offer a product or service that potentially can be delivered online, even in part, are we prepared to offer it online? If we are not yet prepared to do so, will we be prepared before our competitors are, or before an online substitute becomes available?

In addressing these questions, managers will gain efficiencies, improve products, and open markets. And as with traditional competition, first movers have a distinct advantage.

▶ DISCUSSION QUESTIONS

1. What is the difference in B-to-B and B-to-C applications on the Internet? What features of the Internet are more relevant to B-to-B transactions? To B-to-C transactions? Give examples of each type of transaction. What might be the next business model?

2. What are current uses of the Internet for organizations with which you have worked? How might they use the Internet to improve their organizational strategy? Their business strategy?

3. When an organization implements a website, what changes in its organizational strategy should it anticipate? Why?

4. What is your prediction of the next big breakthrough for the Internet? Support your forecast with points drawn from this chapter and from your experience with the Internet.

5. How will e-learning change the business strategy of an organization? The organizational strategy? Support your claims with examples, either hypothetical or from real companies.

AMAZON.COM°

No company exemplifies the new business era of the Internet more than Amazon.com. What started out as a book company, has emerged as a serious competitor to dozens of industries. And if founder and CEO Jeff Bezos achieves his vision, "Amazon.com will be a place where you can find anything." And given the activities, expansions and successes to date, Amazon is making significant headway on its ambitious plans to take over the entire e-commerce e-tailing world.

Amazon.com started in 1996 selling books over the Internet. Since that time, the company has pioneered many of the innovations that define electronic shopping, such as one-click shopping, customer reviews, and online gift wrapping. It was the first site for customers to actually buy anything over the Internet. It is the largest seller of online books, music and videos, with 12 million customers and 1999 sales of $1.4 billion. It went public in 1997, and the stock price has risen from $1.50 to $80 a share. That gives Amazon.com a market cap of $28 billion, making it more than twice as big as that of Sears, the longtime leader in retail sales, and more than 17 times bigger than Barnes and Noble, the brick and mortal book-selling leader.

A customer visiting the Amazon.com site is greeted with a very busy web page showing key specials that day, and giving opportunity to navigate to the type of product the customer wants to buy. If books are the purchase to be made that day, the customer can click on the books link, and search for a book by title, author, or subject. So far, the scenario is not much to get excited about. But the power behind the Amazon.com business model is not yet shown. If a customer searches for a particular book, not only does Amazon.com's site give the details of the book, but potential buyers can read the table of contents, look at comments written by other readers of the book, link to other books of a related topic or by the same author. Comments give a sense of community to the Amazon.com site, since customers can contribute or read comments very easily. Further, the Amazon.com systems have tracked purchases of the book at hand, and can tell the new customer of other books purchased by those who purchased the current book. Their "suggestions" are based on real data culled from an extensive database of transactions, making the suggestions that much more relevant to the current customer.

The purchasing transaction is innovative, too. The standard process lets customers add a selection to their shopping cart and either continue shopping or finish out the transaction. Shipping options are presented and purchases are paid for with credit cards. But if the customer is a repeat customer, the system already has payment and shipping information, and the purchase can be quickly made with a single "click" of the mouse. E-mail is sent to the purchaser at several points along the process, including a confirmation that the order was received, and a notice of the shipping of the order. E-mail is also automatically generated to alert customers of specials related to purchases they made, such as a new book by a favorite author. Being able to combine a transaction system with real time information, customer connections and dissemination systems makes retailing on the web, or e-tailing, a very different experience from traditional buying at the local bookstore or mall.

Bezo's vision is for Amazon.com to be the center of the e-commerce world. That means selling or at least locating books, videos, CDs, electronics, pet food, clothes, or whatever a

° Adapted from Brooke, Katrina, "Amazon vs Everybody." *Fortune Magazine*, November 8, 1999, pp. 120–128.

shopper on the Internet wants to buy. The company offers an online auction, and an online grocery store, drug store, pet store, toy store, electronics store, and clothing store. In mid 1999, Amazon.com announced two more e-tailing options. All Product Search is a product browser that helps customers locate items at Amazon.com, its partners, or anywhere on the net. Z-shops is an online mall where anyone or any company can set up a store, by paying a small monthly fee and commission. In return, these stores have access to the 12 million customers of Amazon.com.

What is next for Amazon.com? Bezos is quoted as saying, "The idea is to let people find anything they might want to buy online. Amazon is a 'Katrina Store' or a 'Jeff Store'. The notion is that you take the customers and put them at the center of their own universe."

Discussion Questions

1. How has Amazon.com and their use of the Internet, changed the retailing industry? Give some specific examples.

2. Many have compared giant bookstore retailer Barnes and Noble with Amazon.com. Barnes and Noble has dozens of bookstores in many local communities. Yet Amazon.com's reach goes anywhere and everywhere with the web. What, in your opinion, should Barnes and Noble do to compete with Amazon.com?

3. How can Amazon.com complete Bezos' vision? What do they need to do to individualize their services to 12 million customers?

CHAPTER 8

THE MANAGEMENT INFORMATION SYSTEMS ORGANIZATION*

Until January 1993, Cisco Systems, Inc. maintained a traditional information systems (IS) department. Considered a cost center, it reported through the finance department. However, in an effort to increase information technology's (IT's) contribution to the bottom line, Cisco made three organizational changes: IS began reporting to Customer Advocacy; it introduced client-funding, charging project costs to the client department and reducing the portion charged to general and administrative expenses; and IT investment decisions that had been made by an IS steering committee were now made by line organizations. Cisco's new budgeting method made each of the business executives think seriously about IT expenses and how they should be allocated.[1]

Cisco still manages IT centrally, and even client-funded projects are managed by the central IT organization. The chief information officer (CIO) has authority over all IT staff and contractors. Cisco management believes that its organizational strategy helped stabilize the company during a period of fast growth.

IS organizations come in all shapes and sizes. Each is built around processes that it performs or supports. These processes fulfill specific needs of internal customers. For instance, a telecommunications company with a large technology infrastructure may require distributed processing capabilities, whereas a regional manufacturing plant may require only back-office support.

Although each IS organization is unique in many ways, all have elements in common. The focus of this chapter is to introduce managers to the typical activities of an IS organization in order to facilitate interaction with management information systems (MIS) professionals. Managers will be a more effective consumer

---

* The author wishes to acknowledge and thank David M. Zahn, MBA '99 for his help in researching and writing early drafts of this chapter.

[1] R. Nolan and K. Porter, "Cisco Systems, Inc." Harvard Business School case 398–127, April 2000.

161

of services from MIS professionals in their organization if they understand, in general, what they do. This chapter examines the roles and tasks of the IS organization. In addition, it addresses recent issues surrounding IS organizations—in particular, outsourcing, return on investment, and decentralization.

▶ UNDERSTANDING THE MIS ORGANIZATION

Consider an analogy of a ship in a regatta to help explain the purpose of an IS organization and how it functions. A ship transports people and cargo to a particular destination, in much the same way that an IS organization directs itself toward the strategic goals set by the larger enterprise. Sometimes the IS organization must navigate perilous waters or storms to win a regatta. For both the IS organization and the ship, the key is to perform more capably than any competitors. This means employing the right resources to propel the enterprise through the rough waters of business. Each of these resources is discussed below.

Chief Information Officer

If an IS organization is like a ship, then the CIO is at the helm. The CIO is an executive who manages IT resources in order to implement enterprise strategy. The Gartner Group defines a CIO as one who is:

> To provide technology vision and leadership for developing and implementing IT initiatives that create and maintain leadership for the enterprise in a constantly changing and intensely competitive marketplace.[2]

This definition may seem clear, but to understand what the CIO does, we should explore the historical origins of this position. The CIO function is a relatively new position when compared to the more established chief executive officer (CEO) or chief financial officer (CFO), which have existed in the corporate structure for decades. In fact, the CIO position did not really emerge until the early 1980s, when there was a perceived need for an executive-level manager to focus on cutting the ever-increasing costs of IT. Cost-cutting measures typically took the form of outsourcing arrangements, which is addressed later in this chapter.

The evolution of the CIO's role closely follows the evolution of technology in business. Throughout the late 1980s and into the 1990s, technology grew from an expensive necessity to a strategic enabler. As technology's role has risen in importance, so has that of the CIO. In fact, many organizations include the CIO as an integral member of the executive-level decision-making team.

CIOs are a unique breed. They have a strong understanding of the business and of the technology. In many organizations they take on roles that span both of these areas. More often than not, CIOs are asked to play strategic roles at some

---

[2] Source: http://www.cio.com/forums/executive/gartner_description.html.

part of their day, and operations roles at other times, rather than spending all of their time on one or the other. Eleven responsibilities define the CIO role:

- **Championing the organization**—promoting IT within the enterprise as a strategic tool for growth
- **Architecture management**—setting organizational direction and priorities
- **Business strategy consultant**—participating in executive-level decision making
- **Business technology planning**—bridging business and technology groups for purposes of collaborating in planning and execution
- **Applications development**—overseeing legacy and emerging enterprise initiatives, as well as broader strategic business unit (SBU) and divisional initiatives
- **IT infrastructure management (e.g., computers, printers, and networks)**—maintaining current technologies and investing in future technologies
- **Sourcing**—developing and implementing a strategy for outsourcing (versus retaining in-house) IT services and/or people
- **Partnership developer**—negotiating relationships with key suppliers of IT expertise and services
- **Technology transfer agent**—providing technologies that enable the enterprise to work better with suppliers and customers—both internal and external—and consequently, increase shareholder value
- **Customer satisfaction management**—understanding and communicating with both internal and external customers to ensure that customer satisfaction goals are met
- **Training**—providing training to IT users, as well as senior executives who must understand how IT fits with enterprise strategy

A CIO must work effectively not only within the technical arena, but also in overall business management. This unique skill set demands a specialized background. The following nine skills are considered essential for success as a CIO:[3]

- A strong orientation towards business in the enterprise industry or through related activities, such as consulting
- Ability to realize the benefits and manage the cost and risks associated with IT
- Ability to bridge any gaps between available technologies and business needs
- Familiarity with the needs of nontechnical internal clients

[3] Some of these skills are adapted from "CIO Position Description," cio.com, http://www.cio.com/forums/executive/gartner_description.html.

- Strong organizational skills to manage localized IS resources and applications as well as broader SBU and divisional resources and initiatives
- Ability to conceive, build, and implement multiple IT projects on time and within budget
- Ability to articulate and advocate for a management vision of IT
- Ability to mesh well with the existing management structure
- A strategic vision for the enterprise that extends beyond IT

Where the CIO fits within an enterprise is often a source of controversy. In the early days of the CIO position, when the CIO was predominantly responsible for controlling costs, the CIO reported to the Chief Financial Officer (CFO). Since the CIO was rarely involved in enterprise governance, this reporting structure worked. But as IT burgeoned into a source for competitive advantage in the marketplace, reporting to the CFO proved too limiting. Conflicts arose because the CFO misunderstood the vision for IT or saw only the costs of technology, or because management still saw the CIO's primary responsibility as controlling costs. More recently, CIOs report directly to the CEO, President, or other executive manager.

Confusion often occurs regarding whether the CIO is more of a strategist or operational manager. He or she is often asked to be both. Since the CIO is the top IS professional in the hierarchy, it is imperative that this person also be a strategist. The title CIO signals to both the organization and to outside observers that this executive is a strategic IS thinker, and is responsible for linking IS strategy with the business strategy. And with the increasing importance of the Internet to every business, the CIO is increasingly asked to assist, advise, and participate in discussions where business strategy is set. However, just as the CFO is somewhat involved in operational management of the financial activities of the organization, the CIO is involved with operational issues related to IS. That includes activities such as identifying and managing the introduction of new technologies into the firm, setting purchasing and vendor policies, and managing the overall IT budget. Actual day-to-day management of the data center, the vendor portfolio, and other operational issues is typically not handled directly by the CIO, but by one of the managers in the IS organization.

However, some organizations choose not to have a CIO. These organizations typically have an individual responsible for running the computer systems, and possibly for managing many of the activities described later in this chapter. But they signal that this person is not a strategist by giving them the title of data processing manager or director of information systems or some other reference that clearly differentiates this person from other top officers in the company. Using the words "chief" and "officer" usually implies a strategic focus, and some organizations do not see the value of having an IS person on their executive team.

What, then, does a CIO do? Although there is no such thing as an average day in the life of a CIO, the following example provides a reference point. In 1996, Levi Strauss & Company sought a new CIO.[4] Although Levi Strauss's IT was in accept-

---

[4] Field, Tom. "Great Expectations: Growing Companies and Changing Times Make Tomorrow a Challenge for Today's New CIOs." *CIO Magazine*, September 15, 1997, p. 245.

able shape, problems existed. First, the IS organization was viewed by many as a stepchild, a necessary component of the enterprise, but one that did not contribute materially to its success. Second, Levi Strauss was working to recover from a massive reorganization earlier in the decade, which had cost millions of dollars and hundreds of jobs, as well as waning morale, lingering resentment, and general ill will. Finally, the role of IT was poorly matched to the strategic goals of the company. The new CIO faced a daunting job: solve Levi Strauss's Y2K problem, deliver new IT tools—such as those that could produce the new custom-fit jeans called Personal Pair to retail outlets—develop new metrics for tracking IT's value, and forge new relationships with external and internal business leaders.[5]

The new CIO, Linda Glick, was a 21-year veteran of Levi Strauss known for her practicality, partnering capabilities, and ability to get the job done. Peter Jacobi, the president of Levi Strauss, described her as fearless. In her job as CIO, Glick tackled the Y2K problem, brought a new attitude to the much-maligned IS department, and began to form the executive-level partnerships required to become an advocate for IT within the Levi Strauss organization. She led Levi Strauss, in late 1998, to enter the world of electronic commerce with an online store. No one could tackle all of Levi Strauss's problems overnight, but Glick's situation typifies the challenges CIOs face.

Chief Knowledge Officer and Other Similar Roles

Although the CIO's role is to guide the enterprise toward the future, this responsibility is too great to accomplish alone. Many organizations have recognized that certain strategic areas of the IS organization require more focused guidance. This recognition has led to the creation of new positions, such as the chief knowledge officer (CKO), chief technology officer (CTO), chief telecommunications officer (also CTO), chief network officer (CNO), and chief resource officer (CRO). See Figure 8.1 for a list of their different responsibilities. Each of these positions typically subordinates to the CIO, with the occasional exception of the chief technology officer. New "chief" roles spring up almost daily as enterprises try to share the complex and growing responsibilities of managing IT. For example, General Motors has established divisional CIO positions that report to the corporate CIO.[6] Other firms have eliminated the CIO altogether in favor of some configuration of the typically subordinate positions. These enterprises hope that flatter organizations will prove more effective.

Other Information Systems Organizational Roles

In addition to the CIO role, MIS organizations are home to many different types of professionals. This section describes some of the most common roles.

---

[5] Ibid.

[6] Paul, Lauren Gibbons. "A Separate Piece." *CIO Magazine*, October 15, 1998.

Title	Responsibility
Chief knowledge officer (CKO)	Create a knowledge management infrastructure
	Build a knowledge culture
	Make corporate knowledge pay off
Chief technology officer (CTO)	Track emerging technologies
	Advise on technology adoption
	Operate in some companies at same level as CIO
Chief telecommunications officer (CTO)	Focus on technology across all MIS functions
	Contribute to strategy formulation
Chief network officer (CNO)	Build and maintain internal and external networks
Chief resource officer (CRO)	Manage outsourcing relationships

FIGURE 8.1 The CIO's lieutenants.

IS Managers

Under the CIO and his or her lieutenants are IS managers. While the strategists set a direction for the enterprise, the managers implement the strategy. IS managers lead systems implementation projects and various IT departmental efforts. They must understand both sides of the technology/business fence and closely align themselves with the general managers of the enterprise. They also must understand both the big picture and the details of the operation. For example, in an Oracle General Ledger implementation project, an IS manager might assume responsibility for budget, progress, problem resolution, and contract issues. He or she would ensure that project operations reflect strategic directions set at the executive level.

The business counterpart to the IS manager is the general manager. General managers set business strategy, identify business opportunities, and, most importantly from an IS perspective, work with IS managers to implement those strategies. A partnership between general managers and IS managers is essential if IT is to fulfill its role as a strategic business enabler. To use the example of the Oracle implementation cited above, a general manager would work with the IS manager to solve such problems as a lack of sufficient detail in the general ledger system or software bugs that prevent the production of key reports.

Systems Developers

Systems developers write new software applications, upgrade existing ones, and maintain current systems. They come with a broad skill set, but typically need programming abilities, an understanding of general business concepts, familiarity with systems development and related lifecycle methodologies, creative problem-solving talents, and cross-technology knowledge. In the Oracle General Ledger implementation project, the systems developer would code modifications to various Oracle application modules and interfaces with legacy systems, as well as solve technical incompatibilities between off-the-shelf software and business requirements.

Business Analysts

Business analysts translate business requirements into implementable IT solutions. They work closely with business leaders and systems developers to ensure coordinated development and maintenance efforts. Business analysts' skills include an understanding of core business requirements, an equivalent understanding of the technological possibilities at hand, and the ability to communicate effectively at all levels of the IS and business organizations. In the Oracle implementation project, a business analyst would manage the defining of operations, the gathering and mapping of business requirements, and the delivery of solutions to the business customer.

Database Administrators

Database administrators (DBAs) implement and maintain the software and hardware that houses networked business applications and data. They keep the systems running smoothly. It is often said that the best DBAs are never seen, since DBAs typically surface when problems occur. A DBA's skill set focuses on technology—specifically, multiple operating systems, hardware products and services, programming languages, networking, telecommunications, and other technologies that utilize databases. In the Oracle implementation project, the DBA would build the relational database management system (RDBMS), install software and server upgrades, develop system backups, and troubleshoot development and production problems.

Operations Personnel

These men and women run, monitor, and maintain the production hardware and software applications within an IS organization. They are often found in data centers, where mainframes or servers are housed. Their skills vary but typically involve specialized knowledge of hardware or software sufficient to monitor and maintain it. Operations personnel often possess such detailed knowledge that they are consulted about the adoption of emerging technologies. In our running example, an operations person would take over most server monitoring responsibilities once the general ledger system was implemented.

Support Personnel

Support personnel fill roles thoughout the IS organization, including the help desk, project management, and desktop services. Their skills vary. In the Oracle example, support personnel might take responsibility for recruiting new project team members, installing new PCs and software for them, and developing a process for providing product support to business system users.

Developers

Most organizations have a group dedicated to developing new processes, methodologies, products, and services. People in these groups often employ multidisciplinary skills to develop or identify next-generation products. They may form cross-functional teams to better meet the needs of a particular development effort. They might develop a new project management system for use in our general ledger implementation effort. This system would feature a software component, but also would include processes, procedures, and support activity.

Webmaster, Web Designer, Web Developer, and Other Web-Based Roles
With the proliferation of the Internet into just about every aspect of business comes a new series of roles for most IS organizations. Many do similar functions to those described above, only they focus on the Web. However, with the Web comes a new type of responsibility for IS organizations, namely to build systems that are both seen by internal employees and external customers, shareholders, and others. That means systems must be designed, developed, and managed differently. And that responsibility falls on the IS organization. A webmaster is typically the top person in the organization who bears the primary responsibility for all web activities. This person is typically one of the early adopters of the Web, and has extensive knowledge in many areas including coding, design, hyper-linking, and web trends. The web designer is the person who designs the interfaces for each web page, and typically has some background in user interface design, graphic arts, or other visual expertise. The web developer is the person who actually codes the web pages since the developer has knowledge of Internet-based languages such as html, Java, and C++ (see Chapter 7 for more on these technologies) and of the technical background needed to put web pages on the servers. Other web-based roles crop up frequently as organizations seek ways to identify the individuals charged with responsibility for their organization's website. Many are given outrageous names, such as czar of the Web (like a CIO only restricted to the Web), content guy (makes sure the content that needs to be on the web page is on the page), digital yenta (makes matches between web specialists and organizations that need them), and vibe evolver (identifies new trends to put on the web).

There are many other roles within an IS organization, including networking specialists, implementation consultants, and vendor-relationship specialists. The simplified IS organization chart shown in Figure 8.2 gives a view of the reporting relationships that can exist.

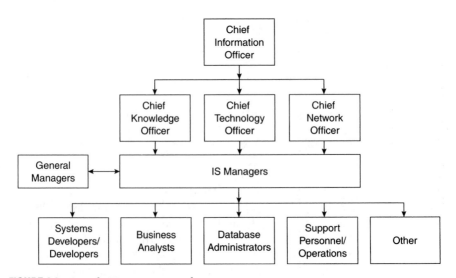

FIGURE 8.2 Sample IS organization chart.

▶INFORMATION SYSTEMS ORGANIZATION PROCESSES

The general manager needs to understand the processes internal to the IS group in order to interact effectively with that group to accomplish business goals. Several processes that typify most IS organizations are discussed in the following section.

Systems Development

The primary processes done by most IS organizations is that of developing systems. Systems development itself will be discussed in more detail in Chapter 10, the chapter on project management. In general, designing and building systems is a core process for most IS organizations. In some cases, it means analyzing needs, designing the software, writing or coding the software, and testing to make sure the software works and meets the business objectives. However, with the proliferation of software companies offering a wide range of packages off the shelf, there is a trend toward buying, rather than making, systems. In that case, systems development processes identify and acquire outside software packages to fill a need for individuals in the organizations. This process also includes installing the package and setting any necessary options and parameters to ensure the system runs properly.

Systems Maintenance

Once installed, systems do not function entirely on their own. Many people work toward their continued maintenance. For instance, once a general ledger system is installed, support personnel or DBAs monitor the daily processing of transactions and reports. Developers and business personnel address post-implementation needs, such as writing additional reports or reconciling system errors. Systems developers provide upgrades as they become available. Business managers interact with process managers to arrange access to new reports, or to report problems they experience with systems functioning.

Data Center Operations

Data centers are common among enterprises that take a more centralized approach to IS organization. The data center typically houses large mainframe computers or rows of servers. Most of the company's data and business applications reside somewhere in the data center alongside remote-access technologies that connect the enterprise to the outside world.

Data center personnel vary in skill, but most maintain familiarity with the nuts and bolts of the installed hardware and software. Often, the most technical of people can be found in data centers due to the mission-critical nature of the technologies that reside there.

General managers rarely have direct contact with data center personnel unless they experience processing problems. Such problems are usually reported to IS managers in processing meetings attended by business and IS representatives.

Although these reports are sometimes made electronically, larger problems often require direct contact. A typical report looks similar to Figure 8.3.

Internet and Networking Services

Such technologies as intranets, extranets, web pages, and e-mail are becoming essential in most business environments. General managers must interact with IS organization members who develop and maintain Internet capabilities. Since levels of these services will vary greatly with each organization, working with the right person is essential. Often Internet business needs remain ambiguous unless the general manager and IS staff can collaborate to develop a strong vision for the enterprise.

In order to implement a successful website, the IS manager and the general manager must agree on a team to support a variety of activities. At a minimum, processes needed by an organization to run a robust web page include the site design process and the site maintenance process. Increasingly, companies are considering outsourcing many of their web-based activities, which means that someone must manage and coordinate these services in order to ensure that the right services are provided. For example, should managers decide to use a web-based ERP system, someone in either the IS organization or the business itself must be charged with managing the vendor, and with ensuring the appropriate level of service is obtained.

Since the early 1980s, networks have grown tremendously, resulting in a growth of networking groups as well. When there are problems connecting to the local area network (LAN), or when a new user needs to set up new PCs for a department, the networking group eventually processes the request. This side of the IS organization is visible to most end users.

Networking groups design network architecture and build and maintain the network infrastructure, keeping abreast of the latest technology and anticipating future needs. Upgrading networks is often expensive and slow, so anticipating future needs is an important concern. Networking people tend to be in high demand. The wide range of technologies on the market and the variable nature of networks

Problem Ticket #	Description of Problem	Resolution of Problem	Contact	Status	Cost of Non-Conformance
PR-17390	Job # 182 ended abnormally due to a disk failure	*2200 hours—* Problem detected *2300 hours—* Bad disk replaced *2310 hours—* Job restarted	Sally Operator	Closed	Delay did not affect processing window

FIGURE 8.3 Morning problem report example.

require personnel who can stay abreast of new technologies and understand how to use them within a given network architecture.

Often the set of processes that manage the physical telephone network is called telecommunications. Although some may not realize that telecommunications falls under the purview of IS, it constitutes a vitally important strategic concern. Telephone systems, certain networking systems, and access to the Internet all may fall under the rubric of telecommunications. And as new wireless technologies become popular, they are managed by these processes. General managers should concern themselves with telecommunications because the quality of service provided will affect the daily operations of the business. Telephones that do not work or voice mail systems that lose messages can affect the bottom line. Moreover, telecommunications costs are typically charged back to the business area cost center.

New Technology Introduction

Staying abreast of new technology is one of the most important functions an IS organization can perform, yet it is sometimes neglected. Missing technology trends gives the competition the chance to capitalize on new costs savings or sources of revenue. IT has assumed such strategic importance in the enterprise that new technology deserves a particular focus within IS.

New technology groups assess the costs and benefits of new technologies for the enterprise. They are the way many innovations formally enter an organization. The new technology group works closely with business groups to determine which technologies can provide the greatest benefit and how the technologies might impact the organization. Technology personnel stay abreast of trends through online newsletters, periodicals, trade shows, product testing, and close relationships with user groups and vendors.

Special Projects

IS organizations are organized to anticipate most business requests, but frequently requests require efforts beyond the scope and capacity of the current organization. These special requests often spur the formation of special project teams. Typically, such teams receive a fair degree of autonomy within the organization, and they focus solely on the project at hand. For example, under most circumstances, the staff who maintains the current general ledger system cannot also implement a new system. A different group can better address the special requirements and workload entailed. Typically, however, maintenance staff will transfer from their current positions to be a part of the special project. A general manager will confer with IS managers to set systems requirements and with project team members to address implementation requirements.

Resource Management

Business projects often require support from personnel with very specific IS skills. On occasions when these skills are not to be found within the IS organization, business managers must still rely on IS colleagues to aid in the search outside the organization. Sometimes, IS personnel directly manage all hiring or contracting for the required services because they can leverage specialized knowledge of contract labor houses or negotiated outsourcing relationships.

General Support

Processes in place to support day-to-day business operations vary depending on the size of the enterprise and the levels of support required. Typically, support requests are centralized so they can be tracked for quality-control purposes. This centralization simplifies the interaction between business and IS. Often, a central support desk dispatches support personnel to address the problem at hand.

Often IS organizations maintain first client contact through a centralized help desk even for such diverse services as networking and telecommunications. The help desk serves as the primary point of contact for technical questions and problem reporting. Centralizing help desk activities allows IS managers to track performance and results more efficiently. It also gives business people a single phone number or e-mail address to remember in times of need.

Help desks are not usually manned by people who will solve the problem. Help desk personnel collect pertinent information, record it, determine its priority, contact the appropriate support personnel, and follow up with the business contacts with updates or resolution information. For help beyond daily support, most organizations also maintain a customer service request (CSR) process. A paper or electronic form is used to allow a business person to describe the nature of the request, its priority, the contact point, and the appropriate cost center. CSRs initiate much of the work in IS organizations.

▶ WHAT TO EXPECT FROM INFORMATION SYSTEMS

Managers must learn what to expect from the IS organization so they can plan and implement business strategy accordingly. A manager can expect six core activities: anticipating new technologies, participating in setting and implementing strategic goals, innovating current processes, managing supplier relationships, establishing architecture platforms and standards, and managing human resources.[7]

Anticipating New Technologies

Technology moves at such break-neck speeds that for an enterprise to leverage state-of-the art tools, IT must keep an eye toward the horizon. Doing so is not as simple as saying, "We need the latest version of WareSoft Version 2.1." IT must weigh the risks and potential benefits of early adoption of technology. IT must understand technology trends so that the enterprise does not invest heavily in new technologies which quickly become obsolete or incompatible with other enterprise

---

[7] Rockart, John F., Michael J. Earl, and Jeanne W. Ross. "Eight Imperatives for the New IT Organization." *Sloan Management Review*, Fall 1996, pp. 52–53.

standards. This situation is not unlike the situation many found themselves in after investing in the Beta format for VCRs, only to find themselves with useless equipment and tapes when the VHS format became the de facto standard. To correctly assess the enterprise's needs, business and IS staff must work closely to evaluate which technologies will advance the business strategy. It is the job of the IS department to scout new technology trends and help the business integrate them into planning and operations.

Strategic Direction

IS staff can enable business managers to achieve strategic goals by acting as consultants or by teaching them about developing technologies. As consultants, IS can advise managers on best practices within IT and work with them to develop IT-enhanced solutions to business problems. For example, Jim Dowling, the director of corporate information systems at Bose Corporation, designated more than 100 of his IT personnel as internal IT consultants.[8] He asked them to fulfill a role similar to that of external consultants in that they understand and address both technical and business issues. As consultants, they act with a degree of autonomy from the current IT organization; their status provides them unusual flexibility in order to move quickly and, ultimately, save money.

IS personnel also educate managers about current technologies as well as IT trends. Sharing business and technical knowledge between groups encourages better, more informed decisions across the enterprise.

Process Innovation

IT staff should work with managers to innovate processes that can benefit from technological solutions. Such solutions can range from installing voice mail to networking personal computers or automating general ledger transactions. Business process reviews usually begin with a survey of best practices. IT becomes an integral component of new processes designed for the enterprise. Thus, IS personnel can play a crucial role by designing systems that facilitate these new ways of doing business.

Internal Partnerships

No longer anonymous techies, IS staff are partners in moving the enterprise forward. IS staff must seek to initiate, foster, and grow strong partnerships with their business colleagues. Greg Walton, vice president and CIO at Carilion Health System in Roanoke, Virginia, for instance, stations his internal consultants within the enterprise business units.[9] Thus, Carilion's IT professionals both represent

---

[8] Horowitz, Alan S. "IS Ambassadors." *Computerworld*, http://www.computerworld.com/home/features.nsf/all/980420mgt, April 20, 1998.

[9] Ibid.

business concerns to the IS organization and IS concerns to the business leaders. This tighter relationship improves integration between systems and business.

Supplier Management

As more companies adopt outsourcing as a means of controlling IT costs and acquiring "best of breed" capabilities, managing these supplier relationships becomes increasingly important. IS must maximize the benefit of these relationships to the enterprise and pre-empt problems that might occur. Failure in this regard could result in deteriorating quality of service, loss of competitive advantages, costly contract disputes, low morale, and loss of key personnel.

One of the most famous illustrations of supplier management derives from the experience of an originator of the concept: the Eastman Kodak Company. In 1989, Kodak outsourced its data center operations to IBM, its network to Digital Equipment Company, and its desktop supply and support operations to Businessland.[10] Kodak managed these relationships through strategic alliances.[11] Kodak retained IS staff to act on behalf of its business personnel with outsource vendors. Vendor contracts created incentives for new investment in technology and provided enough flexibility to encourage quick problem resolution. Vendors made fair profits and received additional business if they performed well. Within a couple of years, Kodak's capital expenditures attributable to computing dropped by 90 percent.[12] Its approach to supplier management became a model emulated by Continental Bank, General Dynamics, Continental Airlines, and National Car Rental.[13]

Architecture and Standards

Given the complex nature of IT in the enterprise, the role of IS in developing, maintaining, and communicating standards is critical. Failure could mean increased maintenance costs due to incompatibilities between platforms, redundant or incorrect data, and slow processing. For example, precise naming standards are crucial in implementing a new data warehouse or accounts payable system. Even small variations in invoice entries—the difference between showing a payment to "IBM," "I.B.M.," or "International Business Machines"—could yield incomplete information when business managers query the data warehouse to understand how much was paid to the vendor in a given period. Inconsistent data undermines the integrity of a data warehouse.

---

[10] Applegate, L. and R. Montealegre. "Eastman Kodak Co: Managing Information Systems Through Strategic Alliances." *HBS* case no. 192030, September 1995.

[11] DiRomualdo, Anthony, and Vijay Gurbaxani. "Strategic Intent for IT Outsourcing." *Sloan Management Review*, June 22, 1998.

[12] Information Systems: A Manager's Perspective, Steven L. Alter, 1996.

[13] Lacity, Mary C., Leslie P. Willcocks, and David F. Feeny. "The Value of Selective IT Sourcing." *Sloan Management Review*, March 22, 1996.

Human Resource Management

IS must manage its own resources. Doing so means providing sufficient business and technical training so that staff can perform effectively and retain their value to the enterprise. Additional human resource activities include hiring and firing, tracking time, and managing budgets, operations, and projects. Since most IS organizations lack their own human resource departments, individual managers bear these responsibilities.

Most IS activities fall within the categories described in this section. In addition, however, business managers can expect the user management activities shown in Figure 8.4.

► WHAT THE INFORMATION SYSTEMS ORGANIZATION DOES NOT DO

This chapter has presented typical roles and processes for IS organizations. Although most IS professionals are asked to do a wide range of tasks for their organization, in reality there are many tasks the IS organization should not do. Clearly, the IS organization does not directly do other core business functions such as selling, manufacturing, accounting, etc. But sometimes managers of these functions inadvertently delegate key operational decisions to the IS organization. When general managers ask the IS professional to build an information system for their organization and don't become an active partner in the design of that system, they are in effect turning over control of their business operations. Likewise, asking an IS professional to implement a software package without partnering with that professional to insure the package not only meets current needs, but future needs as well, is ceding control. The IS organization does not design business processes.

As discussed in Chapter 4, the use of IS for strategic advantage, the general manager, not the IS professional, sets business strategy. However, again, in many organizations, the general manager delegates critical technology decisions to the CIO, which in turn may limit the strategic options available to the firm. There is a role for the IS professional in the discussion of strategy. That role is one of suggesting technologies and applications that enable strategy, identifying limits to the technologies and applications under consideration, and consulting with all those

Traditional IT Activities *(often supplied through alliances with vendors)*	The New IT Activities *(often supplied by MIS organization)*	User's Activities *(Supplied by IS person on payroll in end user department)*
• Data Center Management • Network Management • Application Design, Development and Maintenance • Desktop Hardware Procurement, Installation, and Maintenance	• Architecture, Standards and Technology Planning • IT Strategic Planning • Process Innovation • Vendor Management • Training and Internal Consulting	• Technology scanning and development • Applications Strategy • Choose and maintain Desktop, Laptop, Personal Digital Assistant or other Personal Devices • Implementation

FIGURE 8.4 User management activities.

Adapted from Ownes, J., "Transforming the Informations Systems Organization," CISR Endicott House XXIX presentation, 2–3 December 1993.

involved with setting strategic direction to make sure they properly consider the role and impact of IS on the decisions they make. The IS organization does not set business strategy.

▶ OUTSOURCING AND DECENTRALIZATION

IS managers confront many of the same challenges other managers face in today's business environment. How IS managers address them will directly affect the work of the general managers. The earlier example concerning naming standards illustrates this point. Since small decisions such as a standard spelling for "IBM" on vendor payments can have far-reaching effects, larger decisions, especially strategic ones, will reach even further. This section discusses two key issues: outsourcing and decentralization.

Outsourcing

Since the 1970s, IT managers have turned to outsourcing as an important weapon in the battle to control costs. IT outsourcing means that an outside vendor provides services traditionally provided by the internal MIS department. Over the years, however, certain motives for outsourcing have changed. This section examines the history of outsourcing, models for outsourcing, its advantages and disadvantages, and issues to consider in deciding whether and how to outsource.

The classic model of outsourcing dictates that an enterprise should outsource only those functions that do not give it competitive advantage. For instance, mainframe computer maintenance and monitoring are not often considered core competencies of an enterprise and therefore are often farmed to vendors such as Computer Sciences Corporation or Electronic Data Systems. In the early days of outsourcing, such contracts ran long term—often for 10 years or more. Frequently, outsourcers took over entire IS departments, including people, equipment, and management responsibility. This classic approach prevailed through most of the 1970s and 1980s, but then experienced a decline in popularity.

In the 1990s, outsourcing practices changed such that all IT became up for grabs—including aspects that provide competitive advantage. As relationships with outsourcers have become more sophisticated, companies have realized that even such essential functions as customer service are sometimes better managed by experts on the outside. And the ubiquity of the Internet has spawned a series of new application service providers (ASPs) who perform similar services using web-based applications.

The first choice an enterprise faces about outsourcing is whether to pursue it fully or selectively. As the term "full outsourcing" implies, an enterprise can outsource all its IT functions from desktop services to software development. An enterprise would outsource everything if it does not view IT as a strategic advantage that it needs to cultivate internally. Full outsourcing can free resources to be employed in areas that add greater value. It can also reduce overall cost per transaction due to size and economies of scale.[14] Many companies outsource IT just so their managers are able to focus attention on other business issues. For example, in early 1998, the Connecticut state government outsourced all its IT assets, from desktop PCs to mainframes.[15] The state CIO, Rock Regan, wanted to fix Y2K problems, standardize processing platforms, and cut costs. Regan's particular budget goal was to shrink his $200 million yearly IT expenditure by as much as 15 percent. He chose full outsourcing because he knew that he could not compete in the marketplace for the skilled professionals he needed to accomplish his IT goals. Also, his underperforming IT architecture cried out for a complete overhaul.

With selective outsourcing, an enterprise chooses which IT capabilities to retain in-house and which to give to an outsider. A "best-of-breed" approach is taken in which suppliers are chosen for their expertise in specific technology areas. Although an enterprise can acquire top-level skills and experience through such relationships, the effort required to manage them grows tremendously with each new supplier. Still, selective outsourcing gives greater flexibility and often better service due to the competitive market.[16] To illustrate, an enterprise might retain a web development firm to handle electronic commerce and at the same time select a large outsourcer such as Perot Systems to assume mainframe maintenance. This approach, also called "strategic sourcing," has been adopted by such firms as GM and Southland Corporation.

What factors drive companies to outsource? The most common is the need to save costs. Outsourcing suppliers derive savings from economies of scale. They realize these economies through centralized data centers, preferential contracts with suppliers, and large pools of technical expertise. Most often, enterprises lack such resources on a sufficient scale within their own IS departments. A single company may need only 5000 PCs, but an outsourcer can negotiate a contract for 50,000 and achieve a much lower unit cost.

A second factor driving companies to outsource is that highly qualified IT staff are difficult to retain. An employer must invest in continuous training so that IT staff can keep current with marketplace technologies and also provide them with competitive salaries. Current demand is such that a skilled IT professional need not remain long in a disadvantageous position. Large firms such as CSC, E&Y, PWC, D&T, and Anderson Consulting draw many talented IT professionals, who are then assigned to many different accounts. An outsourcer often can provide greater opportunity for training and advancement in IT than a single MIS organization.

Third, by bringing in outside expertise, management often can focus less attention on IS operations and more on information itself. MIS department personnel manage the relationships with outsourcers and are ultimately still responsible for IS services. But outsourcers are separate businesses, not internal departments.

[14] Field, Tom. "An Outsourcing Buyer's Guide: Caveat Emptor." *CIO Magazine*, April 1, 1997.

[15] Thibodeau, Patrick. "Connecticut Outsources the Works." *Computerworld*, March 30, 1998.

[16] Field, Tom. "An Outsourcing Buyer's Guide: Caveat Emptor." *CIO Magazine*, April 1, 1997.

Managers are freed to devote their energies to areas that reflect core competencies for the business.

Fourth, to the extent that outsourcers specialize in IS services, they are likely to understand how to manage IS staff effectively. An outsourcer often can offer IS personnel a professional environment that a typical company cannot afford to build. For example, a web designer would have responsibility for one website within a company, but for multiple sites at an outsourcer. However, to ensure that staff supporting a particular project are deployed to best advantage, the outsourcer and the management of the client enterprise must maintain a close working relationship.

Fifth, so long as contract terms effectively address contingencies, the larger resources of an outsourcer provide greater capacity on demand. For instance, at year-end, outsourcers potentially can allocate additional mainframe capacity to ensure timely completion of nightly processing, in a manner that would be impossible for an enterprise running its own bare-bones data center.

Finally, outsourcers generally provide access to larger pools of talent and more current knowledge of advancing technologies. For example, many outsourcers had vast experience solving Y2K problems, whereas IS staff within a single company only had limited experience. The vendor's experienced consultants were more readily available to the marketplace than any comparably trained and experienced IT professionals who might be recruitable for in-house employment. It becomes the outsourcer's responsibility to find, train, and retain this talent, not the in-house IS manager's.

Opponents of outsourcing tend to site four disadvantages (see Figure 8.5). A manager should consider each of these before making a decision about outsourcing. Each can be mitigated with effective planning and ongoing management.

First, outsourcing requires that a company surrender a degree of control over critical aspects of the enterprise. By turning over data center operations, for example, a company puts itself at the mercy of an outsourcer's ability to manage this function effectively. A manager must choose an outsourcer carefully and negotiate terms that will support an effective working relationship.

Second, outsourcing decisions can be difficult and expensive to reverse. Unless experienced IT staff can contribute elsewhere in the firm, outsourcing major IT functions means staff will be lost either to the outsourcers or to other companies. If an outsourcing relationship becomes difficult to manage, or if anticipated cost savings are not realized, returning to an "in-sourced" status will require the enterprise to acquire the necessary infrastructure and staff.

Third, outsourcing contracts may not adequately anticipate new technological capabilities. Outsourcers may not recommend so-called bleeding edge technologies for fear of losing money in the process of implementation and support, even

- Abdication of control
- High switching costs
- Lack of technological innovation
- Loss of ownership

FIGURE 8.5 Disadvantages related to outsourcing.

if implementation would best serve the client. Thus, poorly planned outsourcing risks a loss in IT flexibility. For example, some outsourcers were slow to adopt Internet technologies for their clients because they feared the benefits would not be as tangible as the costs of entering the market. This reluctance impinged on clients' ability to realize business strategies involving e-business.

Fourth, by surrendering IT functions, a company gives up any real potential to develop them for competitive advantage—unless, of course, the outsourcing agreement is sophisticated enough to comprehend developing such advantage in tandem with the outsourcing company. However, even these partnerships potentially compromise the advantage since ownership is shared with the outsourcer, and the advantage may become available to the outsourcer's other clients. Under many circumstances, the outsourcer becomes the primary owner of any technological solutions developed. And they allow the outsourcer to leverage the knowledge to benefit other clients, possibly even competitors of the initial client.

Finally, contract terms may leave clients little recourse in terminating troublesome vendor relationships. Outsourcers avoid entering relationships in which they might face summary dismissal. Clients must ensure that contract terms allow them the flexibility they require to manage and, if necessary, sever supplier relationships.

Outsourcing decisions must be made with adequate care and deliberation. The steps outlined in Figure 8.6 are recommended when considering this option.

To illustrate the ins and outs of selective and full outsourcing, consider the case of a company that pursued both approaches. British Petroleum (BP) selected only a few outsourcers with short-term contracts to meet its IT needs.[17] BP awarded Sema Group management of its data center, Science Applications International Corporation its European IT facility management and company-wide applications support, and Syncordia its telecommunications and telex networks. This arrangement was selective in that BP chose each company for its particular expertise, but full in that BP turned over a significant percentage of its IT to outsourcers. Thus, it gained the benefits of best of breed and competitive pricing along with fewer

---

- Do not focus negotiation solely on price.
- Craft full life-cycle service contracts that occur in stages.
- Establish short-term supplier contracts.
- Use multiple, best-of-breed suppliers.
- Develop skills in contract management.
- Carefully evaluate your company's own capabilities.
- Thoroughly evaluate outsourcers' capabilities.
- Choose an outsourcer whose capabilities complement yours.
- Base a choice on cultural fit as well as technical expertise.
- Determine whether a particular outsourcing relationship produces a net benefit for your company.

FIGURE 8.6 Steps to avoid pitfalls.

[17] Cross, J. "IT Outsourcing: British Petroleum." *Harvard Business Review*, May–June 1995, pp. 94–102.

contract management worries and the ability to develop long-term relationships. BP encouraged the outsourcers to work together to provide high-quality services.

What were the results of BP's approach? The company saw its IT costs fall from $360 million in 1989 to $132 million in 1994. At the same time, it gained more flexible IT systems and higher-quality service. BP saw its IT staff shrink by 80 percent. The remaining staff became internal consultants throughout the company. In fact, BP is considering outsourcing its internal consultants to other companies. Not all outsourcing arrangements are so successful, but BP illustrates the best case scenario.

What is the future of outsourcing? Every enterprise faces different competitive pressures. These factors shape how it will view IT and how it will decide to leverage IT for the future. Most will need to outsource at least some IT functions. How each enterprise chooses to manage its outsourced functions will be crucial to its success.

Centralized versus Decentralized Organizational Structures

Organizational approaches to IS have evolved in a cyclic manner over time. At one end of the spectrum, centralized IS organizations bring together all staff, hardware, software, and processing into a single location. Decentralized organizations scatter these components in different locations to address local business needs. Companies' organizational strategies exist along a continuum from centralization to decentralization, with a combination of the two, called *federalism*, found in the middle (see Figure 8.7). Enterprises of all shapes and sizes can be found at any point along the continuum. Over time, however, each enterprise tends to gravitate toward one end of the continuum or the other and often a reorganization is in reality a change from one end to the other.

To illustrate these tendencies, consider the different approaches taken to organize IS. In the 1960s, mainframes dictated a centralized approach to IS because the mainframe resided in one physical location. Centralized decision making, purchasing, maintenance, and staff kept these early computing behemoths running.[18] The 1970s remained centralized due in part to the constraints of mainframe computing, although the mini-computer began to create a rationale to decentralize. The 1980s saw the advent of the PC. PCs allowed computing power to spread beyond the raised-floor, super-cooled rooms of mainframes. This phenomenon gave rise to

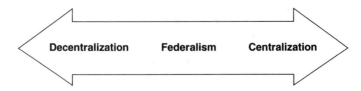

FIGURE 8.7 Organizational continuum.

[18] Laberis, Bill. "Recentralization: Breaking the News." *Computerworld*, June 29, 1998, p. 1.

decentralization, a trend that exploded with the advent of LANs and client/server technology. The Web, with its ubiquitous presence and fast network speeds, has shifted some back to a more centralized approach. What are the most important considerations in deciding how much to centralize or decentralize? Figure 8.8 shows some of the advantages and disadvantages of each approach.

The two approaches amalgamated in the 1990s. Companies began to adopt a strategy based on lessons learned from earlier years of centralization and decentralization. Most companies would like to achieve the advantages derived from both organizational paradigms. This desire leads to federalism.[19] Many companies adopt a form of federal IT, yet still count themselves as either decentralized or centralized, depending on their position on the continuum. Other companies, such as Home Depot, recognize this hybrid approach and actively seek to take advantage of its benefits. Figure 8.9 shows how these approaches interrelate.[20]

Bethlehem Steel has taken a decentralized approach, which mirrors their decentralized business strategy. A global company that traces its roots to 1957, when it was called Saucona Iron Company, Bethlehem Steel has grown its revenues to roughly $4.4 billion and ships 8.6 million tons of steel annually.[21] Bethlehem produces high-quality steel products including hot and cold rolled sheet, carbon and alloy plates, coke, standard rails, forging blooms, billets, flatbars, and large-diameter pipe. The business units themselves are decentralized, with major plants in Steelton, Pennsylvania, Sparrows Point, Maryland, Burns Harbor, Indiana and Lackawanna, New York.

Bethlehem has been challenged to develop new products that respond to alternatives to steel, to implement a capital-intensive facilities plan, to improve quality and cost-effectiveness, and to acquire and maintain human resource competencies.[22] Given these circumstances, Bethlehem and its sole IT provider, Electronic Data Systems, chose a decentralized approach to IT. Bethlehem managers believed that computing power and decision making should be located within local business units. Bethlehem found this approach effective and continues to explore its advantages.

On the other hand, a company that adopted a different approach is Levi Strauss, the company discussed earlier in this chapter. Under the guidance of new CIO Linda Glick, Levi Strauss adopted a centralized strategy. Levi Strauss management wanted to gain better control over strategic IT resources, minimize duplication of resources across its business, and maximize sharing of scarce resources. The managers decided that a centralized approach would achieve this goal.

[20] Eight Imperatives for the New IT Organization, John F. Rockart, Michael J. Earl, Jeanne W. Ross, Sloan Management Review, Fall 1996, pgs. 52–53.

[21] Ibid.

[22] Source: http://www.bethsteel.com.

[23] Conarty, Thomas Jr. "Redefining IS: We are The Business." *Information Week*, p. 1.

Approach	Advantages	Disadvantages	Companies Adopting
Centralized	• Global standards and common data • "One voice" when negotiating supplier contracts • Greater leverage in deploying strategic IT initiatives • Economies of scale and a shared cost structure • Access to large capacity • Better recruitment and training of IT professionals	• Technology may not meet local needs • Slow support for strategic initiatives • Schism between business and IT organization • Us versus them mentality when technology problems occur • Lack of business unit control over overhead costs	Alcoa Levi-Strauss Mobil
Decentralized	• Technology customized to local business needs • Closer partnership between IT and business units • Greater flexibility • Reduced tele-communication costs • Consistency with decentralized enterprise structure • Business unit control over overhead costs	• Difficulty maintaining global standards and consistent data • Higher infrastructure costs • Difficulty negotiating preferential supplier agreements • Loss of control • Duplication of staff and data	Bethlehem Steel VeriFone

FIGURE 8.8 Advantages and disadvantages of organizational approaches.

▶FOOD FOR THOUGHT: CALCULATING RETURN ON INVESTMENT

The Y2K crisis[23] strained IT budgets. Y2K compliance is a business necessity addressed only by implementing new systems or upgrading existing ones. Limited financial resources caused management executives to examine more closely the expected return on other IT investments. A 1998 survey by *InformationWeek* found that "more than 80% of the 150 IS executives at U.S. companies surveyed say their organizations require them to demonstrate the potential revenue, payback, or budget impact of their IT projects."[24]

[23] The Y2 crisis, otherwise known as the Millennium Bug, refers to programs that are unable to interpret years beginning with the year 2000. Some programs will read the year 2000 as the year 1900, others will simply crash, and others will act in some other abnormal manner. The amount of systems and programs that were affected by this problem was enormous. Most government and corporate entities were busy in the latter half of the 1990's addressing this problem.

[24] Violino, Bob. "ROI In the Real World." *Information Week*, April 27, 1998, p. 2.

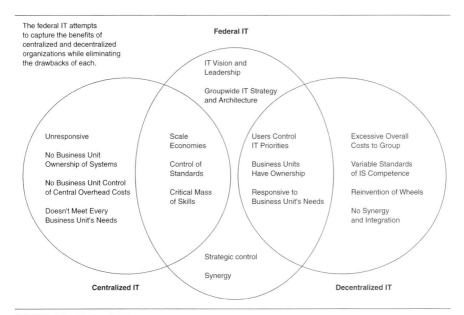

The federal IT attempts to capture the benefits of centralized and decentralized organizations while eliminating the drawbacks of each.

Federal IT

IT Vision and Leadership

Groupwide IT Strategy and Architecture

Unresponsive

No Business Unit Ownership of Systems

No Business Unit Control of Central Overhead Costs

Doesn't Meet Every Business Unit's Needs

Scale Economies

Control of Standards

Critical Mass of Skills

Users Control IT Priorities

Business Units Have Ownership

Responsive to Business Unit's Needs

Excessive Overall Costs to Group

Variable Standards of IS Competence

Reinvention of Wheels

No Synergy and Integration

Strategic control

Synergy

Centralized IT

Decentralized IT

FIGURE 8.9 Federal IT.

Adapted from: Eight Imperatives for the New IT Organization, John F. Rockart, Michael J. Earl, Jeanne W. Ross, Sloan Management Review, Fall 1996, pgs. 52–53.

Thus, a clear need exists to understand the true return on an IT project. But, measuring this return is difficult. To illustrate, consider the relative ease with which a manager might analyze whether the enterprise should build a new plant. The first step would be to estimate the costs of construction. The plant capacity dictates project production levels. Demand will vary and construction costs frequently overrun, but the manager can find sufficient information to make a decision about whether to build.

Most of the time, the benefits of investing in IT are less tangible than those of building a plant. Such benefits might include tighter systems integration, faster response time, more accurate data, better leverage to adopt future technologies, etc. How can a manager quantify these intangibles? He or she should also consider many indirect, or downstream, benefits and costs, such as changes in how people behave, where staff report, and how tasks are assigned. In fact, he or she may not even know who will benefit from an IT investment when making the decision.[25]

Despite the difficulty, the task of evaluating IT investments is necessary. This section outlines some approaches managers can take. Knowing which approaches to use and when to use them are important first steps.

[25] Ford, John C. "Evaluating Investment in IT." *Australian Accountant*, December 1994, p. 3.

Popular Valuation Methods

Return on Investment Analysis

Managers like the return on investment (ROI) metric. They find it easy to use and easy for senior executives to understand. However, this method does lack sophistication in assessing intangible benefits and costs.

Example
Scenario: Accounts payable asks the IT manager to purchase 10 new PCs and appropriate software. Accounts payable is centralizing invoice processing and will have 10 new people to equip. The machines available from the branches where accounts payable functions will no longer exist are too old to support the new software package and consequently will not transfer with the clerks.

Analysis
Costs: 10 PCs at $2,500 per machine total $25,000. TCO suggests an additional $500 per machine, bringing the total purchase cost to $30,000.
Benefits: 10 new clerks, each earning $30,000 per year, cannot perform their duties without new machines to perform data entry and query tasks. The total salary costs equal $300,000 per year. Buying the new machines saves the company $300,000 minus $30,000, or $270,000, in the first year alone! If the IT manager spreads the cost of the machines over three years, the per-year savings is even greater.

Net Present Value

Finance departments typically use net present value (NPV) because it accounts for the time value of money. After discounting and then adding the dollar inflows and outflows, a positive NPV indicates a project should be undertaken, so long as other IT investments do not have higher values. In the example below, however, NPV does not include intangible benefits and costs (see Figure 8.10).

Example
Scenario: The IT department plans to implement a new payroll system. Labor, infrastructure deployment, and licensing costs will equal $100,000 per year over the next two years. Payroll estimates $150,000 in savings per year for three years after the system is implemented, due to reduced staff and reduced system downtime.

A net return of $118,203 makes this investment worthwhile, unless the manager is forgoing other higher-return investments.

Economic Value Added

The economic value added (EVA) model accounts for opportunity costs of capital to measure true economic profit.[26] For example, if a data center at a company receives a return of 15 percent on employed capital, then the managers should expect to receive at least 15 percent on the data center. Otherwise, the company destroys value by underutilizing its assets. This method also revalues historical costs to give a more accurate picture of the true market value of assets. This step enables

[26] Source: http://www.sternstewart.com

	Year 0	Year 1	Year 2	Year 3	Year 4	Year 5
Investment:	0	($100,000)	($100,000)	0	0	0
Expected Return:	0			$150,000	$150,000	$150,000
Net Return:	0	($100,000)	($100,000)	$150,000	$150,000	$150,000
@12% Discount Rate:	0	($89,286)	($79,719)	$106,767	$95,327	$85,114
Net Present Value (The 5-year total):	$118,203					

FIGURE 8.10 Analysis chart.

managers to understand true asset utilization in a company. This method is sufficiently complex that consultants typically are required to implement it. Also, it often features important and expensive IT infrastructure components for measuring asset use. Although useful in valuation, EVA provides no hard and fast rules for intangibles.

Calculating EVA is simple: net operating profit after taxes (NOPAT) minus (capital × the cost of capital).[27] EVA may be an appropriate method if the IT manager's company has adopted it. If so, specific guidelines for using EVA should be available from the finance department. Such companies as Coca-Cola, Sprint, and Hershey Foods use EVA.

How should a manager choose among these three methods? The ROI can be used when detailed analysis is not required, such as when a project will be short lived and its costs and benefits are clear. When the project will last long enough that the time value of money will become a factor, NPV and EVA become useful. EVA becomes particularly appropriate when a project will be capital intensive.

Alternate Valuation Methods

Other valuation methods (see Figure 8.11) become useful under diverse circumstances. Managers should choose one over the other based on the attributes of the project.

Pitfalls in Calculating Returns

An IT manager may encounter a number of pitfalls when analyzing return on investment. First, not every situation calls for in-depth analysis. Some decisions—such as whether to invest in a new operating system to become compatible with a

[27] Source: http://www.sternstewart.com

Valuation Method	Description
Rate of return	Calculation is made to determine the return that the IT investment would have, and then it is compared to the corporate policy on rate of return. If IT investment's rate of return is higher than the corporate policy, the project is considered a good investment.
Weighted scoring methods	Costs and revenues/savings are weighted based on their strategic importance, level of accuracy or confidence, and comparable investment opportunities.
Prototyping	A scaled-down version of a system is tested for its costs and benefits. This approach is useful when the impact of the IT investment seems unclear.
Game theory or role-playing	These approaches may surface behavioral changes or new tasks attributable to a new system. They are less expensive than prototyping.
Simulation	A model is used to test the impact of a new system or series of tasks. This low-cost method surfaces problems and allows system sensitivities to be analyzed.

FIGURE 8.11   Alternate valuation methods.

Adapted from Ford, John C., "Ealuating Investment in IT," *Australian Accountant*, December, 1994, p. 8.

client operating system—are easy to make. The costs are unlikely to be prohibitively high, and the benefits are clear.

Second, not every evaluation method will work in every case. Depending on the assets employed, the duration of the project, and any uncertainty about implementation, one method will work better than another.

Third, circumstances may alter the way a particular valuation method is best employed. For instance, in a software implementation, estimates of labor hours required often fall short of actual hours spent. Accordingly, some managers use an "adjusting" factor in their estimates.

Fourth, managers can fall into "analysis paralysis." Reaching a precise valuation may take longer than is reasonable to make an investment decision. Since a single right valuation may not exist, "close enough" usually suffices. Experience and an eye to the risks of an incorrect valuation help decide when to stop analyzing.

Finally, even when the numbers say a project is not worthwhile, the investment may be necessary to remain competitive. For example, UPS had little choice but to invest heavily in IT. At the time, FedEx had made IT a competitive advantage and was winning the overnight delivery war.

▶ SUMMARY

This chapter has described the components of an IS organization including key job titles found in traditional IS organizations, and typical processes and tasks done by IS organizations. It then discussed two key managerial issues: outsourcing and centralization.

Since each organization will differ depending on the nature of the enterprise, a business manager must know the particular needs of his or her organization—just as the IS manager must educate him or her on the IT available. If neither seeks the other out, then a schism can develop between business and IS. The enterprise will suffer due to missed opportunities and expensive mistakes.

In addition to understanding the structure of an IS organization, a manager should work with IT leaders to develop a lean, competitive enterprise in which IT acts as a strategic enabler. Working as a team, business and IS managers can fruitfully address crucial organizational issues such as outsourcing, centralization, and analyzing return on investment. Such collaboration is essential if the enterprise is to remain afloat amid the difficult waters of business competition.

► DISCUSSION QUESTIONS

1. Using an organization with which you are familiar, describe the role of the most senior IS professional. Is that person a strategist or an operationalist?

2. What advantages does a CIO bring to a business? What might be the disadvantages of having a CIO?

3. The debate about centralization and decentralization is heating up again with the advent of network computing and the increasing use of the Internet. Why does the Internet make this debate topical?

4. The make versus buy decision is important every time a new application is requested of the IS group. What, in your opinion, are the key reasons an MIS organization should make its own systems? What are the key reasons it should buy an application?

► CASE STUDY 8-1

APPLICATION SERVICE PROVIDERS*

Companies like Volvo AB, Monsanto Co., Fleetwood Enterprises Inc., and General Electric have learned that application service providers (ASPs) can add value. An ASP is a company that "rents" the use of an application to the customer. In return, the ASP provides not only the software, but the infrastructure, people, and maintenance to run it. It is different than the traditional outsourcing relationship in which an entire IS shop is run by an outside organization. With an ASP, the outsourcing occurs application by application. The goal is to provide trouble-free operation for the customer. An executive at Monsanto summarized the use of ASPs, "If corporate use of ASPs isn't the trend for most companies, I'd be very surprised."

This model is particularly useful for the IS that are necessary, but not core, to the business. Companies use ASPs to free up IT staff, combine data resources, rapidly deploy new applications, control a widely distributed user base, develop a non-IT-based application, and many other ways. There are many benefits to using ASPs. First, in the age of the shortage of IS professionals, ASPs relieve their customers of the burden of finding and hiring. Second, the ASP is typically responsible for security and maintenance of the systems. That makes it easier to scale and manage systems. And third, ASPs deploy and install new applications,

* Adapted from Morgan, Cynthia, "ASPs Speak the Corporate Language," *Computerworld*, October 25, 1999, p. 74–77

which make it possible to manage the uneven requirements typically associated with these activities. Instead, IS organizations can focus their resources on core business applications that are not only critical to the business, but provide strategic or operational advantages.

Companies exploring Web use often consider ASPs. Typically, building a website for an existing business, or in some cases for a new business, involves specialized hardware, software, and expertise. It is necessary to design and deploy software, hardware, and networking to serve as the infrastructure for the new site. And with the explosive growth of the Web, planning for a company's expansion is virtually unpredictable. Managers want an infrastructure that is scalable, modular, and can grow, contract, or change instantly to accommodate the Web business. Typically building that type of infrastructure is costly in terms of both time and resources, in part because the skills needed to run the Web infrastructure are different than those needed to run the daily operational systems.

Instead, companies turn to ASPs to provide the infrastructure and applications necessary to get the business up and running. Sometimes, the ASPs become critical partners, whose business can make or kill the Web business. For example, the CEO of Barnesandnoble.com commented that his company plans to outsource nearly its entire Web infrastructure. "We're not going to be in the server business. I want to run the interface, the content, and the user experience. But I don't want to have to power it myself," he said.

Premiere Technologies, Inc., a fast growing supplier of communication services in more than 30 countries, provides an example of successful use of an ASP. Premiere began to implement an enterprise resource planning (ERP) system, and found that whenever there was a problem or call to work on a "revenue producing" information system, all resources were diverted from the implementation of the ERP. In Fall of 1998, Premiere decided to outsource the ERP applications. The ASP came in not only to help plan how to best make the ERP system successful, but it bought and maintained the servers on which the ERP runs, installed and configured the ERP software, and staffed the help desk to make the deployment smooth. And when Premiere acquires a new company, something they do regularly, the ASP takes care of incorporating the new acquisition into the ERP. By one estimate, Premiere saved about $3 million over five years by using the ASP instead of doing it themselves.

Discussion Questions

1. When does using an ASP make sense for a large corporation that already has an IS organization?

2. Give an example of when an ASP might make sense for a start-up company?

3. What would determine the application(s) to give to an ASP versus the ones to keep in-house?

CHAPTER 9

KNOWLEDGE MANAGEMENT*

The accounting and consulting firm Ernst and Young (E&Y) implemented a state-of-the-art knowledge management system through which 82,000 people in its global organization can share leading practices and intelligence. This intranet allows access to more than 1200 internal knowledge bases and external sources supplying business knowledge and global news and information. What's more, E&Y developed software tools that rate information in the knowledge bases according to its reliability and that respond to search requests with unsought information that may be relevant to the situation at hand. The firm created a Center for Business Knowledge, a network of subject-matter professionals at 14 strategic locations around the world. The center packages knowledge—from client reports and other forms of internal documentation—for easy assimilation, develops proprietary insight into business situations, and monitors and updates E&Y's knowledge bases. And the firm's Center for Business Innovation fosters strategic thinking on business process, information technology (IT), change management, and knowledge management to develop practical solutions.

Its knowledge management efforts are believed to have contributed to the firm's success. E&Y led the "Big Six" in revenue growth for three consecutive years. In fiscal 1997, U.S. revenues were up 24 percent from the previous year.

E&Y exemplifies a comprehensive, strategic approach to knowledge management. Knowledge management, one of the most popular business solutions, seeks to collect, organize, and distribute knowledge to leverage its value collectively across the organization. Many companies concentrate their efforts on gathering and storing information that may provide continuing value, but they fail to attend to whether and how employees will use it. E&Y has emphasized strategies for organizing information and providing it to employees when it is most useful to them.[1]

---

* The author wishes to acknowledge and thank Ben Ballengee, MBA '93, PhD '01 for his help in researching and writing early drafts of this chapter.

[1] Klimek, Mark, and Nate Hardcastle, "How Winners Do It." *Forbes*, August 24, 1998.

This chapter provides an overview of knowledge management, describes its infrastructure and key elements, functions, and strategies, and briefly examines the role played by technology in managing knowledge. This chapter defines *knowledge management* as the processes necessary to capture, codify, and transfer knowledge across the organization to achieve competitive advantage. Individuals are the ultimate source of organizational knowledge. The organization gains only limited benefit from knowledge isolated within individuals or among workgroups; to obtain the full value of knowledge, it must be captured and transferred across the organization. In this chapter, we focus on knowledge management as infrastructure for business applications, not as an application itself.

Knowledge management is related to information systems (IS) in three ways. First, information technologies make up the infrastructure for knowledge management systems. Second, knowledge management systems make up the data infrastructure for many IS and applications. The knowledge management system provides the source for information needed to run the business. And third, knowledge management is often referred to as an application of IS, much like e-mail, word processing, and spreadsheets. It is increasingly being used as a business application itself.

Another term frequently encountered in discussions of knowledge is *intellectual capital*, defined as knowledge that has been identified, captured, and leveraged to produce higher-value goods or services or some other competitive advantage for the firm. Both knowledge management and intellectual capital are often used imprecisely and interchangeably to describe similar concepts. IT provides an infrastructure for capturing and transferring knowledge, but does not create knowledge and cannot guarantee its sharing or use.

▶ DATA, INFORMATION, AND KNOWLEDGE

The terms "data," "information," and "knowledge" are often used interchangeably, but have significant and discrete meanings within the knowledge management domain. The differences are shown in Figure 9.1. *Data* is a set of specific, objective facts or observations, such as "inventory contains 45 units." Standing alone, such facts have no intrinsic meaning, but can be easily captured, transmitted, and stored electronically.

Information is defined by Peter Drucker as "data endowed with relevance and purpose."[2] People turn data into information by organizing it into some unit of analysis, e.g., dollars, dates, or customers. Deciding on the appropriate unit of analysis involves interpreting the context of the data and summarizing it into a more condensed form. Consensus must be reached on the unit of analysis.

Knowledge is information with the most value. Knowledge is a mix of contextual information, values, experiences, and rules. It is richer and deeper than information, and more valuable because someone has thought deeply about that information and added his or her own unique experience, judgment, and wisdom.

[2] Drucker, Peter F. "The Coming of the New Organization." *Harvard Business Review*, January–February 1988, pp. 45–53.

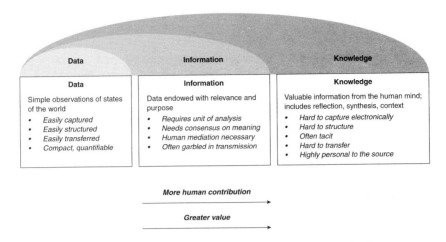

Data	Information	Knowledge
Data	**Information**	**Knowledge**
Simple observations of states of the world	Data endowed with relevance and purpose	Valuable information from the human mind; includes reflection, synthesis, context
• Easily captured • Easily structured • Easily transferred • Compact, quantifiable	• Requires unit of analysis • Needs consensus on meaning • Human mediation necessary • Often garbled in transmission	• Hard to capture electronically • Hard to structure • Often tacit • Hard to transfer • Highly personal to the source

More human contribution →

Greater value →

FIGURE 9.1 The relationships between data, information, and knowledge.[1]

[1] Adapted from Thomas H. Davenport, *Information Ecology* (New York: Oxford University Press, 1997) p. 9.

Values and beliefs are also a component of knowledge, as they determine the interpretation and the organization of knowledge. Tom Davenport and Larry Prusak, experts who have written about this relationship, say, "The power of knowledge to organize, select, learn, and judge comes from values and beliefs as much as and probably more than, from information and logic."[3] Knowledge also involves the synthesis of multiple sources of information over time.[4] The amount of human contribution increases along the continuum from data to information to knowledge. Computers work well for managing data, but are less efficient at managing information. The more complex and ill-defined elements of knowledge (for example, "tacit" knowledge, described below) are difficult if not impossible to capture electronically. Figure 9.1 summarizes these three concepts.

Tacit versus Explicit Knowledge

Knowledge can be further classified into two types: tacit and explicit. Tacit knowledge was first described by philosopher Michael Polyani in his book *The Tacit Dimension* with the classic assertion that "We can know more than we can tell."[5] For example, try writing a memorandum, or even explaining verbally, how to swim or ride a bicycle. *Tacit knowledge* is personal, context-specific, and hard to formalize and communicate. It consists of experiences, beliefs, and skills. Tacit knowledge is entirely subjective and is often acquired through physically practicing a skill or activity.

[3] Davenport, Thomas H., and Laurence Prusak. *Working Knowledge.* Boston: Harvard Business School Press, 1998, p. 12.

[4] Davenport, Thomas H. *Information Ecology.* New York: Oxford University Press, 1997, pp. 9–10.

[5] Polanyi, Michael. *The Tacit Dimension*, 1966 ed. Magnolia, MA: Peter Smith, 1983, p. 4.

IT has traditionally focused on *explicit knowledge*, that is, knowledge which can be easily collected, organized, and transferred through digital means, such as a memorandum or financial report. Individuals, however, possess both kinds of knowledge. Explicit knowledge, such as the knowledge gained from reading this textbook, is objective, theoretical, and codified for transmission in a formal, systematic method using grammar, syntax, and the printed word.

The distinction between tacit and explicit knowledge is important to keep in mind when considering later in the chapter how to capture and transfer knowledge. Figure 9.2 summarizes these differences. Although some experts in the field of artificial intelligence argue to the contrary, most tacit knowledge cannot be captured effectively outside the human mind. Consider the baseball legend Mark McGwire, who, with 70 home runs in 1998, broke the record for number of home runs hit in a single season. Even if it were possible to verbally describe Mark McGwire's home-run swing and put that description into writing, the process would be extremely difficult and ultimately futile. McGwire's swing incorporates so much of his own personal experience and kinesthetic memory that it is impossible to separate that knowledge from the hitter himself.

▶ AN EVOLVING CONCEPT

Managing knowledge is not a new concept,[6] but it has been invigorated and enabled by new technologies for collaborative systems and the emergence of the Internet and intranets, which in themselves act as a large, geographically distributed knowledge repository. The discipline draws from many established sources, including anthropology, cognitive psychology, management, sociology, artificial intelligence, IT, and library science. Knowledge management remains, however, an emerging discipline. There are few generally accepted standards or definitions of key concepts, and it will take time for new capabilities to evolve and for their opportunities to be fully understood. As industry experience is gained, and academics continue to research knowledge management, there will be greater understanding

Tacit Knowledge	Explicit Knowledge
• Knowing how to identify the key issues necessary to solve a problem • Applying similar experiences from past situations • Estimating work required based on intuition and experience • Deciding on an appropriate course of action	• Procedures listed in a manual • Books and articles • News reports and financial statements • Information left over from past projects

FIGURE 9.2 Examples of explicit and tacit knowledge.

[6] The cuneiform texts found at the ancient city Ebla (Tell Mardikh) in Syria, more than 4,000 years old, are some of the earliest known attempts to record and organize information.

and consensus. Persons involved with knowledge management projects should remain flexible, open to new ideas, and willing to view knowledge management as a journey rather than an end.

The most profound aspect of knowledge management is that, ultimately, an organization's only sustainable competitive advantage lies in what its employees know and how they apply that knowledge to business problems. Exaggerated promises and heightened expectations, couched in the hyperbole of technology vendors and consultants, may create unrealistic expectations since knowledge management is not a magic bullet, an appropriate solution for all business problems. While reading this chapter, managers should consider the implications of managing knowledge, but should not believe that knowledge management by itself is the sole answer for managerial success. Knowledge must serve the broader goals of the organization, and managing knowledge must be balanced with other management tasks and the day-to-day issues of running a business.

► WHY MANAGE KNOWLEDGE?

Although knowledge has always been important to the success of organizations, it was presumed that the natural, informal flow of knowledge was sufficient to meet organizational needs and that no explicit effort had to be made to manage that knowledge. The value chain,[7] discussed in earlier chapters of this text, illustrates the need for knowledge in such diverse areas as raw materials handling, operations, manufacturing, sales and marketing, product distribution, customer service, firm infrastructure, human resources, research and development (R&D), and purchasing. Each element of the chain, for example R&D, has also become knowledge intensive: technological developments, market trends, product design, and customer requirements must all be known and managed. In short, information and knowledge have become the fields on which businesses compete. Several trends highlight the need for businesses to manage knowledge for competitive advantage.

Sharing Best Practice

As the workplace has become more complex and chaotic, workers and managers have sought ways to share knowledge. The familiar scenario is that of a guru within a business who has had a lot of experience with a situation and who is sought by others within the organization who want to learn from the guru's experience. Sharing best practice is the concept of leveraging knowledge gained by a subset of an organization. It is increasingly important for organizations whose livelihood depends on applying expertise, such as accounting firms, consulting firms, training firms, architectural firms, and engineering firms. In these types of environment, it is inefficient to have everyone "reinvent the wheel" themselves. Rather, managers set up knowledge management systems to capture best practices and to disseminate that experience thoughout the firm.

---

[7] Porter, Michael E. *Competitive Advantage: Creating and Sustaining Superior Performance*. New York: Free Press, 1985, pp. 39–43.

Problems commonly arise with sharing best practices. Gurus who are rewarded for having specialized knowledge may be reluctant to share it with a knowledge management system, as was the case when KPMG Peat Marwick designed the Shadow Partner, an early knowledge management system to capture and disseminate best practices learned on client engagements. Consultants were hesitant to share their knowledge because in doing so, they were giving away something that was of value. Peers could just tap into the knowledge management system rather than contact the consultants, which decreased the power and rewards the consultants got from their work environment. KPMG Peat Marwick had to carefully manage the diffusion of the Shadow Partner to ensure that the threats of sharing information were minimized in its organization. For more information on this case, see "KPMG Peat Marwick: The Shadow Partner by R. Eccles and J. Gladstone, *Harvard Business School* case study no. 492002, October 1995."

Globalization

Products can be made and sold anywhere around the world. Designing, testing, and manufacturing can occur in parallel at different locations and the results exchanged electronically. The entire supply chain, when organized effectively, can function globally at a lower cost than required to operate in a single domestic economy subject to the vagaries of local supply and demand. New computing and telecommunications technologies allow data, information, and knowledge, albeit explicit knowledge, to flow instantly around the world, resulting in the emergence of an interconnected global economy. Developing countries have rapidly adapted to technological advances and are building competitive production infrastructures capable of manufacturing high-quality goods at lower labor costs than developed nations. Pricing pressures resulting from these new sources of competition preclude inefficient production processes.

In the past, land, labor, and capital gave nation-states their comparative economic advantage. As a greater percentage of economic growth arises from the knowledge sector, comparative advantage derives instead from the collective ability to leverage what people know. Knowledge-based businesses seem to grow according to previously unforeseen patterns, creating new markets, and attracting and producing innovations with little need for the traditional requirements of land, labor, and capital. Figure 9.3, adapted from a similar model at IBM, summarized these forces.

In 1994, Peter Drucker described this trend as follows:

Another implication [of the emerging knowledge society] is that how well an individual, an organization, an industry, a country, does in acquiring and applying knowledge will become the key competitive factor. The knowledge society will inevitably become far more competitive than any society we have yet known—for the simple reason that with knowledge being universally accessible, there will be no excuses for nonperformance . . .

Knowledge has become the key resource for a nation's military strength as well as for its economic strength . . . It is not tied to any country. It is portable. It can be created everywhere, fast and cheaply. Finally, it is by definition changing. Knowledge as the

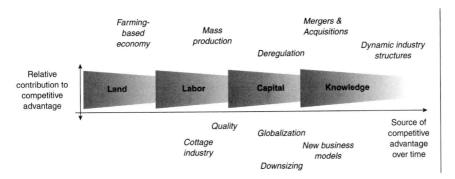

FIGURE 9.3 Forces driving knowledge as the key source of competitive advantage.
© IBM Global Services. Used with permission.

key resource is fundamentally different from the traditional key resources of the economist—land, labor, and even capital.[8]

Rapid Change

Rapid change means that existing knowledge becomes obsolete faster and that employees must learn new skills in less time. New technologies and unexpected forms of competition are announced daily. To keep up, new tools, processes, and strategies must be introduced. Knowledge management provides a way to optimize the use of existing knowledge and streamline the transfer and absorption of new knowledge across the firm. Rather than "reinventing the wheel," firms can customize pre-existing solutions for unique customer needs. The combination of knowledge-intensive businesses, highly skilled knowledge workers, and new and relatively inexpensive computing and telecommunications technologies has created the need to organize and transfer information and knowledge in new ways. Firms must be able to sense and respond to changing trends and markets, encourage creativity and innovation, and help knowledge workers to continuously learn and improve their productivity.

Downsizing

Downsizing initiatives have eliminated employees and removed knowledge, in the form of experience, from the organization. By firing experienced workers and driving away the talented, important knowledge captured in the heads of former employees has been lost. A change in corporate direction can result in the wholesale firing (sometimes incorrectly called a "restructuring") of an entire class of employees with specialized knowledge. As a result, veteran employees with extensive knowledge about an organization and its processes have become increasingly

[8] Drucker, Peter F. "The Age of Social Transformation." *The Atlantic Monthly*, November 1994.

rare. New employees, even if educated in the subject matter, need time and experience to develop specialized knowledge unique to the firm.

Downsizing has also changed the traditional contract between firms and their employees, creating a more mobile workforce than in the past. Workers are prone to change jobs more frequently, another reason to retain knowledge within the organization rather than in the heads of individuals.

By reducing the number of employees, firms have increased pressure on those remaining to accomplish more with less. Fewer employees are available to maintain and update the organization's knowledge, and less slack-time is available for acquiring new knowledge. Concurrently, the speed of innovation is increasing so that knowledge evolves and must be assimilated at an ever increasing rate.

Managing Information and Communication Overload

The growth of information resources along with the accelerating rate of technological change has produced huge amounts of information that often exceed the ability of managers and employees to assimilate and use it productively. Individuals complain of receiving hundreds of e-mail messages, in addition to voice mail messages, faxes, regular telephone calls, and paper mail. As one manager put it, "If I am to keep up with my job I have to spend all of my time, both on and supposedly off the job, communicating. I don't have a life anymore."[9]

Even push technology, with its promise of individualized delivery of information, does not address the issues of limited time and attention, and how to store and manage the information once it is received. Data must be categorized in some manner if it is to be accessed, re-used, organized, or synthesized to build a picture of the company's competitive environment or solve a specific business problem.

Knowledge Embedded in Products

Products and services are becoming increasingly complex, giving them a significant information component. Consulting firms, software manufacturers, and research laboratories all sell knowledge. Managing that knowledge is as important to them as managing inventory is to a manufacturing firm. However, other firms not traditionally viewed as knowledge-based are beginning to realize that much of the value in their products lies in the knowledge embedded in those products. Traditional manufacturing firms differentiate themselves from competitors by offering products that embed specialized knowledge. One classic example is the development of an automatic bread-baking machine by the Japanese firm Matsushita. To design the machine, Matsushita sought out a master baker, observed his techniques, and incorporated those techniques into the machine's functionality.[10] The intangibles that add the most value to goods and services are becoming increasingly knowledge-based, such as creativity, engineering, design, marketing, customer knowledge, and innovation.

[9] Davenport, Thomas H. *Information Ecology.* New York: Oxford University Press, 1997, p. 48.

[10] Nonaka, Ikujiro, and Hirotaka Takeuchi. *The Knowledge-Creating Company.* New York: Oxford University Press, 1995, p. 100.

Sustainable Competitive Advantage

Perhaps the best reason for knowledge management is that it can be a source of lasting and sustainable competitive advantage. It has become increasingly difficult to prevent competitors from copying and improving on new products and processes. The mobility of workers, the availability of powerful and relatively inexpensive technology, and reverse engineering make the advantages of new products and efficient processes more difficult to maintain. The life-cycle of innovation is growing shorter. Competitors can usually meet or exceed the standards of price and quality developed by the market leader in a short period of time. Before that happens, however, the company managing its knowledge can move to new levels of efficiency, quality, and creativity. Unlike raw material, knowledge is not depleted through use. Shared knowledge enriches the recipient while still remaining with the original source. Knowledge is not governed by the law of diminishing returns; on the contrary, the more knowledge that is shared and used, the more new knowledge that is generated. Figure 9.4 summarizes the sustainable competitive advantages.

▶ KNOWLEDGE MANAGEMENT PROCESSES

Knowledge management involves three main processes: the generation, codification, and transfer of knowledge (see Figure 9.5). *Knowledge generation* includes all activities that discover "new" knowledge, whether such knowledge is new to the individual, the firm, or to the entire discipline. *Knowledge codification* refers to the capture and organization of knowledge so that it can be found and re-used. *Knowledge transfer* involves transmitting knowledge from one person or group to another, and the absorption of that knowledge. Without absorption, a transfer of knowledge has not occurred. Generation, codification, and transfer all take place constantly without management intervention. Knowledge management seeks to enhance the efficiency and effectiveness of these activities and leverage their value

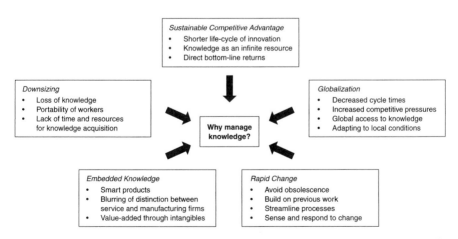

FIGURE 9.4 In an age of increasing competition and unprecedented change, there is only one sustainable competitive advantage: the capacity to learn.
© IBM Global Services. Used with permission.

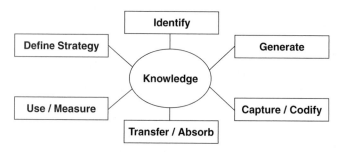

FIGURE 9.5 Knowledge management processes.

for the firm as well as the individual. Knowledge management is a continuous process, as depicted in Figure 9.6. As will be discussed later, identifying the knowledge to be managed, developing strategies to manage it, and measuring the results are also part of knowledge management.

Knowledge Generation

Knowledge generation concerns the intentional activities of an organization to acquire or create new knowledge. In this context, knowledge does not have to be newly created, only new to the organization. This section will discuss ways a firm can generate knowledge. Techniques for knowledge generation include purchase or rental, creation, shared problem solving, adaptation to changing circumstances, and development through informal networks. Facilitating knowledge generation promotes continuous innovation and growth of knowledge in the firm.

Buy or Rent

New knowledge may be acquired by purchasing a firm or hiring individuals, either as employees or consultants, who possess the desired knowledge. Another tech-

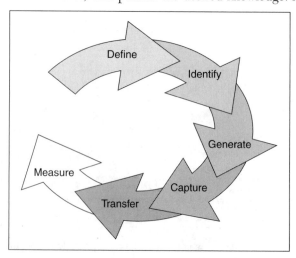

FIGURE 9.6 Knowledge management is a continuous process.

nique is to support outside research in exchange for rights to the first commercial use of the results.

One of the motivations for attempting to place a value on intellectual capital, discussed later in this chapter, is to determine how much the knowledge of an organization is worth in order to determine a fair purchase price. Organizations possessing significant knowledge may be difficult to acquire while keeping the knowledge intact. Uncertainties surrounding corporate takeovers, changes in work environment, relocation, and disruption of internal work processes may cause employees with key knowledge to leave the firm. The acquiring company may also fail to integrate new knowledge effectively. Differences in culture and internal politics may lead to resistance among new employees to share their knowledge, and among old employees to use it. Successful purchase of knowledge requires efforts to protect and integrate newly acquired employees and their knowledge into the acquiring firm.

One example of a successful purchase is IBM's acquisition of Tivoli Systems in 1996. The merger gave Tivoli new resources and global reach, while IBM allowed the firm to continue to operate autonomously without disrupting the firm's internal culture. Since the acquisition, Tivoli has emerged as a leader in the enterprise management software market, and IBM has increased software sales through the success of Tivoli's products.

Research and Development
True creation of knowledge is the rarest form of knowledge generation. Besides funding outside research, another way to create knowledge is through use of a dedicated R&D unit. Financial returns on research often take years to develop. Focusing on short-term profitability makes R&D, in addition to payroll, an attractive target for budget cuts. Such a short-term view may lead to long-term deficits in knowledge and competitiveness. Realizing value from R&D depends largely, however, on how effectively the new knowledge is communicated and applied across the rest of the firm.

Knowledge generated by R&D efforts, or by individuals, frequently arises from *synthesis*. Most new inventions are not based on entirely new ideas, but combine knowledge from different sources in unique ways so that new ideas emerge. For example, the first airplane was an innovative synthesis of three pre-existing ideas: the bicycle, the motor, and the airfoil.[11] Synthesis brings disparate pieces of knowledge together, often from extremely diverse sources, then seeks interesting and useful relationships among them.

Shared Problem Solving
Also called "fusion," shared problem solving brings together people with different backgrounds and cognitive styles to work on the same problem. Although this practice can cause divisiveness, it also provides opportunities for creative solutions. Even the most intelligent individuals can be bound by prior experience and personal style when attacking a problem. The creative energy generated by problem-

---

[11] Ruggles, Rudy. *Knowledge Tools: Using Technology to Manage Knowledge Better*. Working paper, Ernst & Young Center for Business Innovation, July 28 1997. Available:
http://www.businessinnovation.ey.com/mko/pdf/TOOLS.PDF.

solving groups with diverse backgrounds has been termed "creative abrasion."[12] The term "diversity" as used to describe the backgrounds of individuals in the group should not be equated with race- or gender-based diversity as popularly conceived; rather, the key element of diversity for shared problem solving is a difference in cognitive styles. Creative abrasion does, however, require some common ground among group members, namely, a common vocabulary or shared elements of knowledge about the problem and the organization. This overlapping knowledge is sometimes referred to as "knowledge redundancy" and provides a basis for group members to communicate about the problem.[13] Some cultural ideas that can help fusion work more effectively include: (1) fostering awareness of the value of the knowledge sought and a willingness to invest in it; (2) emphasizing the creative potential inherent in different styles of thinking and viewing the differences as positive; (3) clearly specifying the parameters of the problem to focus the group on a common goal.[14]

Adaptation

Firms must often generate knowledge in response to external threats; new products or competitors, changes in economic or social conditions, and government regulation are examples. These outside threats force knowledge generation because if the firm does not change, it will cease to exist.[15] Adaptation is the ability to apply existing resources in new ways when external changes make old ways of doing business prohibitive. A firm's ability to adapt is based on two factors: having sufficient internal resources to accomplish change and being open and willing to change. A firm's *core capabilities*—competitive advantages built up over time that cannot be easily duplicated—can simultaneously be *core rigidities*—the unwillingness to modify tried-and-true business practices. Put another way, past successes can sow the seeds of failure by inculcating managers and employees with an unwillingness to do things differently. For example, Sears failed to even list Wal-Mart as a competitor well into the 1980s.[16] Sears managers thought of Wal-Mart as a discount mass merchandiser and did not think things would change.

Communities of Practice

Informal, self-organizing networks within firms are another source of knowledge generation. Known as *communities of practice*, these groups are composed of workers who share common interests and objectives, but who are not necessarily

---

[12] Dorothy Leonard, *Wellsprings of Knowledge* (Boston: Harvard Business School Press, 1995), p. 63.

[13] Nonaka, Ikujiro and Hirotaka Takeuchi. *The Knowledge-Creating Company.* New York: Oxford University Press, 1995, p. 86.

[14] Davenport, Thomas H. and Laurence Prusak. *Working Knowledge.* Boston: Harvard Business School Press, 1998, p. 62.

[15] Although theoretically related, a discussion of self-organizing, complex adaptive systems is beyond the scope of this chapter. See generally Kauffman, Stuart A., *At Home in the Universe: The Search for the Laws of Self-Organization and Complexity.* New York: Oxford University Press, 1995.

[16] Leonard, Dorothy. *Wellsprings of Knowledge.* Boston: Harvard Business School Press, 1995, pp. 30–31.

employed in the same department or physical location, and who occupy different roles on the organization chart. The workers communicate in person, by telephone, and e-mail to solve problems together. Communities of practice are held together by a common sense of purpose and a need to know what other members of the network know, and their effective collaboration can generate new knowledge.

Managers can nurture knowledge generation by providing sufficient time and incentives for employees to collaborate and exchange ideas. They can also recognize that knowledge generation is an important activity for the firm and encourage employees to engage in knowledge-generating activities. "[Since] it is axiomatic that a firm's greatest asset is its knowledge, then the firm that fails to generate new knowledge will probably cease to exist."[17]

Knowledge Capture and Codification

Generating knowledge by itself is a pointless task. Aside from concerns about intellectual property and proprietary knowledge, once knowledge has been generated, it must be used or shared to be of value. *Capturing* knowledge after it has been generated involves continuous processes of scanning, organizing, and packaging knowledge. *Codification* is the representation of knowledge in a manner that can be easily accessed and transferred. One challenge to knowledge codification is that it is difficult to measure knowledge in discrete units. While data can be compared to a record, and information to a message, knowledge resembles an inventory. It accumulates and changes over time. The boundaries of knowledge are difficult to identify because of context sensitivity; one person's crucial fact is another person's irrelevant trivia. In one respect, capture and codification embody the same idea: although knowledge may be technically "captured" when it resides in a database or on a sheet of paper, that knowledge is unavailable across the firm until it has been codified in a manner that will allow those who need it to find it.

Davenport and Prusak identify four basic principles of knowledge codification:[18]

1. Decide what business goals the codified knowledge will serve (define strategic intent).
2. Identify existing knowledge necessary to achieve strategic intent.
3. Evaluate existing knowledge for usefulness and the ability to be codified.
4. Determine the appropriate medium for codification and distribution.

Defining Srategic Intent
Successful capture and codification require clear identification of the business problem to be solved and alignment of the knowledge to be captured with business

---

[17] Davenport, Thomas H. and Laurence Prusak. *Working Knowledge.* Boston: Harvard Business School Press, 1998, p. 67.

[18] Ibid, p. 69.

objectives. The vague idea of making "knowledge" available to employees is not sufficiently specific. Codification is not an all or nothing proposition, and relevance is more importance than completeness. Through whatever means knowledge is captured, there will inevitably be more knowledge than can be maintained. By implementing capture and codification on a small scale in a narrow, specific problem domain, the techniques can be improved and refined before being applied to other business problems across the organization.

Identifying and Evaluating Existing Knowledge

Determining knowledge requirements can be a difficult problem because it involves understanding how persons make sense of their environment and is an extremely subjective process. At one company, a team created to define information requirements initially asked three questions: (1) What constitutes key information? (2) How should boundaries be placed around that information? and (3) From what sources should the information be obtained? These questions raised significant political, psychological, cultural, and strategic issues within the firm. Potential users disagreed vehemently with content suggestions made by managers. To resolve the problem, the original team was supplemented by consultants, systems analysts, and users, all of whom were required to reach consensus on content. Throughout the process, the team maintained a tightly-coupled connection between content and users' needs. The result combined "hard" information—reports, memoranda, and accounting data traditionally developed internally—with "soft" information such as ideas, gossip, and opinion. By combining both kinds of information, the team developed a knowledge requirements design that offered a rich picture of the competitive environment and was capable of dealing with imprecise and *ad hoc* queries.[19]

Determining Appropriate Media

The appropriate means for codification and transmission will vary with the richness and complexity of the knowledge captured. To contort McLuhan's well-worn phrase, "the message determines the medium." Various kinds of media for codification and transfer will be discussed next.

Scanning. Typically involving a combination of electronic and human approaches, scanning is the first step in capturing knowledge after strategic knowledge has been identified. Electronic scanning can capture relevant information from a particular source (provided the information is available electronically), then filter out redundant or duplicative information. Human analysts, however, can add the most value to the scanning process by using their own knowledge of what is important to the company to provide context, interpretation, comparison, and condensation. Humans are also needed to scan and filter the soft, unstructured information available from experts and through rumor. Organizations usually have no formal or centralized scanning process and leave the scanning up to individual employees. Such individual scanning can be effective, provided the information is shared with

[19] Davenport, Thomas H. *Information Ecology.* New York: Oxford University Press, 1997, pp. 139–140.

others in the organization. The Japanese electronics firm Toshiba maintains a central team which continuously scans news wires, broadcasts, and business and industry publications for information relevant to the firm. The team synthesizes a daily report distributed to selected users, then indexes the source data by subject and archives it to laser disc for later retrieval.[20]

Organizing. This process attempts to take the mass of knowledge accumulated through scanning and structure it into an accessible form. Some structure is necessary to permit rapid access; however, too much structure can effectively hide knowledge from employees whose mental models do not fit those of the organizer. One example would be the index of the Yellow Pages (the real ones, not the knowledge management variety to be discussed later). One person might look under "car sales" and find no entries, while another might look under "auto dealers" and discover a large number of listings. Categorization schemes are always arbitrary and never value-neutral. They necessarily reflect the views of the person creating the taxonomy. To make appropriate decisions about how to categorize information, the following questions should be considered: (1) What business function will be served by the proposed categorization scheme? (2) What individual knowledge behaviors will be optimized by the proposed scheme? (3) Does the information to be categorized have any structure that lends itself to natural categorization? (4) Can an existing, standardized scheme be applied without doing harm to knowledge management objectives? (5) How will the scheme be maintained and updated?[21]

One scheme for categorizing knowledge uses four broad classifications:[22]

- **Process knowledge**. Sometimes referred to as "best practices," this kind of knowledge is useful for increasing efficiency.

- **Factual knowledge**. Basic information about people and things; easy to document, but relatively low-value unless synthesized and placed in context.

- **Catalog knowledge**. Individuals who possess catalog knowledge know where things are. These people are like directories of expertise, and while such knowledge can often be codified into a sort of Yellow Pages, the dynamics within organizations change so quickly that there will always be individuals who are more valuable because they know where to go for the right knowledge.

---

[20] Ibid, p. 143.

[21] Ibid, p. 146.

[22] Ruggles, Rudy, *Knowledge Tools: Using Technology to Manage Knowledge Better*. Working paper, Ernst & Young Center for Business Innovation, July 28 1997. Available: http://www.businessinnovation.ey.com/mko/pdf/TOOLS.PDF.

- **Cultural knowledge**. Knowing how things actually get done in an organization, culturally and politically. The absence of cultural knowledge can reduce efficiency when employees must learn or relearn invisible norms and behaviors.

An *organizational thesaurus* is another term for a categorization scheme. An excellent example of a standardized thesaurus can be found in the American Productivity & Quality Center's (APQC) Process Classification Framework.[23] The framework—originally developed for benchmarking best practices among firms— was developed to allow organizations to communicate across industry boundaries and overcome proprietary vocabularies. It defines generic business processes found in multiple industries and sectors, including manufacturing, service, healthcare, government, education, not-for-profit, and others. The framework provides a common language for organizations to identify their processes. A number of organizations have used the framework to categorize internal and external information. The framework is a living document, regularly updated and maintained at the APQC website.

Another interesting example of a categorization scheme is the *Encyclopædia Britannica*'s "Propædia," or "Outline of Knowledge." The Propædia was originally developed as a framework to classify all knowledge for inclusion in the printed encyclopedia. The designers of the search and retrieval system for *Encyclopædia Britannica*'s CD-ROM edition and website used the Propædia as a benchmark to measure the effectiveness of their system. The written Propædia structure told them which articles, from various parts of the encyclopedia, should be retrieved by a given query. The developers used the results to optimize their search algorithms.[24] The search engine developed from the Propædia is now being used at a website developed by Britannica called eBLAST.[25] A team of editors and indexers scans and identifies high-quality information resources which are then concisely described, rated according to consistent standards, and indexed for retrieval using the organizational hierarchy taken from the Propædia. The eBLAST web navigator uses the Propædia categorization scheme to classify websites indexed in the system.

Designing Knowledge Maps. A knowledge map (see Figure 9.7) serves as both a guide to where knowledge exists in an organization and an inventory of the knowledge assets available. Although it may be graphically represented, a knowledge map can consist of nothing more than a list of people, documents, and databases telling employees where to go when they need help. A good knowledge map gives access to resources that would otherwise be difficult or impossible to find. Maps may also identify knowledge networks or communities of practice within the organization.

---

[23] American Productivity & Quality Center. *Process Classification Framework*. APQC International Benchmarking Clearinghouse, 1997. Available: http://www.apqc.org/download/framewrk.pdf.

[24] Fallows, James. "The Java Theory." *The Atlantic Monthly*, March 1996, pp. 113–117.

[25] Source: http://www.eblast.com/

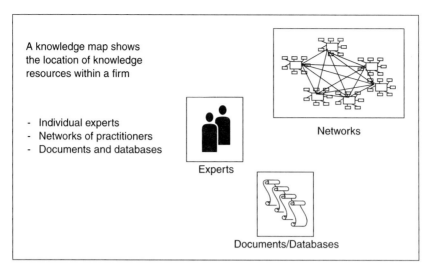

FIGURE 9.7 Contents of knowledge maps.
© IBM Global Services. Used with permission.

Some think a knowledge map is a type of organization chart. But an organization chart is not necessarily a substitute for a knowledge map; job titles can be misleading and an employee's job description or place on the chart may not represent the expertise held by that employee. Moreover, organization charts do not reflect accessibility. Knowledge workers identified on a knowledge map must not only have the requisite knowledge, but must have the time and inclination to share it with colleagues. A knowledge map should focus on a clearly defined need or type of information rather than attempting to list all possible kinds of knowledge held by the firm. Once again, relevance is more important to mapping knowledge than completeness.

There are several schemes to use to map knowledge. A common, but fairly ineffective, way to map knowledge is by its physical location within the firm's IS, identifying the databases, file-servers, document management systems, and groupware locations where it resides. This categorization scheme can help technically astute employees find information quickly because it shows them exactly where to find it. However, *physical mapping* is primarily of use only to those who are interested in learning the IT architecture of the organization.

Qualitative mapping points to information by topic rather than location. Qualitative mapping can be organized around processes, functions, or concepts. *Process mapping* uses a generalized model of how a business functions—such as the APQC framework previously discussed—and maps it to the knowledge contained in the organization. *Functional mapping* is based loosely on the organizational chart and is usually not effective for sharing knowledge across functions, since most workers do not have time to browse through the knowledge assets of other functional areas in hopes of finding something useful. *Conceptual mapping* is the most useful of these methods for organizing knowledge, but harder to design, build, and maintain. Conceptual maps organize information around objects, such as proposals, customers, or employees. These objects or topical areas contain information originally produced in different functional areas which leads to transfer of knowledge across the organization.[26]

The most useful mapping technique in a given situation depends on the individual user's personal preferences, the information required, and pieces of information with which they begin the search. Harking back to the political dilemmas that arose when management tried to define knowledge content without user input, the best method is to reach consensus among users, analysts, and developers before finalizing and implementing any knowledge map design.

Codifying Tacit Knowledge

Narratives. Mapping the identities of experts in an organization does not guarantee access to those experts' knowledge. An expert must have both the time and the willingness to share the knowledge. If the expert is unavailable or leaves the firm, the value of his or her knowledge is lost. A partial answer to this problem is to transfer as much knowledge as possible through mentoring or apprenticeship programs so that important tacit knowledge is not entirely concentrated in one person. Capturing tacit knowledge through narratives provides another answer.

Research has shown that knowledge is communicated most effectively through a good story, told with feeling, that resonates with other people. "War stories" can convey a rich and complex understanding of an event or situation in human context, making them one of the most effective ways to capture tacit knowledge without losing much of its value. Knowledge is most likely to be absorbed if shared in a context that is understood by the listeners. More firms are beginning to circulate videotapes that tell the story, for example, about how an important sale was closed. These narratives "codify" the expert's tacit knowledge of how to close a sale in a way that conveys much of its underlying meaning.[27]

In theory, at least, tacit knowledge can also be codified when it is embedded in a product or service. As with the Matsushita bread-baking machine discussed above, the knower uses his expertise to include some of what he knows in the product or process. This codification can be problematic, however. If the knower departs or is "restructured," deciphering the codified knowledge may require an almost complete reverse-engineering of the product.

Knowledge Transfer

In their book *The Knowledge Creating Company*, Ikujiro Nonaka and Hirotaka Takeuchi describe four different modes of *knowledge conversion*, their term for knowledge transfer (see Figure 9.8). The modes are (1) from tacit knowledge to tacit

---

[26] Davenport, Tom, David DeLong, and Mike Beers. *Building Successful Knowledge Management Projects*. Working paper, Ernst & Young Center for Business Innovation, June 6, 1997. Available: http://www.businessinnovation.ey.com/mko/pdf/KPROJE.PDF.

[27] Davenport, Thomas H. and Laurence Prusak. *Working Knowledge*. Boston: Harvard Business School Press, 1998, p. 82.

		TO	
		Tacit Knowledge	Explicit Knowledge
FROM	Tacit Knowledge	**SOCIALIZATION** Transfering tacit knowledge through shared experiences, apprenticeships, mentoring relationships, on-the-job training, "talking at the water cooler"	**EXTERNALIZATION** Articulating and thereby capturing tacit knowledge through use of metaphors, analogies, and models
	Explicit Knowledge	**INTERNALIZATION** Converting explicit knowledge into tacit knowledge; learning by doing; studying previously captured explicit knowledge (manuals, documentation) to gain technical know-how	**COMBINATION** Combining existing explicit knowledge through exchange and synthesis into new explicit knowledge

FIGURE 9.8 The four modes of knowledge conversion.

Source: Ikujiro Nonaka and Hirotaka Takeuchi, *The Knowledge-Creating Company* (New York: Oxford University Press, 1995) p. 62.

knowledge, called *socialization*, (2) from tacit knowledge to explicit knowledge, called *externalization*, (3) from explicit knowledge to explicit knowledge, called *combination*, and (4) from explicit knowledge to tacit knowledge, called *internalization*.[28]

Socialization is the process of sharing experiences; it occurs through observation, imitation, and practice. Common examples of socialization are apprenticeships, conferences, and casual, unstructured discussions in the office or "at the water cooler." Capturing tacit knowledge requires articulating it in explicit form, such as videotaping a story about closing a big sale to a customer. Copying and distributing the tape converts the knowledge from one explicit form to another, and transferring it to members of the sales force disseminates it so others can benefit from the experience. Internalization is the process of experiencing knowledge through an explicit source. For example, after viewing the videotape and combining the new knowledge conveyed by the narrative with prior experiences, a salesman might close a sale he or she would have otherwise lost.

▶ TYPES OF KNOWLEDGE MANAGEMENT PROJECTS

Although knowledge management projects involve a technology infrastructure, they differ radically from pure IT projects. As Davenport and Prusak point out in their "33⅓% rule," if more than one-third of the time and money spent on a project is spent on technology, the project becomes an IT project rather than a knowledge management project.[29] Figure 9.9 summarizes the contrast between knowledge management and IT projects.

---

[28] Nonaka, Ikujiro and Hirotaka Takeuchi. *The Knowledge-Creating Company.* New York: Oxford University Press, 1995, pp. 62–70

[29] Davenport, Thomas H. and Laurence Prusak. *Working Knowledge.* Boston: Harvard Business School Press, 1998, p. 78.

Knowledge Management Project	Information Technology Project
• Emphasizes valued-added information for users	• Emphasizes accessibility of information for users
• Supports organizational improvement and innovation	• Supports existing operations
• Adds value to content by filtering, interpretation, and synthesis	• Delivers content only
• Requires on-going user contributions	• Emphasizes one-way transfer of information
• Balanced focus on both technology and culture	• Primary focus on technology
• Variety of inputs often precludes automated capture of knowledge	• Assumes capture of all information inputs can be automated

FIGURE 9.9 Contrast between knowledge management and information technology projects.

Source: David DeLong, Tom Davenport, and Mike Beers, *What is a Knowledge Management Project?* Ernst & Young Center for Business Innovation working paper, February 17, 1997, http://www.businessinnovation.ey.com/mko/pdf/KMPRES.PDF.

Knowledge management initiatives can have either an internal or external focus, and have thus far been built around the following four themes:[30] (1) developing knowledge repositories, (2) providing knowledge access, (3) improving the knowledge environment, and (4) evaluating knowledge assets.

Knowledge Repositories

The idea of knowledge repositories is to take documents with knowledge embedded in them, such as memos, reports, or news articles, and store them so they can be easily retrieved. Another less-structured form of repository is the discussion database, in which participants record their own experiences on an issue and react to others' comments. Three fundamental types of repositories have been identified: (1) externally focused knowledge, sometimes called competitive intelligence; (2) structured internal knowledge such as research reports, marketing materials, and production processes; and (3) informal internal knowledge such as discussion databases for "lessons learned" and internal best practices.

Knowledge Access

While capturing knowledge is the objective of the knowledge repository, other projects focus on providing access to knowledge or facilitating its transfer among individuals. These projects are sometimes referred to as corporate "Yellow Pages," and are internally focused with the intent of making knowledge more visible and acces-

---

[30] This taxonomy is derived from Davenport Tom, David DeLong, and Mike Beers. *Building Successful Knowledge Management Projects*. Working paper, Ernst & Young Center for Business Innovation, June 6, 1997. Available: http://www.businessinnovation.ey.com/mko/pdf/KPROJE.PDF.

sible. Yellow Pages map and categorize knowledge and expertise in an organization, allowing identification of expert knowledge sources.

Knowledge Environment

Another type of internally focused knowledge management initiative is aimed strictly at culture, seeking to establish an environment conducive to knowledge creation, transfer, and use. In this category one sees projects that are intended to build awareness and cultural receptivity to knowledge, initiatives that attempt to change behavior relating to knowledge, and attempts to improve the knowledge management process. A consulting firm encouraged creation and distribution of management knowledge by changing its appraisal system so that contributions to the firm's structured knowledge repository were made a significant factor in compensation decisions.

Knowledge Assets

The fourth type of initiative is internally focused on managing knowledge as an asset, sometimes referred to as "intellectual capital." These initiatives attempt to treat knowledge as a balance-sheet asset to persuade investors of the value of the firm's intellectual capital and direct attention towards the effective or ineffective use of intellectual capital over time. Intellectual capital initiatives will be reviewed at length in the next section on measuring the value of knowledge.

▶ FOOD FOR THOUGHT: MEASURING THE VALUE OF KNOWLEDGE MANAGEMENT

No knowledge management effort is likely to be maintained unless there is some evidence of financial return to the organization. As the number of knowledge management projects undertaken grows, so does the pressure to measure the value of those efforts. If the acquisition and management of knowledge cannot be tied directly to bottom-line results, such projects are likely to be abandoned. As the Director of Knowledge Management at McKinsey & Company observed, "The point of a knowledge-based strategy is not to save the world; it's to make money."[31]

Several methods have been advanced to assess the value of knowledge management, intellectual capital, and their relative value to the firm; none has been widely adopted or proven entirely satisfactory, and none relies on traditional accounting methods or permits common-size analysis of knowledge management efforts and intellectual capital at competing firms.

[31] Manville, Brook, and Nathaniel Foote. "Strategy as if Knowledge Mattered." *Fast Company,* April–May 1996, p. 66.

Project-Based Measures

The first and most common method examines the success or failure of specific projects by some metric supposed to be improved through leveraging knowledge. A firm might assess whether production or sales increased, or whether costs and cycle times were reduced. Sometimes called "measurement by anecdote," this technique identifies specific benefits derived from knowledge management projects. Anecdotes are easy to understand, require little expense to gather, and provide good publicity. Inherent in project-based measures is the belief that knowledge adds value, and that specific firm-wide measures are expensive and unnecessary. Some examples of this approach include:[32]

- **Enhanced effectiveness.** The technical support function in one computer firm undertook a number of knowledge management initiatives that reduced the volume and cost of support calls from dealers. Through identifying patterns in support calls, the team preempted many potential problems by alerting customers to frequently asked questions and providing solutions through a discussion database.

- **Generate revenue from existing knowledge assets.** By managing patents more effectively, Dow Chemical saved $4 million in its first year of a review program and expects to generate more than $100 million in licensing revenues that might otherwise have been forgone.

- **Increased value of existing products and services.** To enhance the value of its generic computer-aided design software, one developer has begun including applications designed especially for the energy and chemical industries with its products. Embedding industry-specific knowledge into the software will reduce design time for customers in those industries, significantly differentiating the software from competitors.

- **Increased organizational adaptability.** Filtering, synthesizing, and interpreting competitive intelligence can improve a firm's ability to react to external changes. Threatened by a Japanese competitor that was underpricing them by 50 percent, a major auto parts supplier created a competitive intelligence system to capture a predefined cost model of the business. Using that information, the supplier was able to quickly reposition itself in the market in response to the strategic threat.

- **More efficient re-use of knowledge assets.** Ernst & Young's Center for Business Knowledge tracks the number of consulting engagements in which knowledge captured from previous projects is re-used. One performance measure for the firm's consultants is the amount of re-usable knowledge created.

---

[32] DeLong, David, Tom Davenport, and Mike Beers. *What is a Knowledge Management Project?* Working paper, Ernst & Young Center for Business Innovation, February 17 1997. Available: http://www.businessinnovation.ey.com/mko/pdf/KMPRES.PDF.

- **Reduced costs.** Chevron was able to save $150 million in annual fuel and power expenses through internal knowledge sharing on energy management.

- **Reduced cycle time.** Hoffman-LaRoche was able to reduce filing time for FDA approval for new drugs from 18 months to 90 days, and obtain FDA approval, normally requiring at least 3 years, in 9 months. In the pharmaceutical industry, a single day's delay can represent up to $1 million in lost revenues.

The Intellectual Capital Report

Perhaps the most widely known approach to measuring intellectual capital is the one developed at Skandia, a Swedish insurance company.[33] The Skandia methodology (see Figure 9.10) attempts to define the market value of a company by differentiating between traditional balance-sheet measures of equity and intellectual capital, then further divides intellectual capital into two categories: (1) human capital, which exists in the minds of individuals: their knowledge, skill, experience, creativity, and innovation; and (2) structural capital, which includes both (a) organizational capital, the infrastructure supporting human capital: IS, internal processes, proprietary software and documentation, and traditional forms of intellectual property such as patents, trademarks, and copyrights; and (b) customer capital, the relationships, satisfaction, longevity, price-sensitivity, and financial well-being of long-term customers.

These classifications are used to develop a set of measures for progress in managing knowledge. In its "Intellectual Capital Report," published as a supplement to its annual report, Skandia identifies 111 indices in the following five different groups: (1) *Financial focus*, including income per employee and market value per

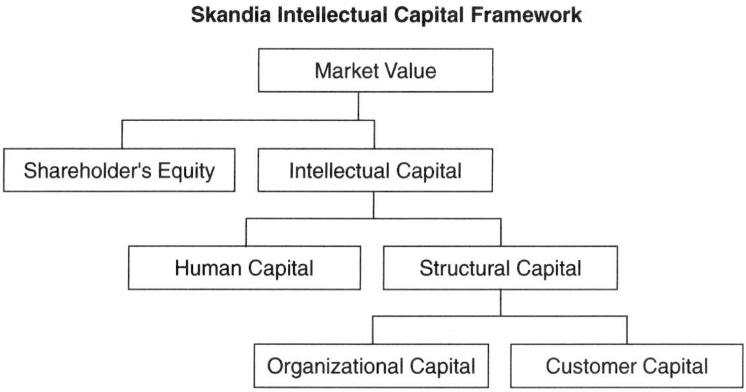

Skandia Intellectual Capital Framework

FIGURE 9.10 Skandia intellectual capital framework.

[33] Edvinsson, Leif, and Michael S. Malone. *Intellectual Capital.* New York: HarperCollins Publishers, Inc., 1997.

employee (2) *Customer focus*, including number of customer visits, satisfied customer index, and lost customers (3) *Process focus*, including administrative error rate and IT expense per employee (4) *Renewal and development focus*, including training per employee, the ratio of R&D expense to administrative expense, and a "satisfied employee index" (5) *Human focus*, including a "leadership index," rate of employee turnover, and IT literacy among employees. Determining a fair market value for such assets, however, remains problematic.

Valuation of Knowledge Capital

If measuring the value of intellectual capital can be considered conventional in any sense, perhaps the most conventional approach has been proposed by Paul Strassmann, a former IS executive in government and industry, consultant, and author. "Knowledge capital" is Strassmann's term for the value a customer places on goods or services over the cost of sales and cost of capital, i.e., the surplus value of corporate knowledge in excess of traditional accounting measures. Strassmann contends that techniques such as those used by Skandia fall short because the data derived cannot be used as an acceptable valuation of assets on the stock market.[34]

Rather than working from the bottom up and estimating the value of knowledge assets to determine intellectual capital, Strassmann works from the top down, examining the capacity of firms to generate additional revenue based on the value added to processes through knowledge. He emphasizes that the costs of acquiring knowledge and the revenue-generating potential of knowledge are unrelated. The value of intellectual capital lies in its use, not in its cost. Thus, any value added through knowledge is worth only what investors are willing to pay for it.

Traditionally, knowledge assets have become reflected in financial reports only after a merger or acquisition at a substantial premium over book value. At that point, such assets are recognized as "goodwill." Allowing companies to record knowledge capital as part of shareholder equity, according to Strassmann, would generate balance sheets that more closely reflect corporate value.

Knowledge capital is the amount an investor is willing to pay for intangible assets, in excess of the cost of capital, for a risk-adjusted interest in the future earnings of the company. Investors cannot differentiate between the price of capital for financial or knowledge investments because those investments are intermingled. "Management value-added" is what is left over after all costs have been fully accounted. Determining management value-added requires subtracting an allowance for the costs of shareholder equity and other adjustments to correct for income taxes from after-tax profits. Knowledge capital then becomes management value-added divided by the cost of capital. This relationship makes it possible to prepare common-size balance sheets for any firm by adding a line item called knowledge capital on the asset side, and increasing (or decreasing) shareholder equity by the same amount.

[34] Strassmann, Paul A. "The Value of Knowledge Capital." *American Programmer,* March 1998, pp. 3–10.

▶ SUMMARY

Following such a broad survey, it seems appropriate to conclude with a few caveats. First, recall that knowledge management is an emerging discipline. Viewing knowledge management as an process rather than an end by itself requires managers to remain flexible and open-minded.

Second, the objective of knowledge management is not always to make knowledge more visible or available. Like other assets, it is sometimes in the best interests of the firm to keep knowledge tacit, hidden, and nontransferable. Competitive advantage increasingly depends on knowledge assets that are hard to reproduce. Retaining knowledge is as much of a strategic issue as sharing knowledge.

Third, knowledge can create a shared context for thinking about the future. If the purpose of knowledge management is to help make better decisions, then it should focus on future events. Through the use of multiple scenarios, organizations can create "memories of the future." The goal is not to know the future, but rather to know what projections influence long-term strategy and short-term tactics.[35]

Finally, people lie at the heart of knowledge management. Establishing and nurturing a culture that values learning and sharing of knowledge enables effective and efficient knowledge management. Knowledge sharing—subject, of course, to the second caveat above—must be valued and practiced by all employees for knowledge management to work. The success of knowledge management ultimately depends on a personal and organizational willingness to learn.

▶ DISCUSSION QUESTIONS

1. The terms "data," "information," and "knowledge" are often used interchangeably. But as this chapter has discussed, they can be seen as three points on a continuum. What, in your opinion, comes after knowledge on this continuum?

2. What is the difference between tacit and explicit knowledge? From your own experience, describe an example of each. How might an organization manage tacit knowledge?

3. What are the steps in the knowledge management process? What IT would you prescribe for each step?

4. How do knowledge maps aid an organization?

---

[35] Fahey, Liam, and Laurence Prusak. "The Eleven Deadliest Sins of Knowledge Management." *California Management Review,* 40.3 (1998), pp. 265–276.

▶ *CASE STUDY 9-1*

McKinsey and Company[*]

McKinsey and Company is perhaps one of the best known management consulting firms in the world. Founded in 1926, McKinsey has built a reputation for creative and innovative strategic solutions for clients. McKinsey and Company's primary clientele are senior managers. The success of this firm is in part due to a narrow focus on problems and issues only relevant to this group of managers. At one point, it was estimated that 80 percent of its business was repeat business from former clients. Its website sums up the firm as follows:

> The nature of the problems we help clients address has changed over the years and has reflected both differences in the relationships between large companies and their governments and the sophistication of management. McKinsey consultants designed the initial organization of NASA (U.S.), advised the Vatican (on its banking system), developed the Universal Product Code (U.S.), specified the systems supporting Frankfurt's stock exchange, and helped the Treuhandanstalt privatize East German companies.

> Given the breadth and depth of this work, there is an intellectual tradition at McKinsey that is very different from what one finds in a university or in a consulting firm that concentrates on a single problem or industry. It is a tradition that first celebrates the complexity and the differences of management challenges, and then presses for practical answers based on both analysis and experience. It is a tradition that recognizes the importance of being able to reach out to colleagues wherever they are in the world.

As part of its organizational support systems, McKinsey and Company has built an extensive knowledge management system. The McKinsey philosophy of knowledge is described on its website.

> Among consulting firms there are very different approaches to building and sharing knowledge. Some believe knowledge of a company or an industry introduces a backward-looking bias into their thinking and instead rely entirely on their consulting skills, e.g., interviewing, coaching, or counseling. Others build depth in a single function or industry and believe their expertise is the primary value they bring to a client. Some rely on a few people, e.g., gurus, to develop a single "big idea," e.g., reengineering, which the rest apply through codified processes. Others try to build capability and expertise throughout their consulting staff.

> We take the position:

> - That knowledge per se is of limited value until people and consulting skills (not merely processes) combine to make it valuable.
> - That both perfection and creativity should result from our knowledge (and our clients').
> - That it is in the intersections of different kinds of knowledge that truly creative and valuable insights often occur.

[*] Adapted from Harvard Business School case, McKinsey and Company: Managing Knowledge and Learning, by C. Bartlett, HBS case no. 396-357, 1996 and McKinsey and Company website, www.mckinsey.com, on October 28, 1999.

- That those intersections are more likely in a team-based, integrative approach to problem-solving enhanced by both a culture of collaboration and a commitment to impact.

McKinsey and Company began their investment in managing knowledge after a 1971 internal study determined that while the consultants were excellent generalists, they often lacked deep industry knowledge or specialization needed to meet clients demands. As a result, McKinsey determined that a focus on continuous development of members of the firm was needed. In addition, consultants were encouraged to supplement their general knowledge with deep knowledge in an industry or specialty. Ultimately, 15 virtual centers of competence were established to develop consultants and to ensure consistent development of knowledge. Management systems were developed to reward practice development, which included the knowledge base, as well as the traditionally well rewarded activities of client development. Building on its culture of self governance and individual initiative, industry and functional networks began to play significant roles in the way the company negotiated and staffed engagements and developed its people.

The knowledge management system is described on the website as follows:

While some kinds of knowledge can be "codified" and "applied," most of them—the most valuable for the kinds of problems top management faces—exist only in people's heads. A consulting firm thus needs its people—not databases—to collaborate. "Knowledge management" is relatively easy. The culture and values that support it are much harder.

McKinsey's consultants share their knowledge and personally collaborate in ways that most organizations and most other consultants find remarkable. We invest in this core competence in several ways:

- Through office transfers and practice development meetings we help each of our consultants build his or her personal networks within McKinsey.
- We look for evidence that the partners responsible for a client have brought others into the team who have depth in an industry or function.
- We avoid any kind of accounting, e.g., making our industry or functional practices profit centers, that would discourage collaboration.
- As stated earlier, we grow our own offices and develop a sense of "one-firm" in all our people.
- We have invested heavily in the information technology and people (researchers, experts) that can support, but not replace, collaboration.

The knowledge infrastructure included technological as well as non-technical initiatives. McKinsey consultants with "big ideas" published some of them in public venues such as newspapers, prestigious business magazines, and trade books. By the 1980s, the firm was actively encouraging consultants to publish their key findings, but doing so required major investments of time and resources. By 1987 a committee reviewed the knowledge infrastructure, and The Knowledge Management Project recommended the firm build a common database of knowledge accumulated from client work in the practices, hire a full-time practice coordinator for each area responsible for the quality of input and assisting consultants with access, and establish career paths for deep specialists that parallel those available for generalists.

The result was an examination of the Firm Practice Information System (FPIS). This database of client engagements typically archived each project, but was overhauled to provide increased accessibility and reliable information useful for current engagements. A Practice Development Network (PDNet) was also built to manage documents representing core knowledge of each practice. Finally, a Knowledge Resource Directory (KRD) was published for internal use with a list of all firm experts and key documents. This directory became instantly indispensable to many consultants.

In the 1990s, the leadership at McKinsey again reevaluated the company's knowledge infrastructure. One partner suggested in a case study published by Harvard Business School that:

> Too many people were seeing practice development as the creation of experts and the generation of documents in order to build our reputation. But knowledge is only valuable when it is between the ears of consultants and applied to clients' problems. Because it is less effectively developed through the disciplined work of a few than through the spontaneous interaction of many, we had to change the more structured "discover-codify-disseminate" model to a looser and more inclusive "engage-explore-apply-share" approach. In other words, we shifted our focus from developing knowledge to building individual and team capability.

Discussion Questions

1. What is the goal of a knowledge management system for a company like McKinsey and Company? How well does its knowledge management system meet this goal?
2. "Traditional" knowledge management systems involve three steps: collection, codification, and dissemination. How do you think the McKinsey system implements each of these steps? How is that implementation different from the "engage-explore-apply-share" philosophy mentioned by the manager at the end of the case?
3. How should McKinsey integrate the Web and its advantages in the area of collaboration and communication in their future knowledge management strategies?

CHAPTER 10

PROJECT MANAGEMENT*

In 1993, Oxford Health Plans Inc. began a project to replace its existing database management system with one by Oracle Corporation. The database was finally completed in September 1996 only to collapse under the load of transactions required by its users. This failure led to serious delays in payment of claims for HMO members and temporarily halted the issuance of thousands of monthly statements. Oxford cited this crucial system failure as a factor in its 1997 third quarter loss of $78 million and in the additional $45 million loss in 1998 first quarter earnings.

This example highlights the possible financial consequences of a failed information systems (IS) project. Such failures occur at an astonishing rate. The Standish Group, a technology research firm, found that 73 percent of all software projects are delivered late or over budget or simply fail to meet their performance criteria. Business projects increasingly rely on IS to attain their objectives, especially with the increased focus to do business on the Internet. Thus, a crucial IS project raises the risk in many business projects. To succeed, a general manager must also be a project manager, and must learn how to manage this type of risk.

In the current environment, businesses face competition from companies equipped to copy existing products and services and then distribute them at lower prices. Often, the quality that differentiates firms in the marketplace—and destines them for success or failure—is the ability to adapt existing business processes and systems faster than the competition. The process of continual adaptation to the changing marketplace drives the need for business change and thus for successful project management. Typical adaptation projects include:

- Rightsizing the organization
- Reengineering business processes
- Adopting more comprehensive, integrative processes

Projects comprise a set of one-time activities that can transform the current situation into the desired new one. Firms seek to compete through new products

---

* The author wishes to acknowledge and thank W. Thomas Cannon, MBA '99 for his help in researching and writing early drafts of this chapter.

and processes, but the work of initially building or radically changing these outcomes falls outside the scope of normal business operations. That is where projects come in. When work can only be accomplished through methods that fundamentally differ from those employed to run daily operations, the skilled project manager plays a crucial role.

Successful business strategy requires executive management to decide which objectives can be met through normal daily operations and which require specialized project management. Virtually all projects involve an information technology (IT) component, including both a computer system and an information flow. Rapidly changing business situations make it difficult to keep both of these IT elements aligned with business strategy. Furthermore, the amount of resources required to complete IT-intensive projects has increased over the years due to their increasing complexity—magnifying the risk that the finished product or process will no longer satisfy the needs of the business. Thus, on most projects the critical element to manage is the IT portion. Executive management no longer has an option but to consider skilled IT project management as fundamental to business success.

This chapter provides an overview of what a project is and how to manage one. It discusses the aspects of IT-intensive projects that make them uniquely challenging. Finally, it identifies the issues that shape the role of the general manager in such projects.

▶ WHAT DEFINES A PROJECT?

In varying degrees, organizations combine two types of work, projects and operations, to transform resources into profits. Both types require people and a flow of resources. The flight of an airplane from its point of departure to its destination is an operation that requires a pilot and crew, the use of an airplane, and fuel. The operation is repetitive: After the plane is refueled, it takes new passengers to another destination. The continuous operation of the plane creates a transportation service. However, the development of the design for such a plane is a project that may require years of work by many people. When the design is completed, the work ends. Figure 10.1 compares characteristics of both project and operational work. The last two characteristics are distinctive and form the basis for the following formal definition:

> [A] project is a temporary endeavor undertaken to create a unique product or service. Temporary means that every project has a definite beginning and a definite end. Unique means that the product or service is different in some distinguishing way from all similar products or services.[1]

To organize the work facing a project team, the project manager may break a project into subprojects. He or she then organizes these subprojects around distinct activities, such as quality control testing. This organizing method allows the

---

[1] Project Management Institute Standards Committee, *A Guide to the Project Management Body of Knowledge*, Project Management Institute, 1996.

Characteristics	Operations	Projects
Labor skills	Low	High
Training time	Low	High
Worker autonomy	Low	High
Compensation system	Hourly or weekly wage	Lump sum for project
Material input requirements	High degree of certainty	Uncertain
Supplier ties	Longer duration	Shorter duration
	More formal	Less formal
Raw materials inventory	Large	Small
Scheduling complexity	Lower	Higher
Quality control	Formal	Informal
Information flows	Less important	Very important
Worker-mgmt communication	Less important	Very important
Duration	On-going	Temporary
Product or service	Repetitive	Unique

FIGURE 10.1 Characteristics of operational and project work.

project manager to contract certain kinds of work externally in order to limit costs or other drains on crucial project resources. At the macro level, a general manager may choose to organize numbers of projects as elements of a larger program, if doing so creates efficiencies. Such programs then provide a framework from which to manage competing resource requirements and shifting priorities among a set of projects.

► WHAT IS PROJECT MANAGEMENT?

Project management is the "application of knowledge, skills, tools, and techniques to project activities in order to meet or exceed stakeholder needs and expectation from a project." Project management always involves continual trade-offs; and it is the manager's job to manage them. Typically one or more of the following are the primary trade-off encountered:

- Scope and Time
- Cost and quality
- Identified requirements and unidentified requirements
- User Needs and user expectations
- Differing needs and expectations of diverse stakeholders

The project manager's role is to develop a system to effectively and efficiently manage these competing demands. Typical activities include:

- Ensuring progress of the project according to defined metrics
- Identifying risks and assessing their probability of occurrence

[2] Project Management Institute Standards Committee, *A Guide to the Project Management Body of Knowledge*, Project Management Institute, 1996.

- Ensuring progress toward deliverables within constraints of time and resources
- Running coordination meetings of the project team
- Negotiating for resources on behalf of the project

A general manager often oversees more than one project, and his role can vary. He may be the customer for any given project, as well as the source of its resources. These dual roles can make it easier for the general manager to ensure attention to both a project's risks and its business value.

Project Modeling

Project work requires in-depth situational analyses and the organization of complex activities into often coincident sequences of discrete tasks. The outcomes of each activity must be tested and integrated into the larger process in order to produce the desired result. The number of variables affecting the performance of such work is potentially enormous. A model can help organize these variables and one such model is shown in Figure 10.2.

Four components essential for any project are a common vocabulary, teamwork, a cycle plan, and management. The common vocabulary is necessary so all those involved with the project understand the project and communicate effectively. Teamwork is necessary to insure that all parts of the project come together correctly and efficiently. The plan represents the methodology and schedule to be used by the team to execute the project. And management is necessary to make sure the entire project is executed appropriately and coordinated properly.

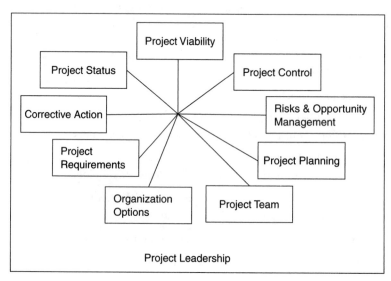

FIGURE 10.2 Project leadership elements model.

It is essential to understand the interrelationships among these elements and with the project itself. Both a commitment to teamwork and a common vocabulary must permeate the management of a project throughout its life. The project plan is the sequential series of steps to organize and track the work of the team. Finally, project management itself comprises a set of tools to balance competing demands for resources and ensure the completion of work at each step and as situational elements evolve through the project plan.

Common Vocabulary

Increasingly, project teams need a growing number of specialists, each of whom may bring a different technical vocabulary. A market research analyst and a software analyst each have many words unique to their specialty; they may also attach different meanings to the same word. Clear thinking requires effective communication and thus a common vocabulary. Each project team should develop its own glossary of terms, and team members should commit to its consistent use.

Teamwork

Business teams often fail because members fail to understand the nature of the work required to make them effective. Teamwork begins by clearly defining the objective of the team and each person's role to help obtain the objective. It is especially important to identify the mutual dependency of the roles on the team. Teams require a common standard of conduct, shared rewards, and team spirit.

Project teams organize people around specific activities. Their staffing can be flexible to allow the assignment of human resources on an as-need basis. Team members often bring specific experiences, such as technical, process, or organizational skills, that can be applied as needed. Team members who represent larger functional units within the organization also serve to transmit information across the boundary of the group. A marketing or research and development (R&D) manager can share departmental information in project meetings. Such information sharing may constitute the first step toward building consensus on critical project issues that will affect the entire organization. Thus, effective project managers use teamwork both to organize and apply human resources and to collect and share information throughout the organization.

Project Cycle Plan

The project cycle plan organizes project activities in relation to time. It identifies critical beginning and end dates and breaks the work spanning these dates into phases. The general manager tracks the phases in order to coordinate the eventual transition from project to operational status, a process that culminates on the "go live" date. The project manager uses the phases to control the progress of work. He or she may establish control gates at various points along the way in order to verify that project work to date has met key requirements regarding cost, quality, and features. If it has not met these requirements, he or she can make corrections to the project plan and adjust the cycle as necessary.

Figure 10.3 compares a generic project cycle plan with one for a typical high tech commercial business and with one for an investigative task force. Notice that while each of these plans has very different phases, all can loosely be described by three periods (shown at the top of the diagram): requirements period, development period, and production/distribution period.

The manager must attend to the following three aspects of the work throughout the project cycle:[3]

- The **technical aspect** includes all activities related to satisfying the technical and quality requirements.

- The **budget aspect** describes all activities related to the appropriation of project funds by executive management and the securing and accounting of funds by the project manager.

- The **business aspect** encompasses all activities related to the management of the project and any associated contracts.

These aspects of a project interrelate as it develops through the cycle. For example, a change in the quality requirements for the project will normally alter the cost and the time involved. The elements of project management presented next provide tools to use in balancing the varying aspects of a project.

Elements of Project Management

The 10 elements described in this section represent management skills that can be organized into a toolbox of sorts. Each addresses a specific factor that affects a project's chances of success. The challenge facing a project manager is to learn and

Requirements Definition Period			Production Period			Deployment/ Dissemination Period	

Investigation Task Force

User requirement definition	Research concept definition	Information use specification	Collection planning phase	Collection and analysis phase	Draft report phase	Publication phase	Distribution phase

Typical High Tech Commercial Business

Product requirements phase	Product definition phase	Product proposal phase	Product development phase	Engineer model phase	Internal test phase	External test phase	Production phase	Manufacturing sales & support phase

Generic Project Cycle Template

User requirement definition phase	Concept definition phase	System specification phase	Acquisition planning phase	Source selection phase	Development phase	Verification phase	Deployment or production phase	Operations/ maintenance or sales/ support phase	Deactivate phase

FIGURE 10.3 Project cycle template. Adapted from: Visualizing Project Management.

[3] Kevin Forsberg, Hal Mooz, and Howard Cotterman. *Visualizing Project Management*. John Wiley & Sons, Inc., 1996.

apply the techniques properly in the situations that require them. The elements are the identification of requirements, organizational integration, team management, project planning, risk and opportunity management, project control, project visibility, project status, corrective action, and project leadership. Figure 10.4 summarizes these elements.

Identification of Requirements. The project manager must determine what the project needs to deliver, and he or she must manage against these project requirements as they change over time. The process of identifying project requirements itself comprises numerous tasks. Some of them are selection in concept, decomposition or analysis, definition, documentation, definitive identification, integration into the project plan, specification, substantiation, validation, and verification.

Managing this process may entail systems analysis and design, establishing the traceability of requirements identified, assigning accountability, and modeling to specification.

Elements of Management	Rational	Major Focus
Requirements	Failure to manage requirements which initiate and drive projects is the major cause of failure.	
Organizing	Putting structure around the key activities, people, and resources is critical to successful management.	Formulate
Project Team	Teams are newly formed for each project and include subcontractors and outsourcing.	Proactive
Planning	Needed to provide roadmap of tasks to be done including schedule, budget, and deliverables.	
Risk and Opportunity Management	Significant cause of project failures if not specifically managed.	
Project Control	When properly implemented, controls identify whether project is proceeding appropriately.	
Visibility	Needed to keep all stakeholders informed.	Variance Control
Status	Need hard metrics, measures, and variances to supplement activity reports.	Reactive
Corrective Action	Innovative actions needed to get back on track with plan.	
Leadership	Creation of team energy to succeed with plan.	Motivate

FIGURE 10.4   Elements of management.
Source: K. Forsberg, H. Mooz, and H. Cotterman, *Visualizing Project Management*. Wiley & Sons, 1996. Used with permission.

Organizational Integration. Ideally, the project manager should start with a structure similar to the organization in support of the project. Doing so might mean revising organizational reporting relationships and reward systems for members of the project team so they can spend time on the project. The following models are helpful to structure simple projects:[4]

- **Pure Functional Structure** (Figure 10.5) works best for a single project that operates with relative independence in terms of organizational interface or technology. This model falls short when an organization must manage multiple projects.

- **Pure Project Structure** (Figure 10.6) works best when performance according to scheduling or product cost considerations is paramount and the cost of development is relatively unimportant.

- **Conventional Matrix Structure** (Figure 10.7) works well when the project manager truly controls the project funds and enjoys clearly defined relationships with supporting managers, including formal commitments and their participation in project planning. This model fails when the project manager is seen as a mere coordinator of activity and the supporting managers perform only on a "best effort" basis.

- **Collocated Matrix Structure** (Figure 10.8) should be considered for very high priority projects that depend on key resources and/or technologies and when ongoing involvement with operating strategy is secondary.

In many organizations the project must simply fit itself into existing structures. Even in this instance, it remains important to understand the trade-offs made by adapting the project to the organizational context.

Team Management. The project manager must acquire and manage the required human resources. Tools commonly available in human resource departments assess professional competencies and skills, as well as personal traits and behaviors. Such assessments can help the project manager select team members with specific roles in mind. As a project progresses through its life cycle, the number of people assigned typically increases, at least periodically. Such growth adds to the need for ongoing management by the project manager.

Project Planning. Project planning involves breaking down the project into discrete activities and sequencing them in steps so that the project delivers according to the requirements of customers and stakeholders. The team assigns tasks and documents the time and resources needed to complete them. Planning is most effective when it continues through the life of a project and when plans are adjusted as events unfold to which the team must respond. Software tools, such as Microsoft Project, Primavera Project Planner, and Timeline, can help manage scheduling and other aspects of planning. These applications enable the definition of tasks at various levels of detail, the delineation of relationships among tasks, the allocation of resources to tasks, and the calculation of the project's critical path.

[4] Kevin Forsberg, Hal Mooz and Howard Cotterman, *Visualizing Project Management*, John Wiley & Sons, Inc., 1996.

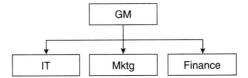

FIGURE 10.5 Pure functional structure.

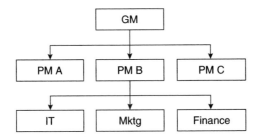

FIGURE 10.6 Pure project structure.

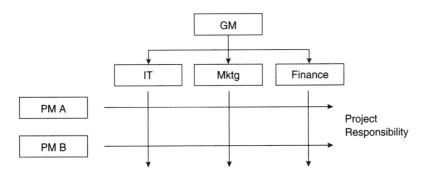

FIGURE 10.7 Conventional matrix structure.

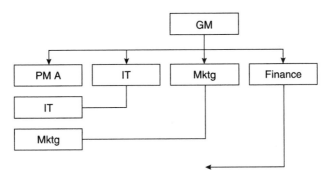

FIGURE 10.8 Collocated matrix structure.

Risk and Opportunity Management. Managing risks and opportunities throughout the project life cycle is a critical task of the team. The first step is to identify risks and opportunities, and assess the probability, potential impact on the project, and any anticipated outcomes. Then it is helpful to compare the outcomes that can be predicted as particular risks and opportunities arise and prioritize them in terms of the magnitude of their effects. Once that is done, strategies can be developed to maximize opportunities and minimize risks, and cost estimates of all alternatives can be made. By comparing costs and benefits of various courses of action, the team can select which sequence of actions to take and obtain agreement from necessary parties. As a precaution, all decisions, and the rationales leading to those decisions, should be documented. That way, when questions arise, there is a way to analyze what the action should have been and why it was chosen.

Risk assessment of projects is an art. There are many frameworks to use to compare projects and to identify potential disasters. For example, the sidebar entitled Project Review Questions for Risk Assessment helps identify project risks by posing a series of questions designed to highlight possible areas where failure begins. Further, Figure 10.9 offers a framework for organizing the answers by categorizing the types of risks they imply.

Project Control

Effective project management requires the exercise of control sufficient to minimize risks and maximize the likelihood of meeting or exceeding requirements. Five variables affect the quality of project control:

- **The nature and number of entities that require control**—Examples include changes in process or project requirements, the roles or performance of key team members, and the schedule for various phases of the work.

- **Control standards**—Which criteria provide the most telling measures of success in any phase of the project?

- **Control authority**—The team must identify those groups or individuals whose requirements define the performance criteria.

- **Control mechanisms**—The project plan must include devices, structures, or events that can track progress or performance against the identified standards.

- **Variance detection**—The team must understand at what point its process has veered substantially from the critical path or performance has fallen significantly short of identified standards, so that it can make needed corrections.

To illustrate, if the management issue is control of the project schedule, the control standard might be the agreed-upon master schedule, and the business manager the control authority. Status review modules in Microsoft Project software might provide the control mechanism, as well as opportunities to detect intolerable variances from the standard. Missing or easily bypassed controls can easily prevent the successful completion of a project.

Cost Analysis (NPV, IRR, Cost/benefit)	Assess whether the project worth the investment.
Opportunity Lost	Assess the cost of inaction or failure.
Vendor Management	Assess the vendor's financial health, marketplace performance, reinvestment tendencies, technology directions, customer relationships, and global capabilities.
Software Development Practices	Assess software development plans and activities to ensure clear business objectives, modular projects, short development cycles, user involvement, and use of off-the-shelf software.
Political Risk	Assess who cares about this project and ask questions, listen, learn, and communicate.
Project Risk Factors	
Investment Size	Assess relative size of investment to be made compared to overall IT budget.
Project Size	Assess the complexity and scope of project and evaluate duration and longevity.
Technical Risk	Assess the newness of the technology to the organization and to the industry as a whole.
Intended Benefit Risk Factors	
Business Impact	Assess how the investment contributes to improvement in organizational performance in specific, outcome-oriented terms.
Customer Needs	Assess how the technology addresses identified needs and demands from internal and external customers.
Return on Investment	Assess whether the figures using benefit-cost analysis thresholds are reliable and technically sound.
Organizational Impact	Assess how broadly the technology investment will affect the organization (i.e., the number of offices, users, work processes, and other systems)?
Expected Improvements	Assess magnitude and ability to obtain expected performance improvements.
Solution Risk Factors	
Flexibility	Assess ability to reorganize, acquire, and divest as needed.
Compatibility	Assess what it will cost to incorporate future technologies.

FIGURE 10.9 IT project risk assessment table.

Adapted from Lynda Radosevich and Cheryl Dahle, 1996, 15 April, "Taking Your Chances," *CIO* magazine website, http://www.cio.com/archive/041596_risk_content.html.

Project Review Questions for Risk Assessment

1. Are we doing the right things?
   - Are project objectives clear?
   - Will the proposed IT solution support business activities?
   - What changes should be considered?

2. Are we doing it in the best way?
   - Have alternative ways been explored?
   - Are there emerging technologies we should consider?
   - What changes would increase the likelihood of success?

3. How do we know how well we are doing?
   - What are the performance standards?
   - Is there regular progress reporting?
   - How will the staff give feedback?

4. What impacts are we having on the business?
   - To what extent have project objectives been achieved?
   - Are the project clients satisfied?
   - Is satisfaction improving or declining?
   - Is support for the project improving, stable, or declining?

5. Is the project cost effective?
   - What significant business costs are influenced by this project?
   - What is the trend of costs?
   - What significant variances from budget have occurred?

6. Is there clear accountability for the project?
   - Are the right people involved?
   - Are lines of responsibility clear?
   - Is senior management supportive?
   - Is performance monitored and on track?
   - Do all those involved with the project understand their roles?

7. Are key assets protected?
   - Will the IT infrastructure handle the deployment of the application?
   - Is IT security adequate?
   - Are risks identified and monitored?
   - How are incidents reported and analyzed?

Project Visibility

It is essential to manage communication among team members and between the team and any project stakeholders. Techniques can usefully range from the old-fashioned approach sometimes called "managing by walking around" to the more technological approaches of video conferencing, e-mail and voice mail. One effective technique to raise visibility uses a project information center comprising physical displays in a central location.

Project Status

Status checks measure the project's performance against the plan to alert everyone to any needed adjustments to budget, schedule, or other business or technical aspects of the project. The status of these elements should be evaluated in a combined format, since they interrelate.

Corrective Action

Corrective techniques can place the project back on track after a variation from the plan is detected. Examples of these reactive techniques include adding work shifts, lengthening work hours, and changing leadership.

Project Leadership

Project leadership is the management quality that binds the other nine elements together. Lack of leadership can result in unmotivated people doing the wrong things and ultimately derailing the project. Strong project leaders skillfully manage team composition, reward systems, and other techniques to focus, align, and motivate team members. Figure 10.10 reflects the fact that the magnitude of the project leader's role varies inversely with the experience and commitment of the team. In organizations that have developed strong processes for project management and professionals trained for this activity, the need for aggressive project leadership is reduced. However, strong project leaders are needed to help the organization develop project competency to begin with.

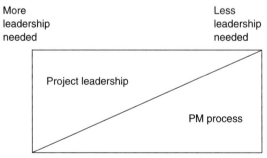

FIGURE 10.10   Project leadership vs. project management process.

▶ WHAT MAKES INFORMATION TECHNOLOGY PROJECTS DIFFERENT?

Today, there is little difference between a non-IT or an IT project since virtually all business projects involve IT at some level. That means that all managers will, at some point, be involved with project management that has a component of IT. However, like all projects, the more complex the IT aspect of the project, the higher the risk of failure of the project. Therefore, this section discusses key aspects of managing the IT component of a project. Sometimes, this is referred to separately as an IT project, not only for simplicity, but because in the business world, there is still a mental split between IT projects and other projects. The general manager needs to understand the issues specific to the IT aspects of projects in order to select the right management tools for the particular challenges presented in such projects.

This section starts with an overview of the systems development life cycle, (SDLC), a popular methodology for developing software and IS. That is followed with a comparison of prototyping and rapid applications development (RAD). Finally, this chapter includes a discussion of various managerial topics including complexity, risk, technology, and communication.

Systems Development Life Cycle

Systems development is the set of activities used to create an IS. The SDLC typically refers to the process of designing and delivering the entire system. While the system includes the hardware, software, networking, and data (as discussed in Chapter 6: Architecture and Infrastructure), the SDLC generally is used in one of two distinct ways. On the one hand, SDLC is the general project plan of all the activities that must take place for the entire system to be put into operation, including the analysis and feasibility study, the development or acquisition of components, the implementation activities, the maintenance activities, and the retirement activities. But in the context of an information system, SDLC can refer to a very structured and formal process for design and development of the software of the system.

SDLC can refer to a specific process to be used by the IS professional so the phases of the project are well documented, and all individuals involved in the project have a full understanding of exactly what the project will consist of, and when deliverables will be made. This approach is much more structured than other approaches, such as prototyping or RAD. However, while it is a very structured approach, there is no one well-accepted SDLC process. For any specific organization, and for a specific project, the actual tasks under each phase may vary. And further, the check points, metrics, and documentation may vary somewhat. This section provides managers with a general overview of the components of SDLC.

SDLC typically consists of seven phases (see Figure 10.11). The first phase is the initiation of the project, where it is initially discussed and scoped. Approval is acquired before proceeding to the next phase. The second phase is the requirements definition phase, where needs and prerequisites are assessed and documented. Again, approval is obtained before proceeding. The third phase is the functional design phase, where the specifications are well discussed and documented. Approval is

Phase	Description	Sample Activities
Initiation and feasibility	Project is begun with a formal initiation and overall project is understood by IS and user/customers.	Document project objectives, scope, benefits, assumptions, constraints, estimated costs and schedule, and user commitment mechanisms.
Requirements definition	The system specifications are identified and documented.	Define business functionality; review existing systems; identify current problems and issues; identify and prioritize user requirements; identify potential solutions; develop user acceptance plan, user documentation needs, and user training strategy.
Functional design	The system is designed.	Complete a detailed analysis of new system including entity-relationship diagrams, data-flow diagrams, and functional design diagrams; define security needs; revise system architecture; identify standards, define systems acceptance criteria; define test scenarios; revise implementation strategy; freeze design.
Technical design and construction	The system is built.	Finalize architecture, technical issues, standards and data needs; complete technical definition of data access, programming flows, interfaces, special needs, intersystem processing, conversion strategy, and test plans; construct system; revise schedule, plan, and costs, as necessary.
Verification	The system is reviewed to make sure it meets specifications and requirements.	Finalize verification testing, stress testing, user testing, security testing, error handling procedures designed, end-user training, documentation and support.
Implementation	The system is brought up for use.	Put system into production environment; establish security procedures; deliver user documentation; execute training and complete monitoring of system.
Maintenance and review	The system is maintained and repaired as needed throughout its lifetime.	Conduct user review and evaluation, and internal review and evaluation; check metrics to ensure usability, reliability, utility, cost, satisfaction, business value, etc.

FIGURE 10.11　SDLC phases.

obtained on the functional specifications before technical design is begun. Phase four is where technical design and construction is done. Here the system is actually built. If the system is acquired, it is at this point where it is customized as needed for the business environment. Following the construction is the verification phase, where the system is tested to ensure usability, security, operability, and that it meets the specifications for which it is designed. Project sign-off and approval signal that the system is acceptable to the users, and implementation, the sixth phase, is begun. This phase is the "cut over" where the new system is put in operation and all links are established. Finally, the system enters the maintenance and review phase, where metrics are measured to ensure the system continues to meet the needs for which it is designed.

Prototyping and Rapid Applications Development

There are several problems with using traditional SDLC methodology for current IT projects. First, many systems projects fail to meet objectives, even with the structure of SDLC. That is often because the skills needed to estimate costs and schedules are difficult to obtain, and each project is often so unique that previous experience may not provide the skills needed for the current project. Second, organizations need to respond very quickly since the business environment changes so quickly. There is not enough time to adequately do each step of the SDLC for each IT project. Therefore, two other methodologies have become popular: prototyping and RAD.

Prototyping, or evolutionary development, is the method of building systems where developers get the general idea of what is needed by the users, and then build a fast, high level version of the system as the beginning of the project. The idea of prototyping is to quickly get a version of the software in the hands of the users, and to jointly evolve the system through a series of cycles of design. In this way, the system is done when the users are happy with the design or the system is proven impossible, too costly, or too complex. Some IS groups use prototyping as a methodology by itself because users are involved in the development much more closely than with the traditional SDLC process. Users see the day-to-day growth of the system and contribute frequently to the development process. The drawbacks to this methodology are first, documentation may be more difficult to write. Since the system evolves, it takes much more discipline to ensure the documentation is adequate. Second, since users see the prototype develop, they often do not understand that a final prototype may not be scalable to an operational system without additional costs and organizational commitments. Once users see a working model, they assume the work is also almost done. And that is not the case.

Another popular methodology for generating systems quickly is called RAD. This process is similar to prototyping in that it is an interactive process, where tools are used to speed up development. RAD systems typically have tools for developing the user interface—called the graphical user interface (GUI)—reusable code, code generation, and programming language testing and debugging. These tools make it easy for the developer to build a library of common, standard sets of code (sometimes called *objects*) which can easily be used in multiple applications. Similarly, RAD systems typically have the ability to allow the developer to simply "drag and drop" objects into the design, and the RAD system automatically writes the code necessary to include that functionality. Finally, the system includes a set of tools to create, test, and debug the programs written in the pure programming language. RAD is commonly used for developing user interfaces and rewriting legacy applications.

There are other development methodologies that a general manager may run into in the course of managing a project. Two other popular ones are object-oriented development, a development methodology utilizing a very different view of IS as a set of objects, and joint applications development, a version of RAD or prototyping in which users are more integrally involved with the entire development process up to and in some cases including coding. There are many good references for systems development, but further detail is beyond the scope of this text. The interested general manager is referred to a more detailed systems development text for a deeper understanding of this critical IS process.

High Complexity Level

What are the managerial level issues associated with IT projects? The first issue is complexity level of the project. Several factors contribute to greater complexity in IT projects. The first is the sheer pace of technological change. The increasing numbers of products and technologies affecting the marketplace cause individuals to have rapidly changing views of any firm's future business situation. For example, the introduction of the JAVA programming language created very different ideas in people's minds about the future direction of Web development. Such uncertainty can make it very difficult for project team members to identify and agree to common goals. This fast rate of change also creates new vocabularies to learn as technologies are implemented. This fact can undermine effective communication.

The development of more complex technologies accelerates the trend toward increased specialization among members of a project team and multiplies the number of interdependencies that must be tracked in project management. Larger numbers of subprojects must be managed and a corresponding number of interfaces developed to integrate the pieces back into a whole.

High complexity played a part in the failure of BAE Automated Systems to provide the City of Denver Airport with a single automated baggage handling system as described in the press and documented in a Harvard Business School case.[5] The original baggage system was scheduled to be completed in June 1993 and was planned to service the concourse of a single carrier: United Airlines. However, during the course of the project the City of Denver asked BAE to expand the system to encompass baggage handling for the entire airport. This project proved to be too complex to be accomplished in the time available. The technology and software systems could not be scaled up to meet the demands of the whole airport, and after

---

[5] For more detail, see Applegate, L., Montealegre, R., Nelson, H. J., and Knoop, C. "BAE Automated Systems (A): Denver International Airport Baggage-Handling System," Harvard Business School Press. Case no. 396311, November 1996, pp. 1–15.

long delays, court battles, and millions of dollars lost, the airport installed two additional baggage systems that had been developed by other firms.

High Risk Level

Complexity contributes to the risk level of a project; the more complex the project, the greater the risk. Should one component of a complex project fail to meet expectations, other components dependent on the outcome of the failed component are going to be affected. Since IT projects in general tend to be highly complex undertakings, the chances of a bug in the code, or an omission of a critical software feature, only increase the risk that a project will fail. Managing the risk of an IT project is more difficult than managing the risk of other types of projects.

The increasing dependence on IT in all aspects of business means that managing the risk level of an IT project is critical to a general manager's job. Organizations increasingly embed IT deeper into their business processes, raising efficiency but also increasing risk. Many companies now rely entirely on IT for their revenue-generating processes, whether the process uses the Internet or not. For example, airlines are dependent on IT for generating reservations and ultimately sales. If the reservation system goes down, that is, if it fails, agents simply cannot sell tickets. And further, while the airplanes technically can fly if the reservation system fails, the airline cannot manage their seat assignments, baggage, or passenger loads without the reservation system. In short, the airline would have to stop doing business should their reservation system fail. That type of dependence on IT raises the risk levels associated with adding or changing the system.

Information Systems Projects Measurements

Some metrics used for IS projects are the same as those used for all business projects: on-time, on-budget, and met specifications. Projects are measured against budgets of cost, schedules of deliverables, and the amount of functionality the final system incorporates.

A lot of attention has been paid on estimating IS projects. At the same time, most software projects fail to meet their schedules and budgets. This is so because estimating techniques are poor, the schedule's progress is often poorly monitored, and when schedule slippage is identified, it is often thought that adding additional people will fix the problem.[6] Not only does this assume that people and months are interchangeable, but if the project is off schedule, it may be that the project was incorrectly designed in the first place, and putting additional people on the project just hastens the process to an inappropriate end. Many projects are measured in "man-months," which is a common unit for discussing the size of a project. For example, a project that takes 100 man-months means that it will take one person 100 months to do the work, or 100 people can do it in a month. There are some problems with this metric. For example, some projects cannot be sped up with addi-

[6] Brooks, Frederick. *The Mythical Man-Month: Essays on Software Engineering*. Reading, MA: Addison-Wesley Publishing Company, 1982.

tional people. An analogy is that of pregnancy. It takes one woman nine months to make a baby, and the process cannot be sped up by putting nine people on the job for one month. Software systems often involve highly interactive, complex sets of tasks that rely on each other to make a completed system. While in some cases additional people can speed up the process, most projects cannot be made more efficient simply by adding labor.

Measuring how well the system meets specifications and business requirements is a more complex set of issues. Metrics for functionality are typically divided along lines of business functionality and system functionality. The first set of measures are those derived specifically from the requirements and business needs that generated the project, such as automating the order entry process or building a knowledge management system for product design. In examples like these, a set of metrics can be derived that measure if the system meets expectations. But there are other aspects of functionality that are also important to measure related to the system itself. An example is usability, or how well the individual using the system can and does use it. Sample measures might be the number of users who use the system, the satisfaction of the users for the system, the time it takes to learn the system, the speed of performance, and the rate of errors made by users. Another common metric is system reliability. For example, one might measure the amount of time the system was up (or running), and the amount of time the system was down (or not running).

Reliance on Consultants and Vendors

Few organizations develop or maintain the in-house capabilities they would need to complete complex IT projects. Risk-averse managers want people who possess crucial IT knowledge and skills. Often that skill set can be attained only from previous experience on similar IT projects. Such people are easier to find at consulting firms because consultants' work is primarily project based. Consulting firms have processes that develop the knowledge and experience of their professionals. Thus, managers often choose to "lease" effective IT team skills rather than try to build them within their own people. However, the project manager must balance the benefits achieved from bringing in outsiders with the costs of not developing that skill set in house. When the project is over and the consultants leave, will the organization be able to manage without them? Having too many outsiders on a team also makes alignment more difficult. Outsiders may have different objectives, such as selling more business, or learning new skills, which can conflict with the project manager's goal of completing the project.

The strategic nature of any given project or project phase can help determine whether a consultant should be used. Operational activities characteristic of the organization are better candidates for consultant work, while crucial strategic activities may be better left to internal people. Figure 10.12 categorizes typical business activities to aid in such decision making.

Organizational Level	Business Activities
Strategic	Develop strategy
	Prioritize business requirements
	Create business plan
	Customer interface management
	Member of business staff/strategy boards
	Resource allocation
	Contract management
	Supplier management
	Technology, architecture, standards
	Systems engineering
	Applications development
Operational	Help desk
	Telecommunications (voice/video/data)
	Distributed computing implementation and support
	Mainframe computing implementation and support
	Desktop implementation and support

FIGURE 10.12   Business activities by organizational level.

Emphasis on the Technical Aspects of the Project

Complex technical issues have the potential to command attention that might be better focused on business and budget issues. General managers who are uncomfortable with technology often either ignore the issues, delegating entirely to the IS organization, or focus inappropriate attention on managing the technology to counter their fear. The technical aspects of IT projects do require special attention, but no more than the people, financial, or other resources of the project.

Many IT projects are built using computer-aided software engineering (CASE) tools. This suite of tools helps minimize the complexity and risk associated with the IS. Two primary software tools used to aid in managing the technical issues are the software development library and an automated audit trail.

The software development library is a controlled collection of software, documentation, test data, and associated tools. Programs, utilities, and other software modules are kept here for several reasons. First is integrity. With multiple copies of a piece of software floating around an organization, it is difficult to know which copy is the actual one for the project. The software library keeps the copy that other modules can use to ensure that the correct version is used. Second is reuse. A software library is useful for programmers who need code, but do not know where to find it. The library is the storage area where programmers would look for code they want to reuse in their module. Third is control. Not only does the library ensure that the software is the right one, but it can make sure that only those authorized to work on the code have access to the code.

Another tool, an automated audit trail, allows the team to track each change made to the code. Each step is recorded in such a way as to capture exactly what was done, making it possible to undo if necessary. The tracing of each step is important should a problem be found. It allows the troubleshooter to retrace and in some cases to regenerate old code to identify where the problem originates. Further, some quality assurance processes require analysis of the generation process, and the audit trail provides that information.

Software metrics are another tool used to manage the technical aspects of the project. The following list serves to identify some of the key terms that a general manager is likely to encounter.

- Source lines of code (SLOC) is the number of lines of code in the source file of the software product.

- Source statement is the number of statements in the source file.

- Function points describe the functional requirements of the software product and can be estimated earlier than total lines of code.

- Inheritance depth is the number of levels through which values must be remembered in a software object.

- Team minimum development time.

- Project minimum development time is always greater than the team minimum development times due to coordination and integration efforts.

- Schedule slip is the current scheduled time divided by the original scheduled time.

- Percentage complete measures the progress of a software product in terms of days or effort.

Taken together, these tools can help the team to manage technical aspects of a project in such a way as to maintain a balance with other business aspects.

Communication Issues

Communication issues are very important for any type of project. But an IT project has special communication needs such as a common project vocabulary. The IT project includes many terms that may be unfamiliar to the general manager and the common project vocabulary documents those terms and their meaning. The combination of having consultants who are new to the organization, a large number of technical members on a team, and business members each with different expertise creates a challenging environment in which to have conversations, meetings, and memos.

The common project vocabulary helps reduce misunderstandings in a couple of ways. First, many terms have multiple meanings. Sorting out, and recording, the exact meaning for the project is done with the common project vocabulary. Second, as with most specialties, there are a large number of cryptic words common to a software project. The common project vocabulary is a place where these words are recorded and explained.

▶ PUTTING IT ALL TOGETHER WITH ORGANIZATIONAL FACTORS

Consider this case example: A general manager has just been given six months and $500,000 to install a corporate website from which customers can order the company's product directly. What should the manager be thinking about as he or she begins organizing a project to accomplish this objective? This section describes how to organize and approach the three key management issues: complexity level, behavioral factors, and success.

Complexity Level

The project's complexity, risk, and size determine how formal the project management system and the planning detail should be. Figure 10.13 shows that as projects grow larger and complexity increases, the need increases for more formal management systems. A small, low risk project can be managed very informally, but a large, complex project will require frequent reporting and tighter performance measurement. Figure 10.14 shows examples of project management tools that the increased sophistication in planning such projects entails. Document management becomes more important as the paperwork increases.

A key variable in measuring complexity is the business objective of the project. If organizational improvement is the business goal, then the IT project may be part of a larger program. This requires evaluation of the IT project in terms of organizational change issues. In our website example, what is the project's complexity level? What additional information might be useful in making this decision?

Complexity can be determined once the context of the project has been established. Questions that might be used to build this context are:

How many products will this website sell?

Will this site support global, national, regional, or local sales?

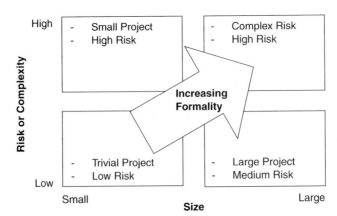

FIGURE 10.13 Increasing formality of project management.
Source: K. Forsberg, H. Mooz, and H. Cotterman, *Visualizing Project Management*. Wiley & Sons, 1996. Used with permission.

FIGURE 10.14   Project management tools for each quadrant.
Source: K. Forsberg, H. Mooz, and H. Cotterman, *Visualizing Project Management*. Wiley & Sons, 1996. Used with permission.

How will this sales process interface with the existing customer fulfillment process?

Does the company possess the technical expertise in-house to build the site?

What other corporate systems and processes does this project impact?

How and when will these other systems be coordinated?

Organizational Factors

Both the project and the project management system must be viewed in the larger context of the organization and the business environment. That means managing project stakeholders, sustaining commitment to projects, and managing organizational and socioeconomic influences.

Managing Project Stakeholders

Stakeholders are individuals and organizations who are actively involved in the project, or whose interests may be positively or negatively affected as a result of project execution or successful project completion.[7] A project management system must be designed to balance the goals of the project stakeholders with the outcomes of the project. And, further, systems may need to be created to specifically manage stakeholders. It is not always a simple task to identify the stakeholders of a project. They may be employees, managers, users, other departments, or even customers. However, failure to do so can lead to costly mistakes later in the project if a particular group is not supportive of the project.

---

[7] Project Management Institute Standards Committee, *A Guide to the Project Management Body of Knowledge*, Project Management Institute, 1996, p. 15.

Key stakeholders on every project include the following:[8]

- **Project manager**—the individual responsible for managing the project.

- **Customer**—the individual or organization who will use the project product. There may be multiple layers of customers. For example, the customers for a new pharmaceutical product may include the doctors who prescribe it, the patients who take it, and the insurers who pay for it.

- **Performing organization**—the enterprise whose employees are most directly involved in doing the work of the project.

- **Sponsor**—the individual or group within the performing organization that provides the financial resources, in cash or in kind, for the project.

Managing the expectations and needs of these people often involves both the project manager and the general manager. Project sponsors are especially critical for IT projects with organizational change components. Sponsors use their power and influence to remove project barriers by gathering support from various social and political groups both inside and outside the organization. They often prove to be valuable when participating in communication efforts to build the visibility of the project.

Sustaining Commitment to Projects

A key job of the project management team is to gain commitment from stakeholders and to sustain that commitment throughout the life of the project. Research has shown that there are four primary types of determinants of commitment to projects (see Figure 10.15).[9] They are project determinants, psychological determinants, social determinants, and organizational determinants. Project teams often focus on only the project factors, ignoring the other three types because of their complexity. But by identifying how these factors are manifested in an organization, project managers can use tactics to ensure a sustained commitment. For example, to maintain commitment, a project team might continually remind stakeholders of the benefits to gain from completion of this project. Likewise, assigning the right project champion the task of selling the project to all levels of the organization can maintain commitment.

On the other hand, projects in trouble often persist long after they should have been abandoned. In part because these same factors can make it difficult to terminate a project. For example, when the penalties for failure within an organization are high, project teams are often willing to go to great lengths to insure that their project persists, even if it means extending resources. Also, if there is an emo-

---

[8] Project Management Institute Standards Committee, *A Guide to the Project Management Body of Knowledge*, Project Management Institute, 1996, p. 15.

[9] See for example, Mark Keil, "Pulling the Plug: Software Project Management and the Problem of Project Escalation", MIS Quarterly, 19(4), December 1995, pg. 421–447. Michael Newman and Rajiv Sabherwal, "Determinants of Commitment to iNformation Systems Development: A Longitudinal Investigation", MIS Quarterly, 20(1), March 1996, pg. 23–54.

Determinant	Description	Example
Project	Objective attributes of the project such as cost, benefits, expected difficulty, and duration	Projects are more likely to have higher commitment if they involve a large potential payoff.
Psychological	Factors managers use to convince themselves things are not so bad, such as previous experience, personal responsibility for outcome, and biases	Projects are more likely to have higher commitment when there is a previous history of success.
Social	Elements of the various groups involved in the process, such as rivalry, norms for consistency, and need for external validation	Projects are more likely to have higher commitment when external stakeholders have been publicly led to believe the project will be successful.
Organizational	Structural attributes of the organization, such as political support, and alignment with values and goals	Projects are more likely to have higher commitment when there is strong political support from executive levels.

FIGURE 10.15 Determinants of commitment for IT projects.
Adapted from Keil, 1995 and Newman and Sabherwal, 1996.

tional attachment to the project by powerful individuals within the organization, the troubled project will often continue well beyond reasonable time limits.

Managing Organizational and Socioeconomic Influences

There are three major organizational influences that the general manager must understand (see Chapter 1 for a discussion of these factors): organizational systems, organizational culture, and organizational structure. The control systems used for non-project-based operations usually do not support project management in an efficient manner. For example, financial reporting systems designed for daily transaction-based operations do not fit well with the reporting needs of a project. Knowing daily profit and loss may not be the best metric for managing a project. A better system would link financial and other metrics with the goals of project stakeholders such as cost of project or completion progress. A consultant who bills monthly based on the percentage of the project that is complete should be monitored with a financial system that tracks resource costs based on percentage complete. The general manager should strive to align the organizational systems with the goals of the project.

The organizational culture influences the communication between team members and the leadership style of the project manager. When selecting a project manager cultural factors should be evaluated. For example, a culture that rewards individual achievement over team participation may hinder a project team.

Members might hoard information instead of sharing it. A leader who sets the example for the team has the opportunity to eliminate or reinforce these barriers. Project time and leadership might also be allocated to help the project team work through these barriers.

Socioeconomic influences on projects include government and industry standards, globalization, and cultural issues. Trends external to the organization, such as changes in industry standards and regulations, will usually affect all projects in varying degrees. An example is the growth of Java as an operating standard for Web developed applications. This factor greatly affected projects written in other languages. Programmers were increasingly difficult to find and many of the best and brightest only wanted jobs in the newest language. In certain cases the standards or regulations may not be known, and managing them means including possible scenarios in the risk management program. Globalization trends create the need for projects that span time zones, oceans, and national boundaries adding to the already complex conditions. Cultural influences, such as economic, ethical, and religious factors, affect the relationship between people and between organizations. All of these factors need to be considered in the project decisions made by the general manager.

▶ FOOD FOR THOUGHT: MEASURING SUCCESS

How does a manager know when a project has been a success? At the start of the project, the general manager should consider several aspects based on achieving the business goals. Care is needed to prevent a too narrow or a too broad set of goals. It is important that the goals be measurable so that they can be used throughout the project to provide the project manager with feedback.

There are four dimensions of success as shown in Figure 10.16. The dimensions are defined as:[10]

- **Resource constraints**—Does the project meet the established time and budget criteria? Most projects set some measure of success along this dimension. This is a short-term success metric that is easy to measure.

- **Impact on customers**—How much benefit does the customer receive from this project? Although some IT projects are transparent to the organization's end customer, every project can be measured on the benefit to the immediate customer of the IS. This dimension includes performance and technical specification measurements.

- **Business success**—How high and how long are the profits? Did the project meet its return on investment goals? This dimension must be aligned with the business strategy of the organization.

- **Prepare the future**—Has the project altered the infrastructure of the organization so that in the future business success and customer impact are more likely? Today many companies are building Internet infrastructures

---

[10] Aaron Shenhar, Dov Dvir and Ofer Levy, "Project Success: A Multidimensional Strategic Approach," Submitted to: Technology and Innovation Management Division, 1998.

Success	Low Tech:	Medium Tech:	High Tech:
Dimension	Existing technologies with new features	Most technologies are new but available before the project	New, untested technologies
Resource Constraint	Important	Overruns acceptable	Overruns most likely
Impact on Customers	Added value	Significantly improved capabilities	Quantum leap in effectiveness
Business Success	Profit Return on Investment	High profits Market share	High, but may come much later Market leader
Prepare the Future	Gain additional capabilities	New market New service	Leadership-core and future technologies

FIGURE 10.16   Success dimensions for various project types.
Adapted from "Project Success: A Multidimensional Strategic Approach."

in anticipation of future business and customer benefits. Overall success of this strategy will only be measurable in the future, although projects underway now can be evaluated on how well they have prepared the business for future opportunities.

What other considerations should be made when defining success? Is it enough just to complete a project? Is it necessary to finish on time and on budget? Are there other important dimensions? The type of project can greatly influence how critical each of these dimensions is in determining the overall success of the project. It is the responsibility of the general manager to coordinate the overall business strategy of the company with the project type and the project success measurements. In this way, the necessary organizational changes can be coordinated to support the new information system.

► SUMMARY

In summary, a general manager has an important role in project management. As a participant, the general manager may be called upon to select the project manager, to provide resources to the project manager, and to provide direction to the project. The key leadership skills in this chapter can be used to evaluate and select a project manager. Understanding the complexity of the project, the environment in which it is developed, and the dimensions used to measure project success will allow the general manager to balance the trade-offs necessary for using resources effectively and to keep the project's direction aligned with the companies business strategy. As a project manager, the general manager would be expected to lead the daily activities of the project in which case, this chapter suggests a management model to be used in managing the technical, budget, and business aspects of the project.

Projects are here to stay and every general manager must be a project manager at some point in his or her career. This chapter offers insight into the necessary skills, processes, and roles that project management requires.

▶ DISCUSSION QUESTIONS

1. What are the trade-offs between cost, quality, and time when designing a project plan? What criteria should managers use to manage this trade-off?

2. Why does it often take a long time before troubled projects are abandoned or brought under control?

3. What are the critical success factors for a project manager? What skills should managers look for when hiring someone who would be successful in this job?

4. What determines the level of technical risk associated with a project? What determines the level of organizational risk? How can a general manager assist in minimizing these risk components?

▶ CASE STUDY 10-1

AVON PRODUCTS, INC. FINANCIAL SYSTEMS*

Avon Products, Inc., founded in 1886, has grown from door-to-door sales in the Northeast United States to a global sales force calling on customers in more than 120 nations. Expansion into emerging markets is growing faster than sales in established economies such as the U.S., Canada, and Western Europe. The door-to-door sales strategy is especially well suited to nations with underdeveloped retail infrastructures since unreliable transportation, inadequate storage facilities, and limited advertising opportunities make traditional types of retailing near impossible.

But global expansion requires integrated and standardized financial systems for efficient operation. These tools are more than profit and loss statement generators; they are operational management tools. And they must be flexible enough to adapt to local market requirements. For example, Brazil has over 200 different district and regional taxing organizations, and each has its own requirements. So Avon must customize its financial statements to address all the laws in each area.

The rollout of the global system required detail planning. This began with a corporate task force made up of financial mangers from several countries, and corporate financial and IS staff. Systems requirements were developed from a detailed study of regulations, taxes, etc. for each country and region. A corporate implementation team of less than 20 people managed 35 divisional teams lead by local personnel. The corporate team developed a single prototype plan as the basic structure for each location. The hardware was standardized on the AS/400 instead of the latest client/server hardware because many regions did not have technical expertise to support the newest technologies. The implementation plans were developed to deploy the system in 40 countries, and documents were translated into local languages.

---

* Condensed from Peter Fabris, "Financial Systems: Global Market Scents," *CIO* magazine, September 1, 1995.

Implementation at each site took about nine months—the first three months were used to plan and install equipment, and the last six months were used for software installation and training. The Global Finance Director assigned his financial accounting manager and two others to work on the implementation full time. The finance department formed an Avon Users Group to provide a mechanism for communication and support. It offered a company-wide bulletin board for sharing tips to make the implementation go smoothly. It was especially useful for sites in Asia, which needed information outside the normal United States business hours.

Local acceptance was critical to the systems success. Local financial directors were in charge of the implementation in their locations to encourage acceptance and to avoid a "top-down" mandate that might have been resisted. The local teams reported weekly on their progress to the corporate team. Problems and potential bottlenecks were identified as quickly as possible and plans made to eliminate them. Problems in one location were used as red flags for other areas. For example, departments in different countries used different formulas for allocating expenses. In response, a common database containing all of these formulas was made so all sites could access them.

The implementation was a success. Locations with antiquated systems have automated tedious manual tasks, such as the Mexico office, which used to type checks by hand. The new system can use electronic funds transfer to pay bills. Best practices were identified from around the world and expanded to include the whole corporation. And unexpected savings came from a variety of sources, such as the Canadian office saving $21,000 per year on computer paper since eliminating the batch processing on their mainframe. Planning and execution minimized culture shock. For example, accountants needed to be convinced that they could accurately keep the books with the new, automated system. But once implemented, the tools that streamlined Avon's financial systems gave them the platform for further expansion into even more remote locations and villages around the world.

Discussion Questions

1. What were the sources of risk for Avon's global rollout of its new system? What do you think the corporate team planned to do to minimize this risk?
2. What were the key roles used to manage this project? What role did the local financial managers play in this project? What might have been used as an incentive to get local managers to align with corporate objectives?
3. How might the corporate team ensure that local best practices from around the world be preserved, and possibly transferred to others in the company?

CHAPTER 11

USING INFORMATION ETHICALLY*

On December 26, 1990 the *Wall Street Journal* carried an article headlined "Coming Soon to Your Local Video Store: Big Brother." The report chastised Blockbuster Video for its plan to sell customer movie preference information to direct mailers and other companies for the purpose of targeted marketing campaigns. Although legality was not at issue, since the law had allowed similar sales of customer data, the article cited many sources who voiced concerns about ethical issues.[1]

> The basic principle is that information collected for one purpose shouldn't be used for another purpose without an individual's consent. Many companies regularly sell their customer lists, but Blockbuster is one of a small fraction using sophisticated computers to keep records of each individual's transactions. Its database promises to raise some especially difficult privacy issues, for the same reason it should be such a gold mine for direct mailers: Video choices are among the most revealing decisions a consumer makes.

Federal law forbids video stores to disclose the names of movies its customers rent. But the law permits stores to tell direct marketers "the subject matter" of movies a customer has rented. Blockbuster—whose members constituted one out of six U.S. households at the time—contended its database was legal because it monitored only video categories, not specific titles. Selling lists of mystery movie renters to mystery book clubs, children's movie renters to toy stores, etc., promised valuable information to direct marketing firms concerned with targeting expensive direct mail campaigns. As Allan Caplan, the Blockbuster vice president overseeing the database project, told the *Journal*, "We not only will know their tastes in movies—we'll know their frequency and that will give us a little more information about their lifestyle." [2]

---

* The author wished to acknowledge and thank Arthur J. Ebersole, MBA '99 for his help in reasearching and writing early drafts of this chapter.

[1] Miller, M.W. "Coming Soon to Your Local Video Store: Big Brother," Wall Street Journal, December 26, 1990, pp.9, 10.

[2] Miller, Ibid.

As in the case of Blockbuster, information collected in the course of business can create valuable competitive advantage. But ethical questions concerning just how that information will be used and by whom, whether they arise inside or outside the organization, can have powerful effects on the company's ability to carry out its plans.[3] As computer networks and their products come to touch every aspect of people's lives, and as the power, speed, and capabilities of computers increase, managers are increasingly challenged to govern their use in an ethical manner. No longer can managers afford to view information systems (IS) as discrete entities within the corporate structure. In many cases, IS are coming to comprise much of the corporation itself.

In such an environment, managers are called upon to manage the information generated and contained within those systems for the benefit not only of the corporation, but also of society as a whole. The predominant issue, which arises due to the omnipresence of corporate IS, concerns the just and ethical use of the information companies collect in the course of everyday operations. Without official guidelines and codes of conduct, who decides how to use this information? More and more, this challenge falls upon corporate managers. Managers need to understand societal needs and expectations in order to determine what they ethically can and cannot do in their quest to learn about their customers, suppliers, and employees and to provide greater service.

Before managers can deal effectively with issues related to the ethical and moral governance of IS, they need to know what these issues are. Unfortunately, as with many emerging fields, well accepted guidelines do not exist. Thus, managers bear even greater responsibility as they try to run their businesses and simultaneously develop control methods that meet both corporate imperatives and the needs of society at large. If this challenge appears to be a matter of drafting operating manuals, nothing could be further from the truth.

In a society whose legal standards are continually challenged, managers must serve as guardians of the public and private interest, although many may have no formal legal training and, thus, no firm basis for judgment. This chapter will address many such concerns. It begins by elaborating the most important issues behind the ethical treatment of information. Next this chapter expands upon the definition of ethical behavior and introduces several heuristics which managers can employ to help them make better decisions. This is followed by a discussion of some newly emerging controversies that will surely test society's resolve concerning the increasing presence of IS in every aspect of life.

This chapter takes a high level view of ethical issues facing managers in today's environment. It focuses primarily on providing a set of frameworks the manager can apply to a wide variety of ethical issues. Omitted is a specific focus on several important issues such as social justice (the impact of computer technology on the poor or "have-nots," racial minorities, and third world nations) nor is there a discussion of intellectual property rights (the ways in which rights extend to the ownership of electronic information). Finally, this chapter does not address social

---

[3] Hasnas, J. and Smith, J. "Ethics and Information Systems: The Corporate Domain." Working paper, 1998, p. 2

concerns that arise out of artificial intelligence, neural networks, and expert systems. Although these are interesting and important areas for concern, in this chapter the objective is to provide managers with a way to think about the issues of ethics and privacy concerns. The interested reader may wish to seek out one of a number of sources for dozens of articles and books on this area of IS management (such as www.isworld.org).

▶ CONTROL OF INFORMATION

In an economy that is rapidly becoming dominated by knowledge workers, the value of information becomes tantamount. Those who possess the "best" information and know how to use it, win. The recent trend in computer prices has meant that high levels of computational power can be purchased for relatively small amounts of money. While this trend means that computer-generated or stored information now falls within the reach of an ever-larger percentage of the populace, it also means that collecting and storing information is becoming easier and more cost effective. Although this circumstance certainly affects businesses and individuals for the better, it also can affect them substantially for the worse. Consider several areas in which the control of information is crucial. Richard O. Mason, in an article published in *MIS Quarterly*,[4] identified four such areas, which can be summarized by the acronym PAPA: privacy, accuracy, property, and accessibility (see Figure 11.1).

Most Americans consider privacy to be the most important area in which their interests need to be safeguarded. Employers can monitor their employees' e-mail and computer utilization while they are at work, even though they have not historically monitored telephone calls. Every time someone logs onto one of the main search engines, a "cookie" is placed in their hard drive so that these companies can track their surfing habits. Currently this information is used only to target advertising, but its future use depends on the discretion of managers. Their view will be formed in part by how much competitive advantage this knowledge can create. Do customers have a right to privacy while searching the Internet? Courts have decided that the answer is no, but as society moves ahead, the right to monitor customer habits will be affected by how managers decide to use the information that they have collected.

The increase in monitoring leads to the question of property. Now that organizations have the ability to collect vast amounts of data on their clients, do they have a right to share data with others to create a more accurate profile of an individual? And if they do create such consolidated profiles, who owns that information, which in many cases was not divulged willingly for that purpose? Who owns images that are posted in cyberspace? With ever more sophisticated methods of computer animation, can companies use newly "created" images or characters building upon models in other media without paying royalties? Mason summarizes the issues,[5]

---

[4] Mason, Richard O. "Four Ethical Issues of the Information Age" MIS Quarterly, 10(1), March 1986.

[5] Ibid.

Area	Critical Questions
Privacy	What information must a person reveal about one's self to others? What information should others be able to access about you—with or without your permission? What safeguards exist for your protection?
Accuracy	Who is responsible for the reliability and accuracy of information? Who will be accountable for errors?
Property	Who owns information? Who owns the channels of distribution, and how should they be regulated?
Accessibility	What information does a person or an organization have a right to obtain, under what conditions, and with what safeguards?

FIGURE 11.1   Mason's areas of managerial concern.

Any individual item of information can be extremely costly to produce in the first instance. Yet once it is produced, that information has the illusive quality of being easy to reproduce and to share with others. Moreover, this replication can take place without destroying the original. This makes information hard to safeguard since, unlike tangible property, it becomes communicable and hard to keep it to one's self. It is even difficult to secure appropriate reimbursements when somebody else uses your information.

The accuracy of information assumes real importance for society as computers come to dominate in corporate record-keeping activities. When records are inputted incorrectly, who is to blame? In a case in Florida, a family whose bank had recently changed from a paper bookkeeping system to a computer-based system found that a mortgage payment that had been made was not credited. As the family attempted to pay the mortgage in subsequent months, the system rejected the payments because the mortgage was listed as past due. After a year of "missing" payments, the bank foreclosed on the house.[6] While this incident may highlight the need for better controls over the bank's internal processes, it also demonstrates the risks that can be attributed to inaccurate information retained in corporate systems. In this case, the bank was responsible for the error, but it paid little—compared to the family—for its mistake. While they cannot expect to eliminate all mistakes from the online environment, managers must establish controls to ensure that situations such as this one do not happen with any frequency.

In the age of the information worker, accessibility becomes increasingly important. Would-be users of information must first gain the physical ability to access online information resources, which broadly means they must access computational systems. Recent trends in computer hardware prices have greatly lowered the barriers to entry on this account. Second and more importantly, the user must gain access to information itself. In this sense, the issue of access is closely linked to that of property. While major corporations have benefited greatly from the drop in computer prices, the same benefit only now is beginning to filter through the rest of

[6] Mason, Richard O. "Four Ethical Issues of the Information Age" MIS Quarterly, 10(1), March 1986.

society. Looking forward, the major issue facing managers is how to create and maintain access to information for society at large. As our society moves toward a service- or knowledge-based economy, managers whose organizations control vast quantities of information will have to weigh the benefits of information control against societal needs to upgrade the knowledge bases of individuals or knowledge workers.

▶ NORMATIVE THEORIES OF BUSINESS ETHICS

The landscape changes daily as advances in technology are incorporated into existing organizational structures. IS are becoming omnipresent as companies look to decrease costs, increase efficiency, and build strategic competitive advantages. Increasingly, however, these advances come about in a business domain lacking ethical clarity. Because of its newness, this area of IT often lacks accepted norms of behavior. Companies encounter daily quandaries as they try to use their IS to create and exploit competitive advantages.

Managers must assess current information initiatives with particular attention to possible ethical issues. Because so many managers have been educated in the current corporate world, they are used to the overriding ethical norms present in their traditional businesses. As Conger and Loch observed, "People who have been trained in engineering, computer science, and MIS, frequently have little training in ethics, philosophy, and moral reasoning. Without a vocabulary with which to think and talk about what constitutes an ethical computing issue, it is difficult to have the necessary discussions to develop social norms."[7]

Managers in the information age will need to translate their current ethical norms into terms meaningful for the new electronic corporation. In order to suggest a workable framework for this process, consider three theories of ethical behavior in the corporate environment that managers can develop and apply to the particular challenges they will face. These normative theories of business ethics—stockholder theory, stakeholder theory, and social welfare theory—are widely applied in traditional business situations. They are "normative" in that they attempt to derive what might be called "intermediate level" ethical principles: principles expressed in language accessible to the ordinary business person, which can be applied to the concrete moral quandaries of the business domain.[8] Below is a definition of each theory followed by an illustration of its application using a recent business example, the Blockbuster Video case outlined at the beginning of this chapter.

Stockholder Theory

According to this theory, stockholders advance capital to corporate managers who act as agents in advancing their ends. The nature of this contract binds managers

---

[7] Conger, S. and Loch, K.D. "Ethics and Computer Use," *Communications of the ACM* (38:12), December 1995, pp. 31,32.

[8] Hasnas and Smith, 1998, p. 5

to act in the interest of the shareholders: i.e., to maximize shareholder value. As Milton Friedman wrote, "There is one and only one social responsibility of business: to use its resources and engage in activities designed to increase its profits so long as it stays within the rules of the game, which is to say, engages in open and free competition, without deception or fraud."[9]

Stockholder theory qualifies the manager's duty in two salient ways. First, managers are bound to employ legal, nonfraudulent means. Second, managers must take the long view of shareholder interest: i.e., they are obliged to forgo short-term gains if doing so will maximize value over the long term.

Managers will want to bear in mind that stockholder theory itself provides a limited framework for moral argument because it assumes the ability of the free market to fully promote the interests of society at large. Yet the singular pursuit of profit on the part of individuals or corporations cannot be said to maximize social welfare. Free markets can foster the creation of monopolies and other circumstances that limit the ability of members of a society to secure the common good. A proponent of stockholder theory might insist that, as agents of stockholders, managers must not use stockholders' money to accomplish goals that do not directly serve the interests of those same stockholders. A critic of stockholder theory would argue that such spending would be just if the money went to further the public interest.

The stipulation under stockholder theory that the pursuit of profits must be legal and nonfraudulent would not limit Blockbuster's plan to sell "broad-based, general" information about clients, because such sales do not violate privacy laws. Moreover, the plan would appear to satisfy the test of maximizing shareholder value because it potentially generates new revenues. On the other hand, if customers stopped renting movies from Blockbuster because they disliked the company's plans to use their personal information in this manner, any lost revenues would weigh against managers' success in meeting the ethical obligation to work toward maximizing value.

Stakeholder Theory

This theory holds that managers, while bound by their relation to stockholders, are entrusted also with a fiduciary responsibility to all those who hold a stake in or a claim on the firm.[10] The term "stakeholder" is currently taken to mean any group that vitally affects the survival and success of the corporation or whose interests the corporation vitally affects. Such groups normally include stockholders, customers, employees, suppliers, and the local community, though other groups may also be considered stakeholders, depending on the circumstances. At its most basic level, stakeholder theory states that management must enact and follow policies that balance the rights of all stakeholders without impinging upon the rights of any one particular stakeholder.

---

[9] Friedman, M. *Capitalism and Freedom*. University of Chicago Press, Chicago, 1962, p. 133.
[10] Hasnas and Smith, 1998, p. 8

Stakeholder theory diverges most consequentially from stockholder theory in affirming that the interests of parties other than the stockholders play a legitimate role in the governance and management of the firm. As a practical matter, due to the high transaction costs entailed in canvassing all of these disparate groups, managers must act as their agents in deriving business solutions that optimally serve their respective interests. Thus, in most cases stakeholders' only real recourse is to stop participating in the corporation: Customers can stop buying the company's products, stockholders can sell, etc.

Viewed in light of stakeholder theory, the Blockbuster plan begins to present more complex ethical issues. Chief among these is how much benefit accrues to stakeholders from an intrusion into clients' privacy. Blockbuster's shareholders stand to gain, but what would be the effects on other stakeholders? Apparently, the only group that stands to lose is the client group itself. Moreover, consumers considered more broadly might benefit by receiving better targeted advertising to replace traditional mass-marketing campaigns. Also, consider the fact that Blockbuster's policy is publicly known, and clients do have recourse: They can stop patronizing Blockbuster, or ask the company to suppress the sale of their own individual information. In general terms, Blockbuster's plan would not violate ethical standards as they are understood under stakeholder theory, unless it could be shown that the costs to clients outweighed the benefits within the larger stakeholder group.

Social Contract Theory

Social contract theory derives the social responsibilities of corporate managers by considering the needs of a society with no corporations or other complex business arrangements. Social contract theorists ask what conditions would have to be met for the members of such a society to agree to allow a corporation to be formed. Thus, society bestows legal recognition on a corporation to allow it to employ social resources toward given ends. This contract generally is taken to mean that, in allowing a corporation to exist, society demands at a minimum that it create more value to the society than it consumes. Thus, society charges the corporation to enhance its welfare by satisfying particular interests of consumers and workers in exploiting the advantages of the corporate form. The corporation must conduct its activities while observing the canons of justice.[11]

The social contract comprises two distinct components: the social welfare term and the justice term. The former arises from the belief that corporations must provide greater benefits than their associated costs or society would not allow their creation. Thus, the social contract obliges managers to pursue profits in ways that are compatible with the well-being of society as a whole. Similarly, the justice term holds that corporations must pursue profits legally, without fraud or deception, and avoid activities that injure society.

Social contract theory meets criticism because no mechanism exists to actuate it. In the absence of a real contract whose terms subordinate profit maximization to social welfare, most critics find it hard to imagine corporations losing profitability

---

[11] Hasnas and Smith, 1998, p.10.

in the name of altruism. Yet, the strength of the theory lies in its broad assessment of the moral foundations of business activity.

Applied to the Blockbuster case, social contract theory would demand that the manager ask whether the plan to sell client information could compromise fundamental tenets of fairness or social justice. If customers were not apprised of the decision to sell information about themselves, the plan could be seen as unethical. It would not seem fair to collect information for one purpose and then use it for another, without informing the parties concerned. If, on the other hand, the plan were disclosed to customers, and if it were clear its implementation would net a benefit to society, the plan could be considered ethical.

While these three normative theories of business ethics possess distinct characteristics, they are not completely incompatible. All offer useful metrics for defining ethical behavior in profit-seeking enterprises under free market conditions. They provide managers with an independent standard by which to judge the ethical nature of superiors' orders as well as their firms' policies and codes of conduct. Upon inspection, the three theories appear to represent concentric circles, with stockholder theory at the center and social contract theory at the outer ring. Stockholder theory is narrowest in scope, stakeholder theory encompasses and expands upon it, and social contract theory covers the broadest area. Figure 11.2 summarizes these three theories.

A similar situation to the Blockbuster case occurred when Lotus Development Corporation launched its Marketplace product in 1990. The product was a marketing database of 120 million U.S. consumers, with demographic information based on publicly available information. Each consumer had personal information, such as name and mailing address. But the value proposition for the product was in the fact that it combined several publicly available databases and the result was

Theory	Definition	Metrics
Stockholder	Maximize stockholder wealth, in legal and nonfraudulent manners.	Will this action maximize long-term stockholder value? Can goal be accomplished without compromising company standards and without breaking laws?
Stakeholder	Maximize benefits to all stakeholders while weighing costs to competing interests.	Does the proposed action maximize collective benefits to the company? Does this action treat one or more of the corporate stakeholders unfairly?
Social contract	Create value for society in a manner that is just and nondiscriminatory.	Does this action create a "net" benefit for society? Does the proposed action discriminate against any group in particular, and is its implementation socially just?

FIGURE 11.2 Three normative theories of business ethics.

a database that made assumptions about lifestyle, income, family and marital status, and several other demographic categories. It was intended to give companies a comprehensive database of individual spending habits for direct-mail marketing. A grassroots outcry on the Internet resulted in over 30,000 letters and phone calls from individuals who wanted their names deleted from the product. The negative press Lotus received combined with the flood of letters from consumers who were concerned about invasion of privacy caused Lotus to cancel the project. With the widespread use of similar tools and concepts found in customer relationship management (CRM) systems, the general manager must become an informed participant in IS designs. More recently, Living.com, a furniture retailer on the Internet made a very public decision not to sell its customer information. Living.com ceased doing business and filed for bankruptcy protection in the fall of 2000. But, while their customer data could be considered an asset and therefore sold to help pay off their debts, managers at Living.com and the U.S. government officials working with them agreed that their customer information was private and it would be inappropriate to sell it for use by someone other than Living.com.

▶ EMERGING ISSUES IN THE ETHICAL GOVERNANCE OF INFORMATION SYSTEMS

Pick up the newspaper almost any day of the week and it will include ethical concerns in the corporate environment. Such privacy issues as the surveillance of employees and their e-mail messages frequently make headlines. How should managers deal with these issues? Managers are rarely expert in better known areas of ethical concern, much less the issues emerging in the information economy. This section highlights several such areas with an eye to exposing those on which managers should focus their attention.

There are two distinct spheres in which managers operate. The first involves the outward transactions of the business and focuses on the customer. To elaborate, consider the issue of privacy raised by the Blockbuster case from the perspective of the consumer, and what steps businesses are taking to ensure the ethical use of information. The second sphere includes the issues related to managing employees and information inside the corporation. This includes topics in internal surveillance and monitoring, the denigration of and bifurcation of IS jobs, and the problems related to the rigidity of IS in the workplace. Figure 11.3 shows these relationships.

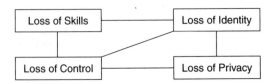

FIGURE 11.3 Some causal connections between identified areas of ethical concern.

Adapted from Fernando Leal, "Ethics is Fragile, Goodness is Not." *Information Society: New Media, Ethics and Postmodernism.* Springer Verlag, 1995, p. 79.

In an age where the Internet and e-mail have become omnipresent, many companies have begun to question the efficacy of such technology in the workplace. Seeking to improve productivity, firms increasingly look to leverage IS to their fullest extent. While e-mail and the Internet have replaced traditional communications and research channels, some companies are seeing corporate networks clogged with excessive traffic, which in turn is leading to lesser productivity gains than anticipated. To combat unauthorized uses of e-mail systems and Internet access, managers are turning to programs that monitor employees' online activities.

A recent *Wall Street Journal* article cited software companies, including Content Advisor of Somerville, Massachusetts, and Secure Computing Corporation of San Jose, California, whose products allow client companies to monitor or restrict the access of employees to certain Internet sites and to prevent them from conducting private business on company time. While the intention may seem both ethical and in the best interest of business, in practice the reverse may actually be true. In many cases employees are not informed that they are being monitored or that information gleaned is being used to measure their productivity. In these cases, monitoring appears to violate both privacy and personal freedoms.[12]

The use of monitoring and surveillance software highlights an increase in the level of control that employers can exert over employees. As employees become aware of these activities, productivity and morale may fall. While the central issue remains with privacy, other potential effects should concern managers, such as undue stress on employees. This issue may seem peripheral, but as technology further intrudes into the workplace and shapes working conditions, its importance can only increase.

Environmental issues previously were the domain of HR professionals and organizational behaviorists. Today, managers must be concerned with creating a work atmosphere amenable to IS. Ethically speaking, managers must address worker health in an increasingly regimented atmosphere. IS by their nature are inflexible. Jobs associated with computer systems demand rigor. As systems come to dominate corporate life, there is an increased risk of sacrificing individuality. Managers rethink job requirements and increase workloads, and depend upon our ability to generate mistake-free work. In an environment where small mistakes can be costly, employees feel greater stress. Managers must be alert to these fundamental changes in the working environment. Ethically, they are obliged to consider the welfare of workers. If, as they create employment opportunities and write job descriptions, managers set out to limit individuality, enforce conformity, and increase demands, they violate their ethical responsibilities as understood under all three normative theories considered in this chapter.

In addition to managing internal ethical concerns, managers must be aware of their relationships with customers. Net purchasers surveyed believed Net retailers should post their policies about how they will use private information. Mary J. Culnan noted in *CIO* magazine that the ease with which consumer information is collected over the Internet makes purchasers increasingly uneasy. "People are

---

[12] Conklin, J.C., "Under the Radar: Content Advisor Snoops as Workers Surf Web." The Wall Street Journal, October 15, 1998, page B8.

balking at giving their information on the Web in a lot of cases because the organization has not made a good case for why they should," Culnan wrote. "If there are no benefits or if they aren't told why the information is being collected or how it's being used, a lot of people say 'Forget it.'"[13] As customers increasingly appreciate the power new technologies put in the hands of retailers, they become skeptical about the wisdom of providing personal information in transacting business online.

Recently the FTC made strides toward requiring web retailers to more fully disclose how they will use customers' private information. The FTC's efforts to foster fair information practices for Net commerce mesh with Mason's PAPA framework. To protect the integrity of information collected about them, federal regulators have recommended allowing consumers limited access to corporate information databases. Consumers thus could update their information and correct errors.

Many Internet industry groups have instituted their own codes of practice in an attempt to avoid regulation. Such companies as Truste Inc. and the Better Business Bureau are licensing members who agree to abide by stringent privacy policies. Compliance earns a medal that can be displayed on the member's website. Transgressors are removed from the program. By creating enforceable standards, the government has begun institutionalizing ethical behavior within corporate IS departments.

Information privacy guidelines must come from above: from the CEO, CIO, and general management. Employees must learn about these issues early in their tenure with a firm to avoid incurring serious problems with FTC oversight.

▶ FOOD FOR THOUGHT: ETHICS AND THE INTERNET

Much debate has been given to privacy and ethics on the Internet. The fact that the Internet crosses state and country boundaries makes these issues extremely complex. Different cultures, laws, customs, and habits of people from different countries ensures that each geographical region will police the Internet in very different ways. This section explores some of the challenges facing managers who must navigate their organizations through the murky waters of ethical use of the Internet.

One area of debate is free speech and censorship. On the Internet, the balance between free speech and censorship is difficult to pinpoint. On the one hand, the First Amendment of the U.S. Constitution guarantees freedom of speech, but that is a United States law, not an international law. The Internet crosses international boundaries, making it a difficult issue to manage. Accompanying freedom of speech is the burden of responsibility. Do websites that host materials of questionable ethics have the responsibility to make sure only appropriate visitors have access to that information? For example, a website with pornography is clearly unsuitable for children. Who is responsible to make sure children do not see it? The web author? The website host? The site where the children access the Web, such as their school or library? Or the children's parents and guardians. In this new world of the Internet, the issues of controlling access, censorship, free speech, and

---

[13] "Saving Private Data" CIO Magazine, October 1, 1998.

responsibility must be reexamined. The astute manager has thought out these issues and addressed them prior to launching the company website.

An Internet Code of Ethics is an issue of much debate by the International Federation of Information Processing (IFIP). IFIP is a nongovernmental, nonprofit umbrella organization for national societies working in the field of information processing. Established in 1960 as part of the United Nations Educational Scientific and Cultural Organization (UNESCO), IFIP has members from all over the world and maintains friendly connections to specialized agencies of the UN System and nongovernmental organizations. This organization's objectives are to help computer professionals and systems designers become aware of the social consequences of their work, to develop criteria to determine the extent to which the public is served with computers, and to encourage designers and users to take human needs into account when making system choices.

IFIP is leading the charge for a discussion of a code of ethics for Internet governance.[14] But consensus among individuals in the United States has not been reached, much less between individuals in different countries. There is general agreement among virtually all IS professionals that safeguarding minors and protecting human dignity is necessary. Virtually all countries have some law or policy related to these dimensions. But beyond that, there is emotional debate on most issues. A well-circulated list of guidelines for computer ethics has been developed by the Computer Ethics Institute. Figure 11.4 summarizes these as the 10 Commandments of Computer Ethics.

Security and Controls

At one end of the spectrum of issues relating to security and control of the Internet is the discussion of issues such as the ones presented earlier: protecting organizational data from unauthorized hackers and undesirable viruses. Managers go to

---

1. Thou shalt not use a computer to harm other people.
2. Thou shalt not interfere with other people's computer work.
3. Thou shalt not snoop around in other people's files.
4. Thou shalt not use a computer to steal.
5. Thou shalt not use a computer to bear false witness.
6. Thou shalt not use or copy software for which you have not paid.
7. Thou shalt not use other people's computer resources without authorization.
8. Thou shalt not appropriate other people's intellectual output.
9. Thou shalt think about the social consequences of the program you write.
10. Thou shalt use a computer in ways that show consideration and respect.

FIGURE 11.4   Ten commandments of computer ethics.

Source: Arlene Rinaldi, Florida Atlantic University, 1998, http://wise.fau.edu/netiquette/net/ten.html verified on September 20, 2000.

---

[14] See, for example, IS World website, www.isworld.org for information on IFIP.

great lengths to make sure their computers are secure from unauthorized insider access, such as an employee seeking data he or she is not authorized to have, and outsider access, such as a hacker who seeks to enter a computer for sport or for malicious intent. At the other end are issues primarily about privacy and protecting individual rights.

Technologies have been devised to manage the security and control issues. Figure 11.5 summarizes four types of tools. These tools, such as firewalls, pass-

Hardware system security and control	Firewalls	A computer set up with both an internal network card and an external network card. This computer is set up to control access to the internal network and only lets authorized traffic pass the barrier.
	Encryption and decryption	Cryptography or secure writing ensures that information is transformed into unintelligible forms before transmission and intelligible forms when it arrives at its destination.
Network and software security controls	Network operating system software	The core set of programs that manage the resources of the computer or network often have functionality such as authentication, access control, and cryptology.
	Security information management	A management scheme to synchronize all mechanisms and protocols built into network and computer operating systems and protect the systems from authorized access.
	Server and browser software security	Mechanisms to ensure that errors in programming do not create holes and trapdoors which can compromise websites.
Broadcast medium security and controls	Labeling and rating software	The software industry incorporates Platform for Internet Content Selection (PICS) technology, a mechanism of labeling web pages based on content. These labels can be used by filtering software to manage access.
	Filtering/blocking software	Software that rates documents and websites that have been rated and contain content on a designated filter's "black list" and keeps them from being displayed on the user's computer.

FIGURE 11.5 Security and control tools.

Adapted from Berleur, J., Duquenoy, P., and Whitehouse, D. "Ethics and the Governance of the Internet," IFIP-SIG9.2.2 white paper, September 1999.

words, and authentication routines, restrict access to information on a computer by preventing access to the server on the network. They provide warning for early discovery of security breaches, limit losses suffered in case of security breaches, analyze and react to security breaches (and try to prevent them from reoccurring), and recover whatever has been lost from security breaches.[15]

Managers must be involved in decisions about security and control measures because they can affect business decisions. For example, a firewall that limits access to an internal network, or intranet, may cause the failure of a work-at-home program a manager seeks to put in place. The firewall may be built in such a way as to completely eliminate gaining access. Likewise, an encryption/decryption system may make future business decisions more expensive. That is because all future applications would have to be built in a manner to accommodate the cryptology. And that additional expense may tip the scales against a future business application the manager sought to implement.

► SUMMARY

The Online Privacy Alliance of Washington, D.C., an industry coalition backed by trade groups and such companies as The Walt Disney Co., Proctor & Gamble, Time Warner Telecom, and IBM, offers its own set of Web privacy guidelines, including the following:

• Have and implement a privacy policy that gives consumers notice, choice, and the ability to correct inaccurate data

• Ensure data security

• Get parental consent before collecting or reselling personally identifiable information from children under the age of 13

Due to the asymmetry of power relationships, managers tend to frame ethical concerns in terms of refraining from doing harm, mitigating injury, and paying attention to dependent and vulnerable parties. As a practical matter, ethics is about maintaining one's own, independent perspective about the propriety of business practices. Managers must make systematic, reasoned judgments about right and wrong, and take responsibility for them. Ethics is about decisive action rooted in principles that express what is right and important and about action that is publicly defensible and personally supportable.

► DISCUSSION QUESTIONS

1. Private corporate data is often encrypted using a key, which is needed to decrypt the information. Who within the corporation should be responsible for maintaining the "keys" to private information collected about consumers? Is that the same person who should have the "keys" to employee data?

2. The Lotus Marketplace case study highlighted the potential of combining otherwise unthreatening databases. In this case, the resulting database showed patterns of spending and placed consumers into categories which reflected personal data the consumers felt was private. But many organizations these days collect individual information, including your

---

[15] Berleur, J., Duquenoy, P., and Whitehouse, D. "Ethics and the Governance of the Internet," IFIP-SIG9.2.2 white paper, September 1999.

credit card provider, your bank, your creditors, and virtually any retail store in which you use a credit card or other identifying customer number. Who owns the information that is collected? Do you, the person who initially provided information to the collector? Or the collecting organization that spent the resources to save the information in the first place?

3. Consider arrest records, which are mostly computerized and stored locally by law enforcement agencies. They have an accuracy rate of about 50 percent—about half of them are inaccurate, incomplete, or ambiguous. These records often are used by others than just law enforcement. Approximately 90 percent of all criminal histories in the United States are available to public and private employers. Use the three normative theories of business ethics to analyze the ethical issues surrounding this situation. How might hiring decisions be influenced inappropriately by this information?

4. The European Community has proposed a set of laws that would strictly limit how database information is used and who has access to it. Some of the restrictions include registering all databases containing personal information with the countries in which they are operating, collecting data only with the consent of the subjects, and telling subjects of the database the intended and actual use of the databases. What effect might these restrictions have on global companies? In your opinion, should these types of restrictions be made into law? Why or why not?

► *CASE STUDY 11-1*

Ethical Decision Making*

Situation 1

The secretarial pool is part of the group assigned to Doug Smith, the Manager of Office Automation. The pool has produced very low quality work for the past several months. Smith has access to the passwords for each of the pool members' computer account. He instructs the pool supervisor to go into each hard drive after hours and obtain a sample document to check for quality control for each pool member.

1. If you were the supervisor, what would you do?
2. What, if any, ethical propositions have been violated by this situation?
3. If poor quality were found, could the information be used for disciplinary purposes? For training purposes?

Situation 2

Kate Essex is the supervisor of the customer service representative group for Enovelty.com, a manufacturer of novelty items. This group spends its work day answering calls, and sometimes placing calls, to customers to assist in solving a variety of issues about orders previously placed with the company. The company has a rule that personal phone calls are only allowed during breaks. Essex is assigned to monitor each representative on the phone for 15 minutes a day, as part of her regular job tasks. The representatives are aware that Essex will be monitoring them, and customers are immediately informed when they begin their

---

* Adapted from short cases suggested by Professor Kay Nelson, University of Utah. The names of people, places, and companies have been made up for these stories. Any similarity to real people, places, or companies is purely coincidental.

calls. Essex begins to monitor James Olsen, and finds that he is on a personal call regarding his sick child.

1. What should Essex do?
2. What, if any, ethical principles help guide decision making in this situation?
3. What management practices should be in place to ensure proper behavior without violating individual "rights"?

Situation 3

Jane Mark was the newest hire in the IS group at We_Sell_More.com, a business on the Internet. The company takes in $30 million in revenue quarterly from Web business. Jane reports to Sam Brady, the VP of IS. Jane is assigned to a project to build a new capability into the company web page which facilitates linking products ordered with future offerings of the company. After weeks of analysis, Jane concluded that the best way to incorporate that capability is to buy a software package from a small start-up company in Silicon Valley, California. She convinces Brady of her decision and is authorized to lease the software. The vendor e-mails Jane the software in a ZIP file, and instructs her on how to install it. At the initial installation, Jane is asked to acknowledge and electronically sign the license agreement. The installed system does not ask Jane if she wants to make a backup copy of the software on diskettes, so as a precaution, Jane takes it upon herself and copies the ZIP files sent to her onto a set of floppies. She stores these floppies in her desk drawer.

A year later the vendor is bought by another company and the software is removed from the marketplace. The new owner believes this software will provide them with a competitive advantage they want to reserve for themselves. The new vendor terminates all lease agreements and revokes all licenses. But Jane still has the floppies she made as backup.

Discussion Questions

1. Is Jane obligated to get rid of her backup copy? Why or why not?
2. If We_Sell_More.com wants to continue to use the system, can they? Why or why not?
3. Does it change your opinion if the software is a critical system for We_Sell_More.com? If it is a noncritical system? Explain.

▶ Glossary

Administrator: An employee who "takes care of" a computer or a number of computers. Administrator duties typically include backing up data (and restoring it if it is lost), performing routine maintenance, installing software upgrades, troubleshooting problems, and assisting users.

ANSI X12: The name of the standard used by EDI applications to allow a software program on one computer system to relay information back and forth to a software program on another computer system, thus allowing organizations to exchange data pertinent to business transactions.

Application: A software program designed to facilitate a specific practical task, as opposed to control resources. Examples of application programs include Microsoft Word, a word processing application; Lotus 1-2-3, a spreadsheet application; and SAP R/3, an enterprise resource planning application. Contrast to *operating system.*

ASP (Application Service Provider): An Internet-based company which offers a software application used through their website. For example, a company might offer small business applications that a small business owner could use on the web, rather than buying software to load on their own computers.

Authentication: A security process where proof is obtained to verify that the users are truly who they say they are.

B2B (Business to Business): Using the Internet to conduct business with business customers. (See B2C).

B2C (Business to Consumer): Using the Internet to conduct business directly with consumers of goods and services. (See B2B).

Bandwidth: The rate at which data can travel through a given medium. The medium may be a network, an internal connection (say from the CPU to RAM), a phone line, etc. For networks and internal connections, bandwidth is typically measured in terms of Megabytes per second (MB/sec) or Gigabytes per second (GB/sec).

Bit: A "binary digit"; the smallest unit of data as represented in a computer. A bit can take only the values 0 or 1.

Bricks-and-clicks: The term used to refer to businesses with a strong business model on both the Internet and in the physical world.

Business Diamond: A simple framework for understanding the design of an organization, linking together the business processes, its values and beliefs, its management control systems, and its tasks and structures.

Byte: 8 bits. A byte can be thought of as a "character" of computer data.

CIO (Chief Information Officer): The senior-most officer responsible for the information systems activities within the organization. The CIO is a strategic thinker, not an operational manager. The CIO is typically a member of the senior management team and is involved in all major business decisions that come before that team, bringing an information systems perspective to the team.

Client: A software program that requests and receives data and sometimes instructions from another software program usually running on a separate computer.

Client/Server: A computing architecture in which one software program (the client) requests and receives data and sometimes instructions from another software program (the server) usually running on a separate computer. In a client/server architecture, the computers running the client program typically require less power and resources (and are therefore less expensive) than the computer running the server program. In many corporate situations, a client/server architecture can be very cost effective.

Co-opetition: A business strategy whereby companies cooperate and compete at the same time.

Coaxial cable (coax): A kind of copper wire typically used in networking. An inner wire is surrounded by insulation, which is surrounded by another copper wire and more insulation.

Complementor: One of the players in a co-opetitive environment. It is a company whose product or service is used in conjunction with a particular product or service to make a more useful set for the customer. (See value net).

Cost leadership strategy: A business strategy where the organization aims to be the lowest-cost producer in the marketplace. (See differentiation strategy and focus strategy).

CPU (Central Processing Unit): The computer hardware on which all computation is done.

CRM (Customer Relationship Management): The management activities done to obtain, enhance, and retain customers. CRM is a coordinated set of activities revolving around the customer.

Cycle plan: A project management plan that organizes project activities in relation to time. It identifies critical beginning and end dates and breaks the work spanning these dates into phases. The general manager tracks the phases in order to coordinate the eventual transition from project to operational status, a process that culminates on the "go live" date.

Database: A collection of data that is formatted and organized to facilitate ease of access, searching, updating, addition, and deletion. A database is typically so large that it must be stored on disk, but sections may be kept in RAM for quicker access.

The software program used to manipulate the data in a database is also often referred to as a "database."

Data Mining: The process of analyzing databases for "gems" that will be useful in management decision making. Typically, data mining is used to refer to the process of combing through massive amounts of customer data in order to understand buying habits and to identify new products, features, and enhancements.

DBA (Database Administrator): The person within the information systems department who manages the data and the database. Typically, this person makes sure that all the data that goes into the database is accurate and appropriate, and that all applications and individuals who need access have it.

Debugging: The process of examining and testing software and hardware to make sure it operates properly under every condition possible. The term is based on calling any problem a "bug"; therefore, eliminating the problem is called "debugging."

Decision Models: Information systems-based model used by managers for scenario planning and evaluation. The information system collects and analyzes the information from automated processes, and presents them to the manager to aid in decision making.

Differentiation Strategy: A business strategy where the organization qualifies its product or service in a way that allows it to appear unique in the marketplace. (See cost leadership strategy and focus strategy).

Digital signature: A digital code applied to an electronically transmitted message used to prove that the sender of a message (e.g., a file or e-mail message) is truly who she claims to be.

DSL (Digital Subscriber Line): A technology used for connecting users to the Internet. The connection is typically offered by a telephone company or other independent company to homes and businesses who desire direct, all the time access. DSL subscribers are able to use the Internet without dialing up a server, and the connection is usually of higher speed than dial up lines.

E-business (Electronic business): Any business activities done electronically within or between businesses. Many use this term to specifically refer to business activities done over the Internet.

E-commerce (Electronic commerce): Transacting business electronically, typically over the Internet or directly with an EDI system.

E-learning: Using the Internet to enable training, learning, and knowledge transfer. E-learning includes distance learning, computer-based training (CBT), on-demand learning, and web-based training.

EDI (Electronic Data Interchange): A mechanism for exchanging business data between two computers over some kind of network.

EFT (Electronic Funds Transfer): The business transaction of sending payments directly from a customer's bank account to a vendor's bank account electronically.

Encryption: The translation of data into a code or a form that can be read only by the intended receiver. Data is encrypted using a key or alphanumeric code, and can be decrypted only by using the same key.

E-marketplaces: A special application of the Internet that bring together different companies to buy and sell goods and services. Sometimes called "net-markets" or "virtual markets."

ERP (Enterprise Resource Planning software): A large, highly complex software program that integrates many business functions under a single application. ERP software can include modules for inventory management, supply chain management, accounting, customer support, order tracking, human resource management, etc. ERP software is typically integrated with a database.

Ethernet: A standard for local area networks. Ethernet specifies software protocols and hardware specifications for creating a LAN to interconnect two or more computers. There are three common versions of Ethernet: 10Base-T, which provides for bandwidths of up to 10 Megabits per second; 100Base-T, which provides 100 Megabits per second; and Gigabit Ethernet, which provides 1 Gigabit per second.

Explicit knowledge: Objective, theoretical, and codified for transmission in a formal, systematic method using grammar, syntax, and the printed word. (See tacit knowledge).

Extranet: A network based on the Internet standard that connects a business with individuals, customers, suppliers, and other stakeholders outside the organization's boundaries. An extranet typically is similar to the Internet, however it has limited access to those specifically authorized to be part of it.

Fiber Optic (or optical fiber): A data transmission medium (and technology) that sends data as pulses of light along a glass or plastic wire or "fiber." Fiber-optic technology is capable of far greater bandwidth than copper technologies such as coax.

Firewall: A security measure that blocks out undesirable requests for entrance into a web site and keeps those on the "inside" from reaching outside.

Focus Strategy: A business strategy where the organization limits its scope to a narrower segment of the market and tailors its offerings to that group of customers. This strategy has two variants: *cost focus*, in which the organization seeks a cost advantage within its segment, and *differentiation focus*, in which it seeks to distinguish its products or services within the segment. This strategy allows the organization to achieve a local competitive advantage, even if it does not achieve competitive advantage in the marketplace overall. (See Cost Strategy and Differentiation Strategy).

Functional view: The view of an organization based on the functional departments, typically including manufacturing, engineering, logistics, sales, marketing, finance, accounting, and human resources. (See Process view).

Gigabit (Gb): 1 billion bits.

Gigabyte (GB): 1 billion bytes.

Groupware: Software that enables a group to work together on a project, whether in the same room, or from remote locations, by allowing them simultaneous access to the same files. Calendars, written documents, e-mail messages, discussion tools, and databases can be shared.

GUI (Graphical User Interface): The term used to refer to the use of icons, windows, colors, and text as the means of representing information and links on the screen of a computer. GUIs give the user the ability to control actions by clicking on objects rather than by typing commands to the operating system.

Hard drive: A set of rotating disks used to store computer data. Since hard drives typically have much greater capacity than RAM, they are often also referred to as "mass storage."

Hypercompetition: A theory about industries and marketplaces which suggests that the speed and aggressiveness of moves and countermoves in any given market create an environment in which advantages are quickly gained and lost. A hypercompetitive environment is one in which conditions change rapidly.

HyperText Markup Language (HTML): The language used to write pages for the Internet. It was created by a researcher in Switzerland in 1989, and is part of an Internet standard called the HyperText Transport Protocol (the "http" at the beginning of Internet addresses), which enables the access of information stored on other Internet computers. "Hypertext" itself is another name for the "links" (or "hyperlinks," "hot links," or "hot spots") found on web pages.

Informate: A term coined by S. Zuboff to imply adding information to a job or task. The alternative to informate is automate, where the tasks done are simply put on a computer to increase speed and accuracy and to cut costs. Informate, on the other hand, means to bring out the information aspects of the job to assist in assessment, monitoring, and decision making.

Information Model: A framework for understanding what information will be crucial to the decision, how to get it, and how to use it.

Information Resource: The available data, technology, people, and processes within an organization to be used by the manager to perform business processes and tasks.

Information Superhighway: U.S. Vice President Al Gore coined the term to describe the vision of a communications network that carries high-speed information all over the world. It encompasses voice, data, telephony, cable television, satellite systems, and other conduits of information.

Information Systems Strategy Triangle: The framework connecting business strategy, information system strategy, and organizational systems strategy.

Intellectual capital: The knowledge that has been identified, captured, and leveraged to produce higher-value goods or services or some other competitive advantage for the firm.

Internet: The system of computers and networks that together connect individuals and businesses worldwide. The Internet is a global, *inter*connected *net*work of millions of individual host computers.

Intranet: A network used within a business to communicate between individuals and departments. Intranets are applications on the Internet, but limited to internal business use. (See Extranets).

IS (Information Systems): The technology (hardware, software, networking, data), people, and processes that an organization uses to manage information.

ISDN (Integrated Services Digital Network): A standard for transmission of digital signals over ordinary telephone lines at up to 128 kilobits per second.

ISP (Internet Service Provider): A company who sells access to the Internet. Usually, the service includes a direct line or dial-up number and a quantity of time for using the connection. The service often includes space for hosting subscriber web pages and e-mail.

IT (Information Technology): The technology component of the information system, usually consisting of the hardware, software, networking, and data.

JAVA: An object-oriented programming language designed to work over networks and commonly used for adding features into web pages.

Kilobit (kb): 1 thousand bits.

Kilobyte (kB): 1 thousand bytes.

Knowledge: Information synthesized and contextualized to provide value.

Knowledge management: The processes necessary to capture, codify, and transfer knowledge across the organization to achieve competitive advantage.

Knowledge map: A list of people, documents, and databases telling employees where to go when they need help. A good knowledge map gives access to resources that would otherwise be difficult or impossible to find. Maps may also identify knowledge networks or communities of practice within the organization. A knowledge map serves as both a guide to where knowledge exists in an organization and an inventory of the knowledge assets available.

Knowledge repository: A physical or virtual place where documents with knowledge embedded in them, such as memos, reports, or news articles, are stored so they can be retrieved easily.

LAN (Local Area Network): A network of interconnected (often via Ethernet) workstations that reside within a limited geographic area (typically within a single building or campus). LANs are typically employed so that the machines on them can share resources such as printers or servers and/or so that they can exchange e-mail or other forms of messages (e.g., to control industrial machinery).

List Server: A type of e-mail mailing list where users subscribe, and when any user sends a message to the server, a copy of the message is sent to everyone on the list. This allows for restricted-access discussion groups: Only subscribed members can participate in or view the discussions, since they are transmitted via e-mail.

Marketspace: A virtual market where the transactions taking place are all based on information exchange, rather than the exchange of goods and services.

Megabit (Mb): 1 million bits.

Megabyte (MB): 1 million bytes.

Modem: A device that translates a computer's digital data into an analog format that can be transmitted over standard telephone lines, and vice versa. Modems are necessary to connect one computer to another via a phone line.

Newsgroup: A type of electronic discussion where the text of the discussions typically is viewable on an Internet or intranet web page rather than sent through e-mail. Unless this page is shielded with a firewall or password, outsiders are able to view and/or participate in the discussion.

Operating System (OS): A program that manages all other programs running on, as well as all the resources connected to, a computer. Examples include Microsoft Windows, DOS, and UNIX.

Oracle: A widely used database program.

Organizational systems: The fundamental elements of a business including people, work processes, structure, and the plan that enables them to work efficiently to achieve business goals.

Outsourcing: The business arrangement where third-party providers and vendors manage the information systems activities. In a typical outsourced arrangement, the company finds vendors to take care of the operational activities, the support activities, and the systems development activities, saving strategic decisions for the internal information systems personnel.

Password: A string of arbitrary characters that is known only to a select person or group, used to verify that the user is who he says he is.

Portal: Easy-to-use web sites that provide access to search engines, critical information, research, applications, and processes that individuals want.

Process View: The view of a business from the perspective of the business processes performed. Typically the view is made up of cross-functional processes that transverse disciplines, departments, functions, and even organizations. (See Functional View).

Processes: An interrelated, sequential set of activities and tasks that turn inputs into outputs, and have a distinct beginning, a clear deliverable at the end, and a set of metrics which are useful to measure performance.

Protocol: A special, typically standardized, set of rules used by computers to enable communication between them.

Prototyping: An evolutionary development method for building an information system. Developers get the general idea of what is needed by the users, and then build a fast, high-level version of the system as the beginning of the project. The idea of prototyping is to quickly get a version of the software in the hands of the users, and to jointly evolve the system through a series of cycles of design and build, then use and evaluate.

RAD (Rapid Application Development): This process is similar to prototyping in that it is an interactive process, where tools are used to speed up development. RAD systems typically have tools for developing the user, reusable code, code generation, and programming language testing and debugging. These tools make it easy for the developer to build a library of a common, standard set of code which can easily be used in multiple applications.

RAM (Random Access Memory): Computer memory that can be accessed at random, read from, and written to by the CPU. Sometimes also called "main memory," it is typically used to store currently running programs and their data. RAM requires power to maintain data.

Reengineering: The management process of redesigning business processes in a relatively radical manner. Reengineering traditionally meant taking a "blank piece of paper" and designing (then building) a business process from the beginning. This was intended to help the designers eliminate any blocks or barriers that the current process or environment might provide. This process is sometimes called BPR, Business Process Redesign or Reengineering or Business Reengineering.

SAP: The company that produces the leading ERP software. The software, technically named "SAP R/3," is often simply referred to as SAP.

SDLC (Systems Development Life Cycle): The process of designing and delivering the entire system. SDLC usually means these 7 phases: initiation of the project, requirements definition phase, functional design phase, technical design and construction phase, verification phase, implementation phase, and maintenance and review phase.

Security Validators: Web sites that validate the security level of other sites, and provide a "seal of approval" that a particular web site is protected.

Server: A software program or computer intended to provide data and/or instructions to another software program or computer. The hardware on which a server program runs is often also referred to as "the server."

Smart card: A plastic card with an embedded microchip that can be loaded with data, used for telephone calling, electronic cash payments, and other applications, and then periodically "recharged" for additional use.

Social Contract Theory: A theory used in business ethics to describe how managers act. The social responsibilities of corporate managers by considering the needs of a society with no corporations or other complex business arrangements. Social contract theorists ask what conditions would have to be met for the members of such a society to agree to allow a corporation to be formed. Thus, society bestows legal recognition on a corporation to allow it to employ social resources toward given ends.

Stakeholder Theory: A theory used in business ethics to describe how managers act. This theory suggests that managers, while bound by their relation to stockholders, are entrusted also with a fiduciary responsibility to all those who hold a stake in or a claim on the firm, including employees, customers, vendors, neighbors, etc.

Stockholder Theory: A theory used in business ethics to describe how managers act. Stockholders advance capital to corporate managers who act as agents in advancing their ends. The nature of this contract binds managers to act in the interest of the shareholders: i.e., to maximize shareholder value.

Tacit knowledge: Personal, context-specific, and hard to formalize and communicate. It consists of experiences, beliefs, and skills. Tacit knowledge is entirely subjective and is often acquired through physically practicing a skill or activity. (See explicit knowledge).

Telecommuting: Combining telecommunications with commuting. This term usually means individuals who work from home instead of commuting into an office. However, it is often used to mean anyone who works regularly from a location outside their company's office.

T-Form Organization: An organizational form where conventional design variables, such as organizational sub-units, reporting mechanisms, flow of work, tasks, and compensation are combined with technology-enabled components, such as electronic linking, production automation, electronic work flows and communications, and electronic customer/supplier relationships.

Thick client: A full function stand-alone computer that is used, either exclusively or occasionally, as a client in a client/server architecture. Thick clients are typically standard PCs equipped with disk drives and their own copies of commonly used software.

Thin client: Computer hardware designed to be used only as a client in a client/server architecture. Thin clients are also referred to as NCs (Network Computers) or NetPCs (Network PCs), and typically lack disk drives, CD ROM drives, and expansion capability.

TQM (Total Quality Management): A management philosophy where quality metrics drive performance evaluation of people, processes, and decisions. The objective of TQM is to continually, and often incrementally, improve the activities of the business toward the goal of eliminating defects (Zero Defects) and producing the highest quality outputs possible.

Value Net: The set of players in a co-opetitive environment. It includes a company and its competitors and complementors, as well as their customers and suppliers, and the interactions among all of them. (See complementor).

Virtual Organization: An organization made up of people living and working from anywhere in the world. The virtual organization may not even have a company headquarters or company building, but functions much like any other organization.

Employees typically use an information systems infrastructure to communicate, collaborate, and carry out company business.

WAN (Wide Area Network): A computer network that spans multiple offices, often dispersed over a wide geographic area. A WAN typically consists of transmission lines leased from telephone companies.

WWW (World Wide Web): A system for accessing much of information on the Internet, via the use of specially formatted documents. WWW is used interchangeably with the term "Internet."

Zero Time Organization: An organization designed around responding instantly to customers, employees, suppliers, and other stakeholder demands.

Index